A LIFE AND DEATH
DECISION

A LIFE AND DEATH DECISION

A Jury Weighs the Death Penalty

S<small>COTT</small> E. S<small>UNDBY</small>

palgrave
macmillan

First published 2005 by
PALGRAVE MACMILLAN™
175 Fifth Avenue, New York, N.Y. 10010 and
Houndmills, Basingstoke, Hampshire, England RG21 6XS.
Companies and representatives throughout the world.

PALGRAVE MACMILLAN is the global academic imprint of the Palgrave
Macmillan division of St. Martin's Press, LLC and of Palgrave Macmillan Ltd.
Macmillan® is a registered trademark in the United States, United Kingdom and
other countries. Palgrave is a registered trademark in the European Union and
other countries.

ISBN 1-4039-6118-2

Library of Congress Cataloging-in-Publication Data
Sundby, Scott E., 1958–
    A life and death decision : a jury weighs the death penalty / Scott E. Sundby.
       p.   cm.
    Includes bibliographical references and index.
    ISBN 1-4039-6118-2 (hardbound)
    1. Jury—United States—Decision making—Case studies.
    2. Trials (Murder)—California.   I. Title.
KF9680.S86   205
345.73'077—dc22

                                                                    2004058692

A catalogue record for this book is available from the British Library.

Design by Letra Libre.

First edition: April 2005
10 9 8 7 6 5 4 3 2 1
Printed in the United States of America.

*To my family for their unwavering support
and to the jurors whose willingness to share
their experiences made this book possible*

CONTENTS

ACKNOWLEDGMENTS

THE FIRST ROUND OF THANKS MUST BE EXTENDED TO THE JURORS who have participated in the Capital Jury Project. These individuals generously gave of their time so that others might begin to comprehend the realities of serving on a capital jury. A special thanks is owed to the jurors on the *Lane* case who first gave so much of themselves during the trial in trying to reach a just verdict under very difficult circumstances, and then in later trying to help me understand what had taken place in the jury room. Ken, Peggy, Frank, and the Chorus members were all individuals who exhibited an intelligence and sincerity that we should hope to find in every juror. By the conclusion of their interviews I had developed a deep respect for each of the *Lane* jurors as individuals and I am extremely grateful to them for sharing such an emotionally trying experience.

Although I am solely responsible for the views expressed and for any mistakes, I have relied heavily upon the expertise and insights of many in writing both this book and the articles that have drawn upon the research of the Capital Jury Project. There are some individuals—Bill Bowers, David Faigman, Calvin Massey, and Chris Slobogin—I have imposed upon time after time and they deserve special mention not only for their input but also for their unflagging patience. In addition, I am grateful to many others who at various times have provided assistance and insight. At Washington and Lee, Darryl Brown, David Bruck, Bill Geimer, Roger Groot, Louise Halper, Brian Murchison, and Julie Woodzicka all have given their time to help keep me pointed in the right direction. I also have benefited greatly from listening over the years to the thoughts of John Blume, Richard Bonnie, Ted Eisenberg, Stephen Garvey, Craig Haney, Joseph Hoffmann, Evan Lee, John Monahan, Marla Sandys, Ben Steiner, Margaret Van Diver, and Penny White.

Because I hope this book will speak to a general readership, I also sought help from individuals whose only crime was that they were friends or family. Many thanks to Chris Arnold, Lucy Buford, Michelle Lyons, Martha Massey, Sloan White, my parents, Elmer and Marilyn Sundby, my brother, Mark Sundby, and his wife, Barb Sundby. I must extend a special thanks to Max Charlesworth who let me take advantage of his kindness and intrude on his time in Paris to read a very rough manuscript; his gentle but stern advice to "let the jurors tell the story" proved invaluable.

I also owe a huge debt of gratitude to the legion of law students from Hastings College of the Law and Washington and Lee School of Law who have assisted over the years with various aspects of the Project. It is not an overstatement to say that my work on the Project never could have occurred without their assistance. Numerous students helped launch the study by identifying cases and interviewing jurors and then by helping process the mountain of data that the interviews generated. Trying to list every student who has helped with the Project would inevitably result in me accidentally omitting someone, so let me simply extend a sincere thanks to every student who has assisted.

A Project of this magnitude could never have been accomplished without the support of the institutions where I have taught. The length of the endeavor can be measured in part by the number of deans under whom I have served while working on the Project. I have been very lucky in that each of them—Mary Kay Kane, Randy Bezanson, Barry Sullivan and David Partlett—has been highly supportive every step of the way. The Frances Lewis Law Center at Washington and Lee has been unfailingly generous in its support by providing funding for research assistants and helping to support my writing during the summers. I also am fortunate to hold a chair named for Frances and Sydney Lewis, two individuals whose lives truly exemplify the phrase "good deeds." Terry Evans, Margaret Williams, and Diane Cochran all exhibited remarkable fortitude in helping prepare manuscripts and deciphering my illegibly scrawled notes and arrows pointing here and there.

A heartfelt thanks to my editor, David Pervin. His suggestions always were right on target and I grew to trust his judgment completely. Although every phone call always resulted in having to spend many more hours of revision, I find myself missing our talks.

In a special category of "those to whom I could never sufficiently express my gratitude" are my wife and children. Katie not only served as a wonderful reader who told me when I was not making sense, she also patiently tolerated my mood swings, picking me up when I despaired that the book would never be finished and celebrating with me as each part took final shape. My children—Taylor, Christopher, and Kelsey—soon learned how to detect from my demeanor how well the writing was proceeding. In the process I fear that I have scared them from ever attempting to write a book, but I am thankful for their senses of humor that got me smiling when I did not think it possible.

When I first started my career, I envisioned writing a number of books and using each one to thank someone special who had served as a mentor in my education or professional life. I realize now that I had better seize the moment while it is here. Thank you Susan Ford Wiltshire for the love of learning you taught to a freshman who had no clue. Thank you Nelson Roth for showing me during law school that a life in the law can be satisfying, exciting, and enjoyable. Thank you Judge Kravitch for allowing me to work for someone who gave me faith that the law can act as a voice for those whose voices otherwise would not be heard. And thank you Bill Bowers for showing me what social science can be at its very best and for becoming a dear friend.

S. E. S.
Lexington, Virginia

FOREWORD

THIS BOOK IS BASED ON INTERVIEWS CONDUCTED AS PART OF A
study designed to understand how jurors decide whether or not to impose the death penalty. Because my purpose is to understand the process
from the juror's point of view, I have not written this book as an argument for or against the death penalty. A reader looking for a polemic on
the death penalty will be disappointed. My subject in many ways is less
the death penalty as a legal topic and more the jurors themselves. The
capital jurors' decision of whether someone should live or die for their
acts is unique to the death penalty context, but the challenges that the
jurors confront as average people faced with making a momentous decision extend across many facets of human affairs.

The study does raise many questions, some quite troubling, about
how the death penalty is imposed, and I hope that these pages will further an informed debate about the future of the death penalty in America. I have tried, though, to keep my personal views about capital
punishment out of the telling of the jurors' stories. Whether I agreed
with the jurors' decisions in a case or not, I have tried to look at how
they reached their decisions rather than to criticize or praise them. After
asking these jurors to talk about what for many of them was the most difficult and emotional decision of their lives, I felt it would be the height
of hubris for me to pass judgment based on my own moral values on
whether they got their decision "right" or "wrong."

Although the book's focus is primarily on the jurors in one particular
case, *The People v. Lane*, its broader perspective comes from interviews
with a large number of jurors who have served on capital cases. I have
conducted or overseen close to 700 hours of interviews with 165 jurors
from 41 cases in which the jury ultimately had to decide between a
death and a life sentence. Approximately half of the jurors served on juries that returned death sentences, and half on juries that handed down

verdicts of life without parole. Almost all of these jurors served on California cases, and unless otherwise indicated, any statistical references are to the responses of California jurors.

These interviews were part of a nationwide study called the Capital Jury Project and headed by William Bowers. By 2005, the Project had interviewed 1,155 capital jurors from 340 trials in 14 states. Not surprisingly, the Project has produced a wealth of quantitative and qualitative data about juries and the death penalty. Although this book has drawn on the Project's discoveries to provide background, it does not attempt to convey the Project's findings in detail. A reader who is interested in a more specific look at a particular area—for instance, a statistical examination of the role of race in the jury's decision making—will want to look at the articles that have been written about the Project listed in the appendix. The reader can consult www.cjp.neu.edu for more information about the Capital Jury Project.

To protect the privacy of those who so generously shared with me their opinions and observations, jurors and cases are not identified by their real names. Some facts also have been changed so that the jurors' identities are protected. In so doing, I have taken great care to not lose the essence of the case or the jurors who decided it. Any quotations are the words of the jurors themselves.

A LIFE AND DEATH
DECISION

CHAPTER ONE

THE IDEALIST

FOR CARLOS CASTILLO, THE NIGHT SHIFT BEGAN LIKE ANY OTHER beneath the bright fluorescent lights that shone like spotlights on the store's stained and scuffed floors. He watched customers pump the coffee dispenser like they were drilling for the last barrel of oil, sold Budweiser by the can to tired-looking men dragging themselves home from work, and helped commuters rushing in to pick up a carton of milk or a loaf of bread as they hurried home to dinner. Carlos himself had eaten supper with his wife and two toddlers just before coming to work, and he soon felt himself slipping into the familiar rhythms of another long night that would see him behind the counter until dawn.

It was still early evening, so Carlos did not even bother to glance up as the door buzzer signaled a new customer entering the store. In a few more hours, when most people were home and safely settled into their nighttime routines, every buzz would draw his attention. As the clock's hour hand moved toward midnight, Carlos's job as a night clerk became one of the most dangerous jobs in America. Carlos might be paid minimum wage because of the job's low expectations, but if his earnings also had reflected risk, he would have been rich: More convenience store clerks and gas station attendants are murdered each year than police officers are killed in the line of duty.

Carlos had quickly grasped what every late-night clerk soon instinctively learns: In the early-morning hours, look immediately into the eyes of whoever comes through the door. This tactic was no poetic tribute to

Cicero's declaration that "the eyes are the window to the soul," but a survival technique of spotting danger in the rheumy eyes of a drug addict or the angry darting eyes of a paranoid individual. No matter how tired a clerk has become, every buzz of the door opening at this hour triggers a momentary jolt of adrenaline, a jolt that lasts until it becomes clear that the person is not there to grab some ready cash for a drug fix.

Still surrounded by the comforting bustle of evening shoppers, however, Carlos never looked up when Steven Lane entered the store. Never made a cautious glance into Lane's eyes. Never noticed Steven Lane glancing edgily in every direction as he walked up to the counter. Instead, a camera mounted up on the wall captured what Carlos did not see. The camera with its blinking red light had been intended to act as a warning to would-be robbers, to scare them off once they realized that they were being recorded. Tonight, however, it would be pressed into service as a filming device, recording a silent movie of the ending of a life.

The gun's report startled everyone in the store, the sound seeming all the louder because no one expected it. Some customers ducked behind shelves full of potato chip bags and bottles of soda; others looked on in paralyzed shock as Carlos fell to the floor, the bloodstain rapidly spreading across his shirt. A few customers took sidelong looks at Steven Lane as he stood there with gun in hand and then watched him as he strode back into the night without having taken any money. Shaken by the suddenness of the murder, the customers might not have made the best eyewitnesses, but they were not really needed. The camera had stared on steadily without blinking.

The murder barely rated a mention in the local newspaper the next day, taking its place alongside the other news capsules that in single paragraphs give a dismaying glimpse of life in a city's harder parts once nighttime falls—a world of gangland shootings and drug deals gone awry. If Carlos Castillo or Steven Lane had been a celebrity or if the killing had been part of a grisly Satanic ritual, the murder would have been splashed across the newspapers. Court TV would have carried the trial, and legal experts would have provided endless color commentary about what had happened that night. As it was, the only national mark that Carlos Castillo's death left was one more number being added to the FBI's homicide totals for convenience store clerks robbed and killed that year.

Although it did not command the attention of teams of reporters huddled by their minicams, Steven Lane's shooting of Carlos Castillo that night not only forever changed his life and that of his victim's family, it also started a ripple that eventually would wash over a number of lives. Carlos Castillo's death might not have caught the media's eye, but the criminal justice system still would have to ask what happened that night and what should be done. The responsibility for answering those questions would lie with twelve ordinary citizens who on the evening of the killing had been going about their own nightly routines, putting up the dinner dishes, helping the kids with their homework, easing onto the sofa to watch a sitcom. None of them knew as they settled in that night that someone named Steven Lane was entering a store and was about to fire a gunshot that would end one man's life and turn theirs upside-down. They were soon to watch a silent movie, and they would have to decide its ending: whether Steven Lane would live or die.

When the twelve jurors in *The People v. Lane* answered their summons to appear at the municipal courthouse for jury duty, they began their participation in an institution that has been lionized as the foundation of democracy and as a bulwark against tyranny. The jury has romantically been declared "the lamp that shows that freedom lives," and school-children are introduced to the jury through Tocqueville's heralding of the American jury as a living lesson in democracy.[1] These lofty accolades may be well deserved, but perhaps it is too easy to forget that the noble goals of the jury must be given life by those who are called to jury duty. In the case of a citizen called to duty as a capital juror, the demands can be especially great.

The *Lane* case was part of a nationwide study designed to examine the many assumptions that have been made about how juries decide whether to impose the death penalty. The United States Supreme Court, for example, has erected an elaborate edifice of rules governing the death penalty based on certain notions of how juries choose between life and death. The study's idea was to gain an understanding of how jurors actually make the most difficult decision entrusted to juries in the criminal law—the decision of whether a defendant lives or dies—by talking to the jurors themselves. Extensive interviews were conducted with a large number of jurors who had sat on capital juries, approximately half of whom had sentenced the defendant to death and half of whom had opted for a sentence of life.

Any hopes that the factors that influence capital jury behavior would be captured easily in colorful pie charts and snappy bar graphs were quickly dashed. What became clear after hundreds of hours of talking to jurors is that every capital case is its own drama with an evolving script and a unique cast of actors. Each trial is full of subtle moments and influences that simply cannot be captured quantitatively but that shape how an individual juror decides whether the defendant deserves to live or die. These are moments no lawyer can anticipate or plan for—a defendant unconsciously straightening his posture in a silent salute when his former Marine colonel testifies on his behalf, a sister's tears touching an emotional chord, a juror recalling her own experiences as the daughter of an alcoholic father. The drama, therefore, is a dynamic changing script. During the first act of the trial itself, each juror develops his or her own story about the defendant and the crime by drawing on the juror's personal experiences. In the next act of the drama, the jurors themselves become actors, bringing their versions of the story into the jury room to argue and bargain with the other eleven jurors over how to edit and merge the stories into a final ending: the verdict of life or death.

This is not to say that common themes and trends do not emerge among capital jurors. Quite to the contrary, the interviews revealed a number of insights into how jurors individually and collectively arrive at their decision of whether to impose the death penalty. In fact, although it sounds odd, predicting whether a jury will sentence a person to die is a lot like predicting whether two people will fall in love. Psychologists have identified factors that increase the likelihood that two people will become lovestruck—factors like comparable physical attractiveness and social status. In the end, however, the intangibles that have kept poets busy for centuries will determine whether Cupid actually finds his mark. The same is largely true with capital juries. Certain facts are likely to swing a jury toward life or death, but any one capital trial will have idiosyncrasies that will elude the sociologist's statistical regressions and can be captured only by listening to the individual jurors' stories.

By following the twists and turns of the *Lane* trial and the jurors who served on it, the door to the jury room can be opened to gain a better understanding of how the death penalty is imposed. Compared to many cases, the *Lane* case was not much as far as murder trials go. Other cases had flashy tabloid facts—severed heads, grotesque tortures, lovers' betrayals, innocent victims lured to their deaths, horrific childhoods that produced killers. *The People v. Lane* had none of these. The case was the generic murder case that has been tried in the quiet of a local courthouse countless times in countless cities: the trial of a nobody-defendant who had killed a convenience store clerk in a robbery gone awry. No glamorous victim. No celebrity defendant. No high-profile prosecutorial team or publicity seeking defense attorneys. In the universe of murder cases, the *Lane* case was the anti-O.J.

More than in any other case, however, the *Lane* jurors' personal struggles and the strife within the jury room underscored the humanness of the death penalty decision. A court clerk's flat intoning of "life" or "death" in reading the verdict form once the jury reaches its decision masks the turmoil, the pleading, the fighting, the praying, the crying that almost always takes place in the jury room as twelve men and women struggle to collectively pass life or death judgment on another person. The jurors' stories force the listener to move beyond a sterile legalistic view of the death penalty to an appreciation of the process as a wrenching human decision made by people who did nothing more than answer a jury summons. Although some remarkable stories emerged, they were not stories of heroes and villains but of ordinary citizens trying to make an extraordinary decision that had been thrust upon them. Certainly this was true of the *Lane* jurors and their struggles in the jury room.

Mark Twain once quipped that jury selection places "a premium upon ignorance, stupidity and perjury," but this is the rare case where Twain's barb misses its mark. The vast majority of jurors interviewed earnestly wanted to carry out the civic duty that had been placed upon their shoulders. Nor was it civic service that earned great rewards, monetary or otherwise. In some cases, jurors served on a jury for as long as a year, being sent home each evening as if they had just spent another day at the office. But this was a job that the jurors could not help but take home with them each night. Forbidden to talk about the case with anyone during the trial, even spouses, they had to struggle on their own with images of autopsy photos that kept them from eating dinner, stories of child abuse that haunted their dreams, frustrations in the jury room that spilled over into family relationships. And then, finally, after they had somehow agreed upon a verdict of "life" or "death" and listened to the judge read it in the courtroom as tears ran down the cheeks of many of them, they were told "good job" and sent back to their everyday lives as if they had been jurors on a dog bite case. As the *Lane* jury's story makes clear, though, for some jurors it was not so easy to step back into everyday life as if a pause button simply had been released.

This book explores the *Lane* case through the contrasting perspectives of those who served on the jury. Each of the first four chapters is dedicated to a different juror or group of jurors. This first chapter introduces the case through the account of Ken, who describes how he perceived the trial as it unfolded. For those unfamiliar with the capital punishment system, this beginning chapter also introduces the reader to the ground rules that are supposed to govern the decision making of capital jurors and to determine who ends up on our nation's death rows.

After providing Ken's detailed description of the case and interweaving his narrative with a brief primer on capital punishment law, we focus intently in the following chapters on how the individual jurors struggled with their consciences in deciding Steven Lane's punishment. The essence of this story is the drama of a jury that convinces a lone holdout to switch her vote from life to death. Listening to the voices of those jurors who earnestly believed they had to reach a unanimous death sentence for justice to be served—and, of course, to the voice of Peggy, the holdout who for days clung to a life sentence—opens a unique window on the struggle of the twelve individuals who had to decide whether Steven Lane should live or die. The final chapters of the book look at the *Lane* jurors' experiences in the broader context of other capital cases, including one case that resulted in a life sentence and, in many ways, mirrored the *Lane* jury's deliberations.

Ken lived in one of the many townhouse settlements that have sprouted up along interstates near large cities. Ten large, identical white buildings, each designated by a microscopically displayed letter, lay off the main drive. A trim and well-dressed man with a touch of gray in his hair, Ken answered the door with a nervous smile. The townhouse was nicely appointed with modernistic furnishings—white, steel, and glass abounded.

Ken had readily agreed to share his experiences as a member of the *Lane* jury. His account of the crime was as succinct, organized, and to the point as a reporter's column for the Local Crime beat. Ken's manner of speaking was cautious and deliberate with a lingering cadence that suggested that each word spoken had been consciously chosen for its meaning. Even his pronunciation reflected thoughtfulness and moderation,

every syllable distinctly articulated, verbal expressions only rarely punctuated by a rise in inflection or a hand gesture. Like most jurors, Ken was
comfortable referring to Lane by either his first or last name, often slipping back and forth between "Steven" and "Lane." It soon was apparent
that Ken was an intelligent and composed individual who was intent on
explaining how the jury had arrived at its decision.

Steven Lane had been a drug addict who supported his habit by
robbing local stores, using the cash to buy his day's fix. Once the drugs
were exhausted, the cycle started anew with a fresh search for money.
Sometimes Steven would involve his girlfriends, almost always prosti-
tutes, Ken noted, who would shoplift from local merchants to help
feed their addictions. Ken stressed repeatedly that "there isn't any
record of him ever holding a job," although Lane was now approaching middle age.

Although he used popular jargon to describe Lane, calling him a "professional criminal" who "knows all the angles," Ken also had clearly
thought of Lane's life in contrast to his own life. He described Lane's
"workday" as one where Lane and his day's companion would get up and
"map out what they were going to do that day to get money for their
drugs." Ken then verbally painted a rather striking image of how "you
would be passing them going to work, possibly, as they would be preoccu-
pied setting up how they would get the cash." When Ken put it that way, it
was easy to see how he had imagined himself driving his Taurus to work,
briefcase nestled next to him, *Morning Edition* on the radio, blowing on a
too-hot cup of coffee as he drove by a street corner where a rumpled and
groggy couple had their heads down together, unwashed hair obscuring
their faces, plotting and laughing over whom they would rip off that day.

As Ken understood it, the night of the killing started off as but one
more in Steven's endless string of nights and days looking for money to
get drugs. Ken recalled that Steven's girlfriend had testified at the trial
that she and Steven had run out of drugs that night, and, after an argument, he had left abruptly, saying "I'm going out to get some money."
Steven eventually found an all-night convenience store. He entered,
even though a number of customers were present, and walked up to the
counter where a young man was awaiting service. At this point, Lane
pulled a gun out of his waistband, poked it into the ribs of the customer,
and said, "Don't move or I'll blow you away." Although the customer's
eyes were bulging in fear, the clerk had his head down filling out a form
and did not notice what was happening. When the clerk eventually
straightened up, Lane trained the gun directly at him, uttered "Open the

till," and then pulled the trigger, shooting the clerk at point-blank range. The clerk fell to the floor and started crawling back toward the office, at which point Lane told him, "Don't move." Lane then put the gun back in his waistband and, in Ken's words, "calmly walked out the door." Lane did not take any money because only the clerk, who was on the floor dying, was able to open the till—a fact, Ken added, that made the killing "really dumb."

Ken's remarkably detailed sequencing of the robbery and killing and very visual descriptions might normally arouse suspicions of embellishment, except that the sequence was captured on tape by a surveillance camera. The prosecutor played the tape for the jury and also presented testimony from several customers, including the young man at the counter who found Lane's gun poking into his side. Ken also was darkly impressed by the testimony of a drug dealer who had been outside the gas station arranging a deal when the killing took place. At trial he had identified Lane as the killer. When challenged on cross-examination about whether he would have been paying sufficient attention to make an accurate identification, the drug dealer, to Ken's morbid amusement, pointed out that he had thousands of dollars on him at the time and thus was paying very keen attention when he heard a gunshot. Finally, the girlfriend with whom Lane had argued earlier in the evening testified that Lane had declared "I really fucked up this time" upon returning to the apartment.

As Ken described the case up to this point, it seemed pretty much a prosecutor's dream: multiple eyewitness testimony, the defendant captured on film, even an "inside" look at Lane's motives and actions through the girlfriend confidante. Nor did Lane's demeanor help his cause, as Ken said the jury found him more and more frightening in appearance as the trial progressed, "a mean-looking guy, a scowler."

Ken saw the defense's efforts to counter this growing mountain of evidence of Lane's guilt as surprisingly weak. Lane's defense was built on a claim that his was a tragic case of mistaken identity and that the killing actually was a "who-done-it?" mystery. Unfortunately for Lane, the jury was quick with the answer to the mystery, having little trouble concluding that it was indeed Lane who was depicted on the video committing the robbery and killing. Lane was represented by two attorneys, one of whom handled most of the questioning of witnesses and presentation of evidence throughout the case. Ken bluntly and succinctly summarized the defense as "not very good" and could only speculate that the defense had not anticipated how strong the prosecution's evidence would be identifying Lane as the robber. For Ken, not a shred of doubt existed about Lane's guilt.

If the prosecution had not been pursuing the death penalty, the *Lane* jury's task would have been fairly straightforward and focused on whether Steven Lane was guilty of murder and, if so, what degree of murder. This does not mean that the jury necessarily would have been spared fireworks in the jury room, as juries often have fights over whether a murder is first degree or second degree. In deciding between first- or second-degree murder, for instance, a jury might be required to decide if the defendant's killing of the victim was premeditated or not, the type of mind-reading about which jurors can easily disagree. But even if jury members had clashed over Lane's mental state at the time of the killing, once they had reached agreement on what level of murder to convict him of, their duty would have been finished and they would have gone home while Lane would have been sent to the state penitentiary.

A capital trial, however, consists of two distinct phases. Not only is there a guilt-innocence phase, as in a regular murder trial, but there also is a penalty phase during which the jury chooses between a life-or-death sentence. And to even reach the penalty phase in a state like California, the jury has to determine at the guilt-innocence phase not only that the defendant committed first-degree murder—for example, because the killing was premeditated—but also whether an additional legal factor has been proven, a factor known as a special circumstance or, in some states, as an aggravating factor. A special circumstance or aggravating factor is supposed to be a circumstance that marks the killing before the jury as an especially egregious murder.

Only if the jury finds at the guilt-innocence phase that at least one special circumstance has been proven beyond a reasonable doubt will the defendant become "death eligible." The phrase "death eligible" sounds as if the defendant has won something ("Mr. *Lane, you are now eligible . . .*"), but its meaning is far more ominous: The trial now can move into the penalty phase, during which the jury will be asked whether the convicted defendant should live or die.[2]

Special circumstances, therefore, are intended to identify those circumstances that single out the crime and the criminal as among the "worst of the worst." The jury is not even allowed to debate whether to impose the death penalty unless it finds that a special circumstance exists. In theory, therefore, special circumstances act as a factual sieve, sorting out only those individuals whom society can agree have done a crime so horrible that it might deserve the death penalty. And it is critical that the factual sieve work properly, as the United States Supreme Court has ruled that the death penalty can be used constitutionally only if the special circumstances provide "a meaningful basis for distinguishing the few cases in which [death] is imposed from the many cases in which it is not."[3]

Legislatures, however, have not had an easy time specifying what special circumstances or aggravating factors should make a defendant eligible for the death penalty. Many legislatures have used words and phrases that are intended to describe the most terrible murders and murderers. Juries are required to find, for instance, that the murder was "vile" or "atrocious" or "horrible or inhuman" or "heinous." Such descriptions have created their own problems, though, because some jurors might reasonably believe that any killing is "vile" or "heinous," assuming, of course, that they understand the word's meaning in the first place. As a juror in one case said with exasperation, "What does 'heinous' mean? There was not one juror on our jury who could define heinous." The vagueness of such phrases has troubled the courts and sometimes has led a court or legislature to add a further layer of definition in an attempt to clarify.

These further efforts, however, can border on the verbally surreal as courts and legislatures try to figure out how to say in legalese that "we mean not just that the defendant was bad, but really, really bad." The end result often gives the appearance of a court or legislature simply looking in a thesaurus to find more words conveying a sense of abhorrence and sprinkling in muscular adjectives and adverbs such as "especially" or "exceptionally." California, for instance, has tried to make its "heinous, atrocious or cruel" special circumstance constitutional by adding into the statute that "the phrase 'especially heinous, atrocious or cruel, manifesting exceptional depravity' means a conscienceless or pitiless crime that is unnecessarily torturous to the victim." And that is one of the better efforts. The Supreme Court of Virginia has tried to cure the vagueness of the phrase "depravity of mind" by adding the further definition that "depravity" means "a degree of moral turpitude and psychical debasement surpassing that inherent in the definition of ordinary malice and premeditation."[4] Undoubtedly, the reader is now left thinking, "Oh yes, that clarifies matters." The difficulty of providing clarification for descriptive special circumstances or aggravating factors such as "vile" and "heinous" have led some to question whether they really do separate out the worst from the worst.

In addition to these descriptive types of special circumstances, legislatures will use special circumstances that identify specific fact patterns to determine who is eligible for the death penalty. Again, the challenge is in identifying factual events that consistently and objectively cull out the "worst of the worst" murders. Typical are factors such as murdering a police officer, a prosecutor, or a judge because of his or her duties. Perhaps showing an unusual dedication to the First Amendment, or else a rather strong newspaper lobby, the state of Washington includes the murdering of a newspaper reporter to keep the reporter from carrying out his or her job.

Fact patterns such as murdering a police officer do help narrow who is death eligible, but such killings are relatively rare. Far more common is the "felony-murder" special circumstance, which arises when a killing occurs during the course of a felony, such as a robbery, arson, rape, or burglary. The felony-murder circumstance is the most commonly used basis for making defendants eligible for the death penalty; it accounts for more than 80 percent of the defendants on death rows.[5] Indeed, the difficulty with the felony-murder factor is that it encompasses such a large range of killings that it brings within its sweep a large number of people acting under widely divergent circumstances.[6] Like the descriptive aggravating factors, the felony-murder factor has been criticized as not providing a sufficiently fine sieve to reliably sift out who should be death eligible as the worst of the worst.[7]

Thus, on paper the states' various capital punishment statutes seem to list a limited number of very specific aggravating factors that make a defendant subject to the death penalty. In practice, though, the two most elastic factors—felony-murder and the catch-all factor that the killing was "vile" or "heinous" or whatever term the state uses to mean "really, really bad"—explain why the vast majority of death row inmates nationwide face the death penalty. And in the case of *The People v. Lane*, it was the felony-murder special circumstance that the jury was asked to find at the guilt-innocence stage to see whether Steven Lane would be eligible for the death penalty.

Ken described the jury deliberations at the guilt-innocence phase as fairly open and shut. According to Ken, the jury was quickly unanimous on a verdict that the defendant was guilty of basic first-degree murder (in Lane's case, a killing during the course of an attempted robbery). The only real discussion was over whether the defendant also was guilty of the robbery-murder special circumstance, which also required that the killing be intentional.[8] Unless the jury found the special circumstance, the trial could not move to the penalty phase and Lane would not be eligible for the death penalty; indeed, without a special circumstance finding, Lane might have become eligible for parole at some point.

The killing's circumstances as captured on tape created some dissonance among the jurors in deciding whether Lane had intended to kill: He had shot the only person who could open the cash register almost simultaneously with his demand that it be opened. Because the defense had pursued an all-or-nothing defense that Lane was not the robber at all, the jury ended up having to work its way through the issue of intent pretty much on its own. According to Ken, three jury members initially were reluctant to find the special circumstance, but eventually they were persuaded that Lane must have killed the clerk intentionally. Particularly persuasive to the jury was a ballistic expert's testimony that the gun did not have a hair trigger but required a deliberate application of pressure to the trigger to make it fire. Ken also mentioned that the evidence showed that Lane had entered the store with the gun readily accessible—a fact suggesting that he intended to use it from the start. Ultimately, the jury solved the evidentiary puzzle by deciding that Lane must have killed the clerk to show that he meant business without realizing that it also meant that he would then be unable to open the register. With the jury unanimous that Steven Lane was guilty of murder with special circumstances, they were ready to announce their verdict in court, an announcement that Ken noticed seemed to take Lane by surprise: "He became more intense, I think reality started to set in—hey, you know, this might go beyond life."

As Ken had described how the jury had worked its way through the evidence to find the special circumstance, the overarching depiction was of a conscientious jury rationally and unanimously resolving the issues as required by law. This description was very much in harmony with Ken's view of his role as a juror. He had seen jury service as a civic duty to be embraced, and he had wanted to serve in a way that brought to life his ideal of what a jury should be: twelve community members from different walks of life who in a spirit of civility reasoned their way to the correct answer. His personality was particularly well-suited for this view of jury service; Ken was a problem solver and teacher by nature, someone who believed that a solution existed and that with sufficient effort everyone could be made to see the answer. And because he was likeable and intelligent, the other jurors were naturally inclined to listen to him as he worked at achieving this vision.

Indeed, much of Ken's discussion of the guilt deliberation process centered on how he had convinced the jury to devise a list of "norms" to govern the jury's deliberations:

> I thought it would be a good idea, because they don't give you a whole lot of direction. So I said, "We should write a paper and title it 'norms.'" I felt it was real important that we equally decide in the decision over the life of an individual. My vote isn't any more important than yours—so let's establish norms, how we are going to operate. I'm going to give you some ideas and you're going to give me some ideas. . . . So then we worked on developing trust. One norm was that we wouldn't attack any individual personally. We had a rule that if emotions got out of hand, we would break for five minutes, and that really helped when it happened. It was a wonderful calming device. So we kept those norms on the wall and we would always refer to them. It was good because it put everybody on equal footing. It seems like it would be a model. I've used it in conducting meetings.

Ken's understandable pride in devising a framework for model jury deliberations trickled into his comments at various points. At one point he offered that "it seems like the norms might even be a template or model that would be extremely helpful to other juries. Everyone on the jury bought into it."

By Ken's telling, the jury deliberations seemed less like *Twelve Angry Men* and more like a corporate decision-making model that should be studied at the Harvard Business School. It did seem a bit odd that for a jury working so well together, the guilt deliberations had taken four days. This was an unusually long time for electing a foreperson and deciding guilt in an open-and-shut case, even accounting for the need to tie up the loose ends on the special circumstance. Overall, though, the jury seemed to have made it through the guilt phase with relatively little turmoil. And now that the jury had found Steven Lane guilty of first-degree murder with a special circumstance, he was "eligible" for the death penalty. The trial was ready to proceed to the one of the most unique legal proceedings in the law: the death penalty phase of a capital murder trial.

If, as is often said, criminal trials are a form of drama, then death penalty trials are Shakespearean drama. Literally. To understand the modern-day capital trial, the best place to begin is not the statute book or the maze of Supreme Court rulings over the past quarter century dealing with capital punishment, but with the *Merchant of Venice*. At bottom, all of these legal efforts to make the death penalty a fair procedure are an effort to balance the value of "justice," the understandable desire to have the defendant punished for his or her heinous act and to protect society, with the value of "mercy," the need to understand that not everyone who kills deserves the death penalty. A defendant, for example, may have suffered through a brutal childhood that will lead a jury to find that he or she never really had the opportunity to avoid a life of crime.

This tension between justice and mercy is what Portia captures in her famous plea to Shylock after he demands the pound of flesh from Antonio to which he is legally entitled under their contract. Portia, disguised as a learned Doctor of Laws, does not deny that Shylock has "justice" on his side in the sense of having a legal right under the contract. But, as she continues in trying to dissuade Shylock from his demand, insisting on one's legal right does not necessarily make a person right, because "[t]he quality of mercy is not strain'd. It droppeth as the gentle rain from heaven [u]pon the place beneath. . . . It is an attribute to God himself [a]nd earthly power doth then show likest God's [w]hen mercy seasons justice."[9]

The criminal justice system's challenge is translating Shakespeare's wonderful poetic phrase—"when mercy seasons justice"—from iambic pentameter into workable legal doctrine that can be used in the courtroom and applied by the sentencer. That a jury must have a chance to season justice with mercy is in a sense what the United States Supreme

Court has found to be constitutionally required under the Eighth Amendment's ban against "cruel and unusual punishments." The Court has held that the Eighth Amendment embodies a principle of "individualized consideration," a principle that requires that before a sentence of death can be imposed, the jury must first consider a defendant's individual circumstances. The principle of individualized consideration means that a capital defendant must be allowed to present to the jury what are termed "mitigating factors," which, according to the Supreme Court, are "*any*" facts about the defendant or the crime that might serve "as a basis for a sentence less than death."[10]

It takes only a little imagination to realize that possible mitigating factors can cover a huge expanse of evidentiary territory. A small sample of potential mitigating evidence includes psychological evidence that the defendant was mentally ill, a prison guard's observations that the defendant conforms well to the structured setting of a prison, a mother's testimony that the defendant was a good son growing up, and accounts by siblings of the abuse that the defendant suffered at the hands of a parent. In one case the defendant's artistic ability—his ability to draw well—was recognized as proper mitigating evidence. It should be added, however, that the prosecution in most states will be allowed to counter the mitigating evidence by introducing aggravating evidence that argues against showing mercy. The prosecution might present, for example, testimony from victims of the defendant's prior violent crimes or a diagnosis by a psychiatrist that the defendant is likely to kill again.

The effect of allowing great leeway in presenting mitigating and aggravating evidence to the capital jury is essentially to put the defendant's entire life on trial. Not wholly unlike the popular image of the Pearly Gates where St. Peter reviews one's life from birth to death, weighing good deeds against malevolent acts, the capital jury is likely to hear about the defendant's life from infancy (or even prenatally if a condition such as fetal alcohol syndrome is involved) on through the defendant's incarceration awaiting trial.

Unlike St. Peter at the Pearly Gates, however, the trier of fact is not all-knowing and depends entirely on the attorneys and witnesses to learn about the defendant. Consequently, the attorney representing a capital defendant faces one of the most daunting tasks in the law, a task for which law books provide little guidance: how to become a master storyteller and explain to the jury why, despite this terrible crime, they should give greater heed to their Portia-like instincts than to their desire for retribution or their concerns over future dangerousness. As would be expected, not all mitigating factors carry the same persuasive power with the jury. The constitutional right guarantees only the right to present mitigating evidence; it is up to the attorney to convince the jury that the mitigating evidence sufficiently "seasons" justice to warrant a sentence less than death.

And, of course, the Pearly Gates analogy fails in one other critical way: Not being archangels with divine guidance, the twelve individuals of the jury will have to make the death penalty decision confined by the limits of human knowledge and emotion. As a general rule, the criminal justice system tries to avoid asking juries to make direct moral judgments about the defendant, attempting instead to limit the jury's role to determining whether certain facts are true: Did the defendant *in fact* kill the victim? Did the defendant *in fact* intend to kill?[11] The death penalty decision, however, confounds such factual formulations, because the decision is unavoidably a moral judgment.

Granted, in trying to keep with the idea that the jury's discretion in imposing the death penalty must be "guided," the legal system attempts to provide an overlay of legal guidance.[12] Statutes, for example, will tell the jury to "weigh" the aggravating and mitigating evidence and if the aggravating evidence "outweighs" the mitigating evidence to then impose a death sentence. The metaphorical image of weighing may comfort by providing a scientific-sounding veneer, but the metaphor does not change that one cannot in chemist-like fashion simply tote up Column A of mitigating circumstances, compare it to Column B of aggravating factors, and then see which one "outweighs" the other. Even the most finely calibrated laboratory scale does not lend itself to weighing the abuse that a defendant suffered at the hands of an alcoholic father against the victim's suffering as he pleaded for his life.[13]

That it is almost impossible to guide the death penalty decision with any detailed precision is not to say that death penalty trials are the Wild West of the legal world where everything and anything goes. Indeed, the United States Supreme Court has attempted to construct an elaborate structure of rules governing how the death penalty decision is to be made. The rules cannot change, however, the fundamental fact that, in the end, we ask jurors in death penalty cases to draw on their own senses of morality, outrage, and mercy in deciding whether the defendant deserves to live or die.

If "all the world's a stage," nowhere is it more true than at the death penalty trial. The defense attorney must strive to tell the defendant's story in a way that will make the jurors glimpse enough humanity in the defendant, grasp enough understanding of the factors beyond his control that shaped his life, that they will decide to spare him from execution.

Often the penalty phase commences almost immediately after the defendant is convicted at the guilt stage, sometimes on the same day. Because of other court matters, though, the *Lane* case recessed for three weeks before the penalty phase began. Ken said that he gave little thought to the upcoming penalty phase during the recess, but concentrated on taking care of matters that he had let slide during the two months it had taken to try the guilt stage. Although Ken did not dwell on the trial while the court was on break, he knew that he was leaning strongly toward a death sentence based on what he had seen and heard at the guilt phase. As Ken candidly recalled, he had favored death during the guilt-innocence phase as soon as "the evidence came in that, hey, he was there, he pulled a gun on the individual, didn't give the individual any chance and just blew him away." Ken knew that he was likely to vote for the death penalty then, "unless the defense came up with something real strong on the penalty side—and I was hoping for that. But otherwise, you take somebody's life, you pay with yours."

Ken's account of what the prosecution and defense had argued at the penalty phase exhibited the same ability to capsulize and summarize with detail and precision that he had shown in his description of the guilt phase. The prosecution began the penalty phase by introducing aggravating evidence of Lane's numerous prior robbery convictions. The jury had not heard about the prior convictions at the guilt phase, because generally the fact that the accused has committed other crimes in the past is not seen as relevant to showing that he or she committed *this* crime. At the penalty phase, however, prior violent crimes are seen as relevant, because they bear on the defendant's future dangerousness and arguably show that the current crime was not an isolated incident. The introduction of Lane's prior record had a pyrotechnic effect on Ken: "This is what I became the most angry about. These individuals are continuously released on society and all of us are paying for it. I was blown away by his priors. This wasn't just one sort of whimsical, impulsive evening—this guy has a master plan of how to go counter to society."

The prosecutor, anticipating the defense's strategy, also started chipping away at the idea that the defendant would be safely locked away if given a sentence of life without parole rather than being sent to the death chamber. He called police officers who had arrested Lane for an earlier robbery, and they related how Lane had gotten hold of one of the officers and was "beating the pulp out of him." It had taken three officers to subdue him. The testimony scored a direct hit in shaping Ken's image of Steven Lane: "This guy was just amazing. I saw a real violent, angry individual there. A dangerous individual." Given Ken's reaction to this testimony, it is not surprising that he found Lane to be increasingly frightening in appearance as the trial had progressed.

Most devastatingly, a corrections official from the local jail described how guards had found evidence in Steven's cell indicating that he was planning a jail break. During this testimony, an image must have flashed through every juror's mind of stumbling bleary-eyed into the kitchen some early morning in the future, flicking on the radio as the coffee began to brew and hearing a reporter talk about the midnight escape of a convicted murderer named Steven Lane. With this testimony hanging in the air, the prosecution concluded its part of the penalty phase and the presentation of evidence arguing for a death sentence. From Ken's perspective, the prosecution had created a strong evidentiary and emotional momentum in favor of a death sentence by the time the defense's turn arrived to present its case for a life sentence.

Ken had no trouble understanding the defense's story or the moral that the defense wanted the jury to take away. Ken proceeded to tell succinctly how Steven Lane had come from a home with little parental supervision "so that he was pretty much on his own," except for one brother to whom he was particularly close. When Steven was in junior high, he and his brother were supposed to attend a religious meeting. Instead, they skipped the meeting and went out drinking. After they had become drunk, matters took a tragic turn. The brother became ill from the alcohol and died.

According to Steven's mother and one of his sisters, although Steven had been religious and caring before his brother's death, after the accident he changed and "went the other way." Ken then ticked off landmarks on Steven's journey "the other way": Trouble in high school, never graduated, dishonorable discharge from the military, unable to hold a job, and then the spiral into a life of drugs and crime. The down-ward plunge finally had culminated in the murder of the store clerk.

Ken was willing to attribute some of Steven's troubles to his life's events, commenting that "Steven's background definitely contributed to the final killing." Ultimately, though, Ken found the mitigation theme emotionally and logically tepid. Ken took particular umbrage at the idea that Steven was "a victim of his past," believing strongly that Steven "knows right from wrong, his was a life of poor choices." Ken's response to the question of whether Steven knew his place in society was, after a pause, "He *found* his place in society." For Ken, Steven Lane had made choices, was responsible for them, and deserved the consequences.

The free-will prism through which Ken viewed Lane's life led him to reject out of hand the psychiatrist who testified for the defense. The psychiatrist tried to develop the idea that the traumatic loss of his brother made Steven turn away from his family and societal structures, eventually leading him into a life of drugs and crimes. Ken did not have difficulty in articulating his assessment of the expert: "I thought you're crazy to blame his past—as a justification for his lifestyle, just forget it."

The psychiatrist also revealed to the jury that during the recess between the guilt and penalty stages, Steven had admitted the killing to him but also had said that the shooting was accidental and that he was very sorry for it. Ken was distinctly unmoved by Steven's confession and profession of remorse as filtered through the psychiatrist, characterizing the testimony as "extremely damaging," because "see, it really confirmed for those who might not have been 100 percent sure about his guilt—now here he has confessed. I could sense a sigh of relief on the part of the jury that we did indeed identify the person who did indeed do this."

The final witnesses in the mitigation phase were several prison guards who testified that Steven had been a good prisoner during his various periods of incarceration and that he had been given positions of trust as a prisoner. The defense even introduced a letter from a civilian who explained that Steven had come to his assistance a number of years earlier when Steven had been on a prison work detail.

"Good prison behavior" testimony by prison guards usually is highly persuasive with jurors. Because the only alternative to a death sentence is life without parole, such testimony can assure the jury that, if it chooses life, the defendant will not pose any future danger and may even make some positive contributions if allowed to live. In Lane's case, though, the testimony fell flat, given the earlier aggravation evidence that he had viciously fought arresting officers and had tried to escape. Even the civilian's letter backfired when it came out on cross-examination that Lane had solicited the civilian to write the letter, further painting Lane as a manipulator. It also was very damaging that a corrections officer from the work detail—the incarceration experience that the defense was trying to use to establish that Steven functioned well in prison—testified on rebuttal that Lane had caused trouble at the camp and had to be removed. All of this led Ken to laugh sarcastically as he described how the defense had argued that Lane had become a "model prisoner."

By the time the presentation of evidence at the penalty phase concluded, Ken had moved from being "pretty sure" after the guilt stage that Steven deserved the death penalty to "absolutely convinced." It was now time to see how the rest of the jury members felt as they retired once again to their cubbyhole of a jury room to begin debating whether Lane should receive the death penalty.

The jury began its deliberations at the penalty phase by reviewing the norms and having the jurors agree to abide by them. One of the jurors was designated as "recorder," and the jury then taped two posters up on the wall—one for aggravating evidence, the other for detailing mitigating circumstances. The first day no vote was taken as the jurors discussed the lists, the recorder adding items and striking others as the discussion moved in different directions. Finally, on the morning of the second day, the discussion started to stall for new ideas, and everyone agreed it was time for a vote.

As each slip was unfolded and announced as "death" or "life," it became evident that a substantial majority of the jury was leaning toward death. Nine jurors had written "death," only three "life." Now that the three "dissenters," as Ken called them, had formally declared their positions, the discussion became lively again. Some of the discussion returned to whether the killing had been premeditated, or, even if it had been, whether it was sufficiently planned to justify putting Lane to death. Several jurors also tried to argue that a sentence of life would accomplish the goal of ensuring that Lane would never be able to commit another crime, an argument that the jurors favoring death swiftly and strongly responded to by pointing to Lane's earlier planned escape.

From Ken's viewpoint, the hesitations of the jurors in favor of life were not founded on substantive concerns of whether Lane morally deserved to die or whether he was dangerous. Ken saw little room for disagreement on these issues if they were looked at rationally and methodically. Rather, he attributed the dissenters' position to a basic reluctance to shoulder the responsibility of "making the decision of whether someone should live." For Ken, the challenge became a matter of making the life jurors understand that "it was really not us deciding it, but the law. We are just confirming what the law says. We explained to the dissenters that it was the circumstances that took place sending him to death, not you or I. The dissenters were taking it more personally, like, I am sending this person to the death chamber. The rest of us were trying to help them see that the decision was separate from the person. We worked on that a lot."

The work began to pay off fairly quickly. By early afternoon of the second day, the vote had shifted to ten for death and only two against, and that was where the tally stood as the jury broke off deliberations at the end of the day. After a brief discussion to start the third day of deliberations, the jury held another vote. The results showed that the second "dissenter" also had decided to switch his vote to death, leaving a sole juror in favor of life. Although Ken had hoped that this lone juror—a woman named Peggy—could be persuaded quickly now that she stood alone, she was to prove quite an obstacle to reaching the unanimous verdict required by law.

Ken's description of the jury's efforts to change the holdout's vote resonated with the image of a teacher trying to lead students to the right answer: "We didn't feel like we were coercing her, it was just that she did not have all the information." Ken saw Peggy as someone who was unable to separate out her own emotions from her duty to evaluate the evidence. He attributed this in part to her being younger and to her job as a social worker. Ken's assumptions were ones widely shared by many jurors (and also by many trial attorneys) that younger individuals and those with certain jobs, such as social workers, nurses, humanities professors, and elementary school teachers, tend to be soft-hearted. (High school teachers, on the other hand, because they have to deal with adolescent hormones all day, are not seen as likely to take an overly charitable view of human nature.) Ken, thus, saw the holdout as someone who had fallen for the defense's case hook, line, and sinker—"she really got into the life of Steven Lane, extremely so, emotionally so, psychologically so"—and now needed to be brought back the realities of the facts and the law.

Ken took care to stress that the jury had kept on a fairly even keel. If a juror responded to Peggy's talk about giving Lane another chance with a heated challenge of "And what chance did he give the victim?," Ken was usually the juror who intervened to tamp down the emotion, sometimes invoking the norms. Ken stated that by the fourth day, "People were getting frustrated without verbalizing it—like, 'Come on, Peggy, get with the program, goddammit'—but again we tried to stay away from this." Ken made one allusion to a potentially incendiary confrontation, saying "We had one guy explode. A former military guy, big burly guy, rides a Harley, you know? He went wild, and I said, 'Wait a second here, this isn't going to work.'" The episode had a peaceful ending, because "We came back and the military guy started off by saying, 'I'm sorry, it really just got to me.' So it was good."

From Ken's perspective, the jury finally began to make headway by asking Peggy whether she had been completely candid with herself when answering questions on *voir dire* (an Old French phrase that means "to speak the truth"), the pretrial procedure during which prospective jurors are questioned to see if they can be fair jurors. In every death penalty case as part of *voir dire*, prospective jurors are asked questions along the lines of whether their views on the death penalty would prevent or substantially impair them from following the law.

These inquiries are called *Witherspoon* questions, named after the 1968 Supreme Court case of *Witherspoon v. Illinois*, which first addressed their constitutional legitimacy.[14] The questions are intended to cull out jurors who are so opposed to the death penalty that they *never* would be able to impose it even where the law allowed it to be imposed; otherwise, a single person—the juror who did not believe in the death penalty—could effectively veto the legislature's intent of making the death penalty a possible punishment for those convicted of capital murder (in the same way, for instance, that someone cannot sit on a jury in a drug trial who believes that the government has no right to criminalize drugs and thus would never vote to convict someone of a drug crime). Potential jurors for whom the prospect of the death penalty would "substantially impair" their ability to follow the law are dismissed from the jury pool "for cause," the "cause" being their inability to follow the law.[15]

Potential jurors are also asked the opposite question, known as the reverse-*Witherspoon* question, of whether they would *automatically* impose the death penalty on someone convicted of murder no matter what mitigating circumstances were proven. As with the juror who always opposes the death penalty, a juror who always would impose the death penalty is also incapable of following the law and must be dismissed "for cause," because the law requires that individualized consideration be given to the defendant's circumstances before the death penalty can be imposed. The *Witherspoon* genre of questions thus theoretically sifts out potential jurors at the two ideological poles of the jury pool regarding the death penalty—those who would never impose the death penalty and those who would impose it in all cases of murder.

Although designed to solve one problem, *Witherspoon* questions have brought about their own troubles.[16] Trial judges have found that implementing *Witherspoon* in the courtroom is no easy task. The difficulties arise because the trial judge must walk a legal tightrope when asking jurors the *Witherspoon* questions. On one hand, judges *must* exclude those whose views on the death penalty mean they cannot follow the law, but they also *must not* exclude those who, although troubled by the death penalty, still can impose it. Again, such a rule makes sense in theory, because if anyone merely "troubled" by the death penalty could be excluded, even if ultimately he or she could vote for death, one would end up, in the Supreme Court's words, with "a jury uncommonly willing to condemn a man to die."

The judges' tightrope—they must exclude those whose beliefs would "substantially impair" their ability to follow the law but not those whose beliefs would only "affect" their deliberations—is made even more treacherous by the inherent difficulty that potential jurors often have in answering the *Witherspoon* questions. As with most of the great controversies of our time—abortion, school prayer, affirmative action—many individuals are conflicted about their views of the death penalty, and giving a ready "yes, I could impose a sentence of death" or "no, I could not" is not easy. This is especially true when the question is asked not by a Gallup pollster on the street, but by a judge in the solemnity of the courtroom with the defendant seated ten feet away. Not surprisingly, therefore, the *Witherspoon* questions often elicit much stream-of-consciousness vacillation among potential jurors, like the following exchange in a case:

> PROSECUTOR: [So,] no matter what the facts or circumstances of this case might be, you do not believe that you could follow the instructions of the court to consider the death penalty and vote to impose it, is that right?
>
> MRS. MELTON: No, sir, as I said before, I feel there are times when the death penalty is warranted. I do not believe that I with my conscience could vote to impose the death penalty.
>
> PROSECUTOR: No matter what the facts or circumstances of the case might be?
>
> MRS. MELTON: In some cases I might.
>
> JUDGE: Let me ask her my question, too. Then, are you so conscientiously opposed to capital punishment that you would not vote for the death penalty under any circumstances?
>
> MRS. MELTON: As I said before, I believe there are circumstances where the death penalty is warranted. I do not believe that I could vote for it.

The trial judge's decision to excuse Mrs. Melton was later reversed on appeal, because, at most, Mrs. Melton had expressed only "serious reservations" about applying the death penalty.[17]

The back-and-forth "yes, I could—no, I couldn't" wavering is often further exacerbated when the defense attorney and district attorney are allowed to ask follow-up questions. Indeed, the questioning by the attorneys frequently has an upside-down feel because the defense attorney and district attorney will be seeking answers that seemingly are contrary to their positions. The defense attorney, for example, who is fighting the death penalty will be delighted to have jurors who are "troubled" by the death penalty on the jury. To get such a juror seated, however, the attorney must first convince the judge that the juror in fact *could* impose the death penalty. Consequently, the defense attorney will ask questions of the "troubled" juror like "Now, Mrs. Jones, you would be able to impose the death penalty on Adolf Hitler, for instance, wouldn't you?" The prosecutor, on the other hand, will not want such a hesitant juror on the jury, but to get the person struck for cause will try to have the juror state that, when push comes to shove, he or she *could not* sentence another person to die. As a result, the prosecutor, who will be arguing strenuously for the death penalty at trial, will sound extremely sympathetic to the juror's problems with the death penalty: "Mrs. Jones, it sounds to me that after much soul searching [pause], as much as you'd like to follow the law, you really could not sentence another human being to the gas chamber, wouldn't you agree?"[18]

For Ken and the other jurors in favor of sentencing Lane to death, the *Witherspoon* questions offered a way to acknowledge the strength of Peggy's beliefs while at the same time undermining their legitimacy as a reason to not impose the death penalty on Lane. The jurors began to ask Peggy whether she had been completely candid with herself in answering the *Witherspoon* questions. They stressed to her that they were not implying that she consciously lied in saying that she could impose the death penalty, but perhaps she understandably had not foreseen the difficulty of actually facing someone and saying "You deserve to die." The power of these questions to Peggy was no doubt magnified by the fact that, according to Ken, the other jurors sincerely believed this was what had happened to her: "So, then I would ask, 'Peggy, in your mind, what would it take to sentence somebody to death? What would he have to do—cut off the victim's arm? I mean, because you were asked, if this person killed beyond a shadow of a doubt, could you give this person the death penalty? I mean, there was no way the prosecution would have even accepted you if you didn't have an open mind.' It gave her pause for thought. I don't think in all candor that she was completely honest when she had said she could give death. I think she thought she was being honest, but then she became extremely emotionally involved." This tack reopened the dialogue with Peggy. Rather than arguing to her that she was mistaken in her emotional and moral belief that Lane did not deserve the death penalty, it suggested that, however hard it might be, she had to set those feelings aside because they welled up from an illegitimate source: her inability to follow the law and actually sentence someone to death.

For Ken, these types of arguments were not an attempt to browbeat Peggy into a decision, but a necessary way of keeping her from straying from the evidence into what he believed was an improper consideration of sympathy for Lane. Ken was unwavering in his belief that there was only one "right" sentence once all factors were considered. He viewed it as part of his responsibility to make sure that the holdouts, especially Peggy, overcame their emotional distractions and focused on what he fervently believed was the only "fact" that mattered: that Lane's long history of crime and lack of remorse meant he would always pose a danger. Ken's voice gave no hint of disingenuousness when he said with a touch of passion, "It would have been very important to me if he could have been rehabilitated—but, don't you see, he just couldn't be."

Peggy had held firm as the sole holdout for life through days three and four, but Ken sensed some weakening in her position in response to the majority's questioning. And although Ken insisted that the atmosphere never turned hostile, the frustration in the jury room was palpable as the fourth day's deliberations closed.

On the morning of the fifth day, as the jury settled in around the table with brimming coffee cups in hand and readied itself for another long day, Peggy said, "I didn't sleep last night." She paused and then added, "I'm ready to vote." Ken said, "people were like"—at this point Ken gave a deep sigh—"finally."

Slips of paper were passed around, quickly scribbled on, and collected. The verdict of "death" was read out twelve times. At this point, according to Ken, the jurors turned to Peggy and asked if she was ready to go downstairs and be polled—the process during which the judge asks each individual juror to announce his or her vote in open court—because, Ken warned her, "If you don't really believe this, don't vote or it will all blow up." Peggy replied, "The eleven of you want this, so it must be so," at which point Ken recalled exclaiming to her with frustration, "You're still undecided!"

The jury's response was to go back over the evidence for the rest of the morning, after which Peggy again stated that she was ready to vote. The others thought, however, that it was best to wait until after lunch just to make sure that she had fully thought through her vote. Lunch seemed to take forever as the jurors ate their court-ordered sandwiches and made small talk to spackle in the tension-filled moments of silence. After lunch, the familiar ritual of passing out the ballots and writing "life" or "death" was repeated. Each slip was opened and read out loud, the anticipation building as the pile of opened slips with "death" written on them grew until there were no more slips left to open. It was Ken who then turned to Peggy and said, "We're back to the same place. Don't do this for me or the others. Do you really believe it? Are you really going to be able to look Steven Lane in the eyes and say 'death'?" Peggy said, "Yes."

The jury was brought into the courtroom and seated in the jury box where they had spent so many of their waking hours for the prior half year. The judge asked if the jury had reached a verdict. The foreperson announced, "Yes," and handed the verdict form to the bailiff, who handed the form up to the judge. The judge read the form silently, looked at the jury, nodded, and handed it to the clerk of the court. The clerk faced the courtroom and read: "We, the jury in the case of *The People v. Steven Lane*, sentence the defendant to death." During this entire process, Ken was acutely aware of Peggy and wondering if she was going to hold together.

The time had arrived for the judge to ask each juror individually whether he or she joined in the verdict. Peggy's turn came and went in a second, her "Yes, I do" uneventful except to the other jurors, who exchanged glances of relief among themselves. They had made it. The jury's work was done: The holdout had been persuaded, Steven Lane had been sentenced to death, and the verdict was in.

Well, almost. Ken revealed with the relish of a mystery writer springing an unexpected plot twist on the reader that Peggy contacted the judge after the verdict was announced and attempted to withdraw her vote for death. The judge refused to speak with her, referring her instead to the district attorney and defense attorneys. Ken did not know much about what transpired after this point, except that the death penalty still stood despite Peggy's efforts to change her vote. Although Ken's tone revealed some exasperation with these events, the overarching tenor was one of sympathy. Her efforts to undo the verdict were proof to him of what the jury had suspected all along: She had not been emotionally up to sitting on a capital jury and had come to identify too strongly with Steven Lane. Ken suggested that Peggy may have identified so strongly with Lane because apparently she at some point had undergone a separation from a sister to whom she was close—"her suffering was his suffering"—but, in any case, the jury's task had been to help Peggy separate her feelings and emotions out from what could properly be considered. And this, Ken believed, the jury had accomplished, even if Peggy's vote for death only had lasted for the slice of time that it had taken for the jurors to reach a unanimous vote, walk into the courtroom, and announce their verdict.

Ken's account of the case had made clear that he had felt a strong sense of personal responsibility for how the jury had deliberated, a feeling that was common among jurors who had assumed leadership roles on their jury. Ken had not been blind to the fact that conflicts had arisen within the jury room (unlike, for instance, the juror in one case who described his jury's deliberations as if they were another Woodstock, only to have other members of the same jury reveal that the juror had been at the center of bitter exchanges that had almost flared into fist-fights). Despite the conflicts with Peggy, however, Ken had done as much as he personally could to make the deliberations live up to his ideal of the jury as a group that reasons together to reach the right conclusion. In looking back at the experience, therefore, Ken had tended to focus on how the jury had finally reached agreement rather than on the disagreements themselves.

Ken's narrative proved invaluable in providing an articulate description of the *Lane* case and the issues that had confronted the jury. To fully understand any jury's decision, however, it is essential to hear from a number of the jurors. Not surprisingly, jurors from the same case often will describe events from a different perspective and provide another angle from which to understand the jury's deliberations. And in the *Lane* case, a number of jurors were willing to share their perspectives.

CHAPTER TWO

THE CHORUS

IN ANCIENT GREEK TRAGEDIES, THE CHORUS EXPRESSED THE COL-
lective sentiments of the community about the unfolding action and
provided a sense of continuity in theme. In the *Lane* case, a group of five
jurors came to play a similar role in the drama that had played out in the
jury room. This group of five jurors was remarkably similar in their reasoning and descriptions of the process. Their concerns also largely
echoed the themes that capital jurors as a whole most commonly identify as influencing them in their decision making.

   The jurors who comprised the Chorus shared a number of characteristics. They were all white women between the ages of forty-six and
seventy with grown children. All had been married, although two
were now divorced. Of the five, one was a college graduate, three had
attended some college, and the fifth had graduated from high school.
All were currently working and had been steadily employed for a
number of years in positions ranging from clerical work to business
management. Although none of the group was affluent, their house-
holds all enjoyed comfortable incomes. Four of the five had owned
their homes for over fifteen years. And although all five identified
themselves as belonging to a church, none of them professed to be
particularly religious or involved with their churches. Indeed, the
only juror of the group who said that her religious beliefs had a significant impact on her decision was the one who no longer attended
church at all.

As a group, the Chorus presented a picture of stability and middle-class sensibility whose lives largely revolved around their families and their jobs. This is not to say, of course, that they were interchangeable. Each of the Chorus members had faced her own travails and moments of personal crisis, giving her a uniqueness in worldview and experiences that she brought to the jury room. Each juror had her own way of expressing her thoughts, ranging from one juror's occasionally salty vocabulary to another juror whose stoic attitude and frugal use of words made it appear that she had stepped straight out of the pages of Lake Wobegone.

Overall, though, it was striking how the Chorus jurors echoed the same motifs and concerns in explaining how they had struggled with the question of whether Steven Lane deserved to die. If political elections often are determined by swing voters who approach each election without a predetermined candidate or party, the Chorus members were the swing voters on the *Lane* jury. They all believed the death penalty was justified in certain cases or else they could not have served on the jury, but they also shared a deep ambivalence over personally having to sentence someone to death. And although all of the Chorus members ended up believing that Steven Lane should receive a death sentence, each had experienced points during the trial where she was uncertain if death was the proper outcome, and they remained troubled after the trial that they had played a role in condemning a person to die. Even the Chorus member who most strongly favored a death sentence continued to wrestle afterward with the emotion of having sentenced Lane to death and had discovered that the experience left her with serious doubts about capital punishment.

The Chorus thus felt considerable consternation as the sentencing phase began to unfold and they started to hear from the wide range of witnesses presented by the prosecution and defense. Their description of the evidence and testimony was quite consistent with Ken's. Because they had not shared Ken's early certainty that Steven Lane should die, however, they had grappled with the evidence in different ways. Their reactions helped fill out the picture of what had happened in the jury room and cracked the door a bit further on how much the jury had struggled to persuade Peggy to end her holdout for life.

In trying to navigate the maze of evidence and legal instructions that was presented to them, the Chorus members used two fundamental questions as compass points to get their bearings: How could they best prevent Steven Lane from ever killing again? Did his actions and life story justify a sentence of death? Or, to phrase the questions in the more down-to-earth terms of the philosopher-journalist Hunter S. Thompson, the jurors asked themselves how much they feared Steven Lane and how much they loathed who he was and what he had done.[1] And in trying to answer the fear and loathing questions, the jury looked at and reacted to a variety of facts and issues.

When the Chorus members first filed into the courtroom knowing that they would see someone accused of murder, they brought with them Hollywood-created expectations that, although sinister music might not be playing in the background, the defendant at least would look "criminal." Much to their surprise, their first impression upon seeing Lane was rather positive. Several noted that when they first saw Lane, they thought that *he* was one of the attorneys because he appeared so normal and was nicely dressed, even more presentable than the lead attorney: "I actually thought he might be one of the attorneys as he stood up and waved, like, 'howdy.'" Another Chorus member had undergone a similar reaction: "When I first saw the defense attorney, I thought he was the defendant! (*Laughs.*) We all did!"

Lane's clean-cut appearance, however, soon began to work against him. While Lane sat just yards away, appearing as if he would be at home in a corporate boardroom, the Chorus watched the prosecution show "pictures of [Lane] when they hauled him into jail, and he was a totally different person—long hair, tattoos everywhere." The Chorus was taken aback by the contrast between Lane's "real-life" look prior to trial and his courtroom appearance. A perception began to take root that he was trying to deceive them.

The perception rapidly strengthened as the trial proceeded, with the Chorus members paying as much attention to Lane's demeanor and reactions during the trial as they did to the evidence being introduced. After seeing his arrest pictures, the Chorus members started to notice that Lane always wore long-sleeved shirts or sweaters and kept tugging on the sleeves to "hide" the tattoos on his forearms. The Chorus's reaction to his changed appearance soon blossomed into a belief that Lane was remorseless and completely unrepentant for his actions. Particularly

galling to the Chorus was Lane's nonchalant attitude, a perceived arro-
gance that led one of the Chorus members to describe him as "cocky,
very cocky . . . throughout the entire trial he was trying to smile and
elicit responses, to establish eye contact." She continued: "Some days I
thought he didn't know what he was there for. It was amazing. As we'd
come in, he'd look like anybody going to work that day. I was amazed."

This growing sense of anger over Lane's apparent lack of emotion
was further heightened when the prosecutor showed them the videotape
of the killing. Unlike many cases where juries had to stare for the entire
trial at grisly autopsy and crime photos depicting in vivid Kodachrome
color the victim's horrible fate, the photographic evidence in Lane's case
was not especially gruesome. The Chorus jurors did not characterize the
murder as particularly "gory" or "bloody," primarily because the killing
had been by a single gunshot and the autopsy photos were not very
vivid. Nor was the video of the actual killing particularly graphic, as it
was the grainy picture of a surveillance camera with a far less detailed
picture than if the crime had been filmed with even the basic camcorder
found in most people's closets. But if the video evidence lacked the visual effects of an Oliver Stone movie, what the Chorus members saw still
made them extremely angry.

For them, the images unfolding on the video seemed like a morality
play, and the play they saw acted out was one of an utterly "senseless"
killing. What particularly angered them was that Lane seemed to have
no cognizance of the brutality of what he had done. Not only did Lane
shoot the clerk, who "was as innocent as a child," without any provoca-
tion, but he did so without even giving the clerk a chance to comply
with the demand for money: "It was cold-blooded. There was no warning. He just walked in and shot the guy. The victim had no chance at all,
and it was on videotape." For another Chorus member, the single most
important factor in her decision on punishment was "the fact that he
could go up to someone and point a gun right at a person's chest and pull
the trigger for no reason, without giving him a way to give the money he
wanted." All of which led her to conclude that Lane "was a guy who was
used to getting what he wanted with a gun." Another Chorus member
summed up her feelings in this way: "After hearing all of that stuff about
him, I felt disgusted, I found him disgusting."

And, of course, further spurring the Chorus's members growing sense
of loathing was that they could see that the morality play was having no
apparent effect on Steven Lane as he sat at the defense table. Watching

Lane out of the corner of their eyes, the Chorus was in a perfect position to see if the lessons being taught were having any impact. One Chorus member recalled looking over at Lane as the videotape of the killing was being shown and seeing that "it didn't faze him at all." She then gave a laugh of astonishment and added, "I can't imagine that if I saw a picture of me shooting someone that I wouldn't have had some reaction." In later explaining why they voted for the death penalty, the Chorus members frequently came back to their angry bewilderment that during the trial Lane never showed the slightest sign of sorrow or repentance for his acts. One Chorus member stated, "I think if he had shown any remorse, if he had started crying, it would have been all over, we never could have voted for death."

The Chorus's belief that Lane felt no remorse for Carlos Castillo's death stemmed not only from his appearance and actions at trial, but also because he had tried to convince them that the whole case was one of mistaken identity in the first place. In arguing to the jury that the prosecution had not proven beyond a reasonable doubt that Steven Lane was the person on the videotape pulling the trigger, Lane and his attorneys were not doing anything out of the ordinary for a criminal trial. Every criminal defendant is presumed innocent until the prosecution proves him or her guilty beyond a reasonable doubt, a legal concept dating as far back as Aristotle and reflecting the popular saying that "it is better to let ten guilty people go free than to convict one innocent person." (A nineteenth-century English judge, on the other hand, once mused that "everything depends on what the ten guilty have been doing," a sentiment shared by a number of observers of the O. J. Simpson trial.) By making the prosecution go through its paces and arguing to the jury that a reasonable doubt existed that Lane was the killer shown on the surveillance tape, therefore, Lane's attorneys were simply exercising their client's constitutional right to be presumed innocent.

Lane's problem, however, was that a death penalty trial is no ordinary criminal trial and invoking one's presumption of innocence can prove deadly. By claiming that the prosecution had not proven him guilty, Lane placed the jury in the position of having to look at the evidence on its own and decide whether the prosecution or defense was telling the "truth" (even if Lane's "truth" was not an outright statement "It wasn't me," but simply "the prosecution has not proven it was me"). Consequently, once the Chorus members had decided that Lane was guilty, they also had started to become personally and emotionally invested in the prosecution's view of Steven Lane and his crime. One Chorus member's comment was quite revealing: "Lane's lawyer never really said he wasn't there, *we just had to prove it was him*." As a matter of legal theory, it was the prosecutor, of course, and not the jury who "had to prove it was him," but as a practical matter, Lane's defense strategy had placed the jury in the position of actively looking at the evidence from the prosecutor's vantage point and seeing Lane as their antagonist.

By making the jury come to its own conclusion that he was guilty, Lane also created an image for the Chorus of someone who willingly would try to do whatever he could to take advantage of the system and see if he might get off. In Lane's case, this was to prove particularly harmful given the later evidence the Chorus was to hear at the penalty phase of Lane's extensive history of being in and out of jail. When the Chorus members heard the evidence of his criminal past it confirmed in their minds that he was a manipulator who knew how to work the criminal justice system for his own benefit. As one Chorus member said, "He was like a con man. He is a guy who has been a crime person and who knew how to get things done."

When Lane contended, therefore, that a reasonable doubt existed, despite the existence of a videotape and a number of eyewitnesses, it created a perception of him as someone "you can't trust." To a lawyer, Lane simply may have been exercising his right to be presumed innocent, but to the Chorus it looked a lot like someone who was willing to exploit any possible loophole, to roll the dice that the jury might find a reasonable doubt even where the prosecution's evidence was quite strong. A Chorus member described her reaction to Lane's defense as bordering on incredulity by the end: "Their whole case was based on false identification of that tape. They were just saying he wasn't there. And did they have proof he wasn't there? No, because [*laughter*] he *was* there. It was surprising. I mean, throughout all this lead-up I was waiting for this grand defense, thinking 'Now, keep your options open,' and then [*laughter*] they said, "We rest," and I about died. I went, 'Really?' They really hung their hat on beyond a shadow of a doubt—that was their whole case. I had kept saying 'Don't judge, don't judge, keep an open mind,' but then the defense had nothing." And for a jury that was perpetually fingering its worry beads that Lane might someday find a way to get back on the streets if given a life sentence, this image of Lane trying to pull a fast one only heightened the sense that, in the words of one Chorus member, "If Lane got a chance to get away, he would."

But not only did Lane's reasonable doubt defense at the guilt phase push the Chorus members in the direction of the death penalty by further casting him as a remorseless manipulator, it also chilled their receptiveness to his later claims of mitigation and regret at the penalty phase. The Chorus felt that for Lane to have first denied guilt and then to turn around and claim that he had committed the crime only because of extenuating circumstances was to say hypocritically, 'Okay, we tried to bluff you into thinking that I was not responsible for the killing, but since you found me guilty, let me now try to hoodwink you into thinking that I am not fully responsible for becoming the killer that I claimed I wasn't.' The Chorus members frequently brought up this shift in Lane's defense, making comments such as, "The attorney argued at the penalty phase that others were worse than him—Hitler, Manson—*assuming, of course* [*laughter*], that he had done it." Having refused to accept responsibility at the guilt phase, the defense's presentation of mitigating evidence on matters such as hardships in the defendant's upbringing struck the Chorus as just another example of "There he goes again, placing blame on everyone but himself." The Chorus even saw Lane's demeanor during the penalty phase as highlighting the insincerity of his lawyers' efforts to suggest that he now was sorry for what he was done. As one Chorus member commented, "His manner showed no remorse, no regret, he was still acting like he wasn't at the crime."

Lane's lawyers may have had very good reasons for arguing during the guilt-innocence phase that Lane was not the culprit. Quite possibly Lane himself, facing a minimum of a lifetime in prison if convicted, insisted on trying for an acquittal no matter how slim the chances. And if this was the case, then such a monumental decision properly rested with Lane, the person who would have to live with the consequences, rather than his attorneys, even if they had misgivings.[2]

Whatever his lawyers' reasons for arguing that Steven Lane was not the person shown on the video, though, the strategy essentially turned Lane into a gambler in the criminal justice system hoping for a lucky draw that the jury would acquit him. Like most gamblers, he lost, and the Chorus came to see Lane as someone who was remorseless and manipulative. The Chorus's perceptions of these traits in Lane, however, not only increased feelings of loathing toward him, they added to the other major concern that deeply troubled the Chorus members: the dread that if they did not sentence Lane to death, he might find a way to kill again.

The extent of the Chorus's fear of Lane was poignantly highlighted by several members who expressed a worry that Lane actually would get free and come after them. Although jurors in other cases occasionally expressed a fleeting concern that someday they might be targeted by defendants if they ever got free, several of the Chorus members saw it as a distinct possibility, even as a contingency for which to plan: "I always wondered what I would do if I saw him in a crowd, because I just have this feeling he's going to get out. He's that kind of guy, that somehow he'll figure a way to get out. What would I do? What would my game plan be? Would he recognize me? He has access to all the information about the jury." Another Chorus member described the fact that the jury list is a public record as "pretty scary," adding, "During the case I didn't know if he had a group of friends there checking me out." Yet another Chorus member said that she "wanted to be incognito" and revealed that she periodically called the prosecutor to make sure that Lane was still in prison.

For the Chorus members with their palpable fear of Steven Lane, the debate among academics, policy wonks, and lawmakers about whether capital punishment generally deters murder was far removed from their deliberations. The Chorus had a far simpler, more basic question when it came to deterrence: Was the death penalty necessary *to prevent Steven Lane from ever killing again?* And like most jurors, the Chorus members were strongly risk-averse in answering the question. Because the consequences were so grave if they were wrong in imposing a life sentence, their strong inclination was to opt for the "safer" route of a death sentence unless they could be completely assured that Lane could be controlled in prison.

One might assume that the Chorus members' foreboding that their lives might become a real-life remake of *Cape Fear* would have been allayed by the judge's instructions that Lane would be sentenced to life without parole if the jury did not impose a death sentence. The promise of a life sentence, however, fell far short of providing the assurances that the Chorus required. Foremost was the concern that whatever his sentence, Lane would attempt to escape at any possible opportunity. This concern was given frightening emphasis by testimony that during a "shakedown" of Lane's cell, guards had discovered a tool made out of a mop handle that he apparently had been using to chip away at the window. That Lane evidently had been hatching an escape attempt even while the trial was going on convinced the Chorus that if Lane "just got life, he would kill again to get away or to get his way, without a doubt."

Yet even if the Chorus members had been persuaded that Lane would have been physically unable to burrow out of jail, they would have remained extremely worried that clever lawyers and a lax judiciary would burrow him out legally. The Chorus viewed the legal system's promise that Lane would never be eligible for parole with a skepticism usually reserved for used car salesmen. For starters, the criminal justice system's prior handling of Lane's criminal activities had not exactly inspired confidence. Like Ken, the Chorus had been astounded by Lane's revolving door with the courts for his prior crimes. One Chorus member remarked, "He had been on a crime spree since the age of thirteen"; another stated, "It stuck in my mind during the trial how this man had been let out on the streets after all his crimes and each was progressively worse until finally it came to murder." Moreover, the prosecutor introduced evidence that when in jail for his prior offenses, Lane had not behaved—"jail break tries, injuring guards, that sort of thing." The Chorus's confidence in the prison and parole system to keep Lane in check, therefore, was not bolstered by what it had heard concerning his "string of crimes" leading up to the killing and his behavior during his earlier prison stays.

The Chorus's skepticism that a sentence of "life without parole" could guarantee that Lane would remain in prison, however, went beyond how the system had handled him previously. The Chorus believed—and this belief was widely shared among jurors in many of the cases studied—that even a prisoner serving a sentence of life without parole might be released someday. Although expressly told that the only sentencing choice was between death and life without parole, a mere 36 percent of the California jurors replied that they believed that a capital defendant who is not given the death penalty will in fact be in prison for "life."[3] Jurors sometimes justified their skepticism by pointing to periodic media reports that notorious murderers such as Charles Manson and Sirhan Sirhan had just received another parole hearing. One Chorus member gave voice to this underlying mistrust when she worried out loud that a sentence of life without parole would "still give him a chance to be free."

The Chorus's mistrust actually had little factual basis. Although more than 2,500 inmates have been given sentences of life without parole since 1978 in California, no one has ever had a life sentence commuted to a lesser sentence.[4] Moreover, if convicted under today's laws, individuals like Manson and Sirhan no longer would have parole hearings.[5] The Chorus, however, was operating with little information on how a sentence of life without parole worked and, consequently, felt a distinct tug-of-war between what they were told they were to assume by the judge and what their general impressions were of reality. As a Chorus member stated with marked ambivalence, "You have to go by what the law says that he would not be eligible for parole, but you read and hear all these stories—but—but we tried to follow the law."

The Chorus's effort to sort out whether the legal system could be trusted to keep Lane in prison was complicated by one more undercurrent of mistrust running through its deliberations. The Chorus's skepticism that life does not mean life was coupled with a corresponding belief, as one phrased it, that "death doesn't mean death." Like the overwhelming majority of California jurors who were interviewed, the Chorus believed that the state of California would never carry out many death sentences.[6] As the Chorus pondered whether to sentence Lane to death, therefore, the members held in the backs of their minds the thought that the odds were very slim that Lane would ever walk to the death chamber even if they did impose a death sentence.

In contrast to their assumptions about a life sentence, the Chorus's perception about the small likelihood that Lane would be executed did have a historical basis. The execution of Robert Alton Harris in 1992 was the first execution in California since 1967. Since 1977 when the death penalty was re-instituted, only 10 of the 717 defendants sentenced to death in California between 1977 and 2004, including Harris, have been executed. More death row inmates committed suicide during this time period—13—than were executed. By contrast, during that same time period, the fact that 128 defendants have had their death sentences overturned or commuted, has fostered a perception that the judiciary is undoing a large number of death sentences.[7] Given these figures and events, it is not surprising that the Chorus members would express views along the lines that "This being the state of California, I never thought he would be executed anyway, no matter what we said."

The Chorus's sense that "death doesn't mean death" made it slightly easier for several members to vote for a death sentence. One confessed that she had "personally hated" having to vote for death and that "part of me was banking on the fact that the system could get caught up with this for so long that he may just die in prison." When coupled with their doubts that a life sentence would keep Lane in the penitentiary, such thoughts allowed Chorus members to vote for a death sentence comforted by the belief that it was highly unlikely that their vote actually would result in Lane walking to the death chamber. For these Chorus members, a vote for a death sentence was like an insurance policy, more of a vote for a "life-plus" sentence than a condemnation to die: Lane was unlikely to ever be put to death, but by placing him in a cell on death row, at least he would be subjected to the harshest prison conditions possible and also would be less likely to escape or cause trouble.[8]

When it came to trying to ensure that Lane would never pose a danger to society again, therefore, Chorus members found themselves choosing between sentences that were, to them, shrouded by uncertainty and dubious assumptions: How confident could they be that a life sentence truly would mean that Lane would never again walk the streets? Could they safely opt for death as a way to lock him as far away within the prison as possible but without having to confront the reality that he actually might be put to death?

In forcing the Chorus to ponder these questions with very little factual evidence, the legal system had acted as if the Chorus members had been in a lifelong slumber until they arrived on the courthouse steps and now could be awakened and counted on to be the proverbial blank slate. As the members made clear, however, they were not Rip van Winkles who suddenly woke up when placed in the jury box. They were ordinary people bringing bits and pieces of information to their roles as jurors and who now were unsure how to meld what they had heard prior to the trial with what the judge told them they were to assume without question. Their unalterable bottom line was that they had to make sure that Lane never killed again, but what appeared to be a simple either–or choice between life and death was anything but simple.

As the Chorus members contemplated their options against this backdrop of uncertainty, they found themselves particularly affected by the testimony of several witnesses who had been victims of Lane's prior crimes. The image of Lane shooting Carlos Castillo had been shocking, but Castillo had largely remained a two-dimensional figure depicted on a video clip. Chorus members were outraged by what they had seen, but had not felt the intensely gripping anger or sorrow that wells up when one feels that one knows the victim and can personalize the victim's terror.

The victims from Lane's earlier robberies, however, quickly filled that void. Emerging like ghosts from the past, their descriptions brought his rap sheet to life in very human and frightening terms. The Chorus was especially affected by a victim who recounted how Lane had held her at gunpoint during a robbery of the store where she was working. When a police officer had entered the store, Lane had pressed the gun against the nape of her neck and yelled, "Drop the gun, pig, or I'll kill her." Even more than the store clerk's words, the Chorus was affected by how, a full ten years after the robbery, the clerk could not bring herself to look at Lane when she was on the witness stand. This unconscious reenactment of the trauma that Lane had caused, all the more powerful because it was unintended by the witness, added an immediacy to crimes that otherwise might have faded in impact because they were a decade or more old. Having watched the emotional toll that testifying took on the victims, one Chorus member felt guilty that the witnesses had been required to come in and recall their experiences: "What I felt bad about was that all those victims over the years are never going to be able to forget, because ten to twelve years later, they have to come in and testify against this guy."

The victims' descriptions, however, not only gave a human face to the pain that Lane had caused, but also highlighted how he tended to choose victims much like the jurors themselves. Lane's victims had been minding their own business, working at their jobs or filling their cars with gas, when he had appeared out of nowhere and turned their worlds horribly upside-down. The randomness of the crimes led the Chorus members to identify strongly with the victims and made it easy for them to vividly picture themselves as one of Lane's victims. The Chorus's sense of identification with the victims was an experience that was frequently shared by jurors from other cases that also had randomly chosen victims. Indeed, jurors from cases with random victims sometimes described themselves as having a there-but-for-the-grace-of-God-go-I response when they learned that the victim had been doing something that everyone has done hundreds of times, such as withdrawing money from an ATM, stopping at a public restroom, or placing a classified in the newspaper but not expecting Hannibal Lecter to answer the ad. Because jurors in such cases tend to see defendants as particularly menacing criminals who can attack anyone at any time, cases with randomly chosen victims strongly correlate with a sentence of death.[9]

The Chorus members' ability to readily imagine themselves as one of Lane's victims also led them to react violently against one of the defense's arguments for life in the closing argument of the penalty phase. It is fairly standard fare for defense attorneys during their closing argument to argue that the death penalty is meant to be reserved for the "worst of the worst." The lawyer then stresses to the jury that while the defendant committed a highly regrettable murder, his crime still was not at the level of a Hitler, a Charles Manson, a Ted Bundy, a Son of Sam, a Timothy McVeigh, or whoever is the embodiment of pure evil *du jour*. In Lane's case, the attorney used Ricardo Ramirez ("the Nightstalker" who was convicted of thirteen brutal murders), Ramon Salcido (who killed seven people, including his wife and two daughters, while leaving his third daughter for dead at a dump with a slashed throat), and the perennial favorite, Charles Manson (a popular comparison in part because he is serving a life sentence despite his notorious crimes). Lane's lawyer no doubt was hoping that the jurors would agree that the death penalty should be reserved only for killers so horrible that their names instinctively induce a collective gasp of horror and that Lane did not belong among such elite evil company.

The Chorus, however, not only was unpersuaded by the he's-not-a-Hitler-Manson-Bundy comparison, they actually became angry. Like jurors from other cases who also had strongly identified with the victim, the Chorus bristled at what they perceived as the implicit argument that the death penalty should be reserved only for murders so spectacular or gruesome that the perpetrator becomes infamous. The Chorus members essentially heard the defense's argument of "Lane's murder of Carlos Castillo wasn't so bad compared to . . ." as a callous suggestion that Castillo's murder somehow could be discounted because he had not been dismembered by a notorious killer but dispatched by a garden-variety criminal. As one Chorus member put it: "[The defense attorney] tried to compare Steven's crime with crimes by mass killers, Ramirez [the Nightstalker], the guy that killed up in the wine country [Salcido]. He brought those up and said Steven's crime was not as bad as them, so maybe they should have the death penalty, but not Steven. And in my mind, and the mind of a lot of jurors, any murder, even if it's one murder, is bad, you know. So I think the defense attorney by his closing testimony hurt his own case." Another Chorus member grudgingly agreed with the defense attorney that "the Manson case was worse than this," but disagreed that it mattered, because "the law does not break it down to say if you kill six or one you get or don't get the death penalty, it just didn't."

Perhaps, then, if Lane's victim had been someone with whom Chorus members were less able to envision as themselves or a loved one, they might have felt less anger or might not have seen Lane as an omnipresent danger when on the streets. As it was, though, the Chorus felt an emotional kinship with the victims from Lane's prior robberies and had come to see Lane as fitting the profile of the defendant that jurors feared most: someone who chose his victims randomly and could be standing behind you the next time you walk up to a 7-Eleven counter to buy a cup of coffee and a chocolate glazed doughnut.

By the time Steven Lane's lawyers turn arrived to present their case for life, a number of currents had started to converge carrying the Chorus in the direction of a sentence of death. A perception of Lane as a remorseless manipulator was rapidly hardening, originally spurred by his claims of innocence and then exacerbated by his seeming indifference to the horrors of the crime. The Chorus members also believed that their initial concerns over Lane's dangerousness had been vividly confirmed as they watched his earlier victims tell their stories with voices still faltering with fear after many years. Further pushing them in the direction of a death sentence was an innate distrust of the ability of the criminal justice system to keep Lane in prison even if they did impose a life sentence. If anything, the Chorus members' distrust had deepened as they heard that Lane had been in and out of prison at what seemed to them an almost dizzying pace. And, of course, all of these concerns and doubts were being played out against the backdrop of a visual image of Lane firing his gun into an innocent victim whose only mistake was showing up for his minimum-wage job to support his family.

Making the challenge to Lane's attorneys even more demanding as they tried to pull the Chorus back in the direction of a life sentence was the fact that the Chorus had entered the jury box with a world view that strongly embraced a presumption of free will. Reports about cases such as the trial of the Menendez brothers or the case involving the "Twinkie Defense" have raised concerns that juries nationwide are being duped by what has been termed "abuse excuse" and are acquitting defendants in epidemic proportions based on "psychobabble" that blames a defendant's actions on factors beyond his or her control.[10] At least when it comes to capital juries, though, belief in free will appears to be alive and well in the jury room. The Chorus members very much shared the belief that individuals control their own destiny and generally should be seen as capable of making their own choices even under adverse circumstances. Consequently, any attempt to convince the Chorus that Lane somehow was not fully responsible for his own actions was going to be a hard sell and was going to be scrutinized with a jaundiced eye.

With these currents creating a strong tug toward a death sentence, Lane's attorneys had to create a case for life that would lead the Chorus to understand Steven Lane as someone other than a two-dimensional killer who felt no remorse. The key would be whether the Lane defense could convince the Chorus members to suspend their horror over the crime and their anger with Lane long enough that the lawyers could present a portrait of Lane that would move them away from a death sentence. The story that they needed to present was one that explained that when Steven Lane found himself with his finger hooked around a trigger that night in the convenience store, the tragedy that ensued was but the final act of a series of life events that had hurtled him into a downward spiral beyond his control.

Although a daunting task, the challenge of convincing jury members to put aside their initial outrage over the crime is not always as impossible as it might first seem. The Chorus's feelings of revulsion and anger toward the defendant as the prosecution concluded its case were commonly felt reactions among jurors who sat on capital cases—even among jurors whose jury eventually voted for a life sentence. In the cases that ultimately ended in a life sentence, however, the jury later heard something in the defendant's case that led them to look beyond the outrage of the crime and more closely at the defendant's life story. As a juror explained in a case that had involved a double killing but still resulted in a life sentence: "It took a long time for us to really put aside the photographs, they were very gruesome, to put aside the gun, and *really look at this as a human factor*." And while no single element of a capital case can fully explain or predict the final sentence, whether jury members are willing to "put aside" their sense of loathing and "look at [the] human factor" largely depends on the strength of the defendant's case in arguing for life.

In trying to persuade the Chorus to "look at [the] human factor" in Steven Lane's case, his attorneys called an array of witnesses to try to fill in a third dimension to Lane beyond the remorseless killer the Chorus saw sitting at the defense table. Like most defense attorneys in capital cases, Lane's defense believed that calling a psychiatrist would lend a greater credibility to their effort of explaining how Lane had ended up trapped inside a life of crime. After all, a psychiatrist should command special respect based on advanced degrees and expertise about human behavior gained from years of study.

When called to the stand, the psychiatrist told how Lane had suffered a great trauma with the loss of his brother and how Steven had never really been able to overcome the sense of guilt that he felt over his brother's death. He also was able to tell the jury how Steven had suffered from never receiving counseling or help after the loss. In the psychiatrist's opinion, therefore, Steven had never been given the chance to recover from such a severe blow at such a vulnerable age. The psychiatrist also said that Steven had told him that he was sorry for the killing of Carlos Castillo.

Not only were Chorus members unimpressed by the psychiatrist, they were quite harsh in their judgment. In his cross-examination, the prosecutor had followed standard textbook strategy for cross-examining a professional expert witness and asked the psychiatrist about his fees. The questions had their intended effect: The psychiatrist's answers immediately led the Chorus to view him as a "hired gun" who would say whatever the highest bidder requested. As one Chorus member saw it, the psychiatrist came across not as a professional expert but as "a professional witness." Like many jurors who first hear how much money the expert was charging—which in capital cases often is quite high—this Chorus member was taken aback by what she heard: "The prosecution did an excellent job of showing that this guy made his money by going around and testifying in cases like this, totally disqualifying him as a credible witness. Because it looked as if he were out for the money, and that, coupled with his poor performance—he couldn't remember dates, had lost papers, was totally absentminded—he really backfired as a witness because it looked like he was just out for the money. They brought out just how much money he had made the last year alone from this kind of testimony."

Nor did the psychiatrist's actions on the stand help dispel the Chorus's view of the psychiatrist as a hired gun. When asked by the prosecutor how much he was being paid, the psychiatrist pulled papers out of his briefcase and proceeded to figure out the sum in front of the jury. The Chorus viewed this action as highly unprofessional, and watching him tote up the bill while seated in the witness chair seemed to visually confirm for the Chorus their perception that "he did it for the money."

That the psychiatrist was getting paid by the defense had the Chorus in a distrustful mood, and his testimony did nothing to change their minds. The Chorus members disliked his style of communication, commenting that he "came off as a self-centered egotist" and describing his performance as "poor." Particularly devastating in their eyes was how the psychiatrist was willing to testify expansively on direct examination about his expert opinion of Steven's condition, only to have it come out on cross-examination that he had first interviewed the defendant and his family only several days before trial. That he had not revealed this when testifying on direct examination led one Chorus member to state that the "whole testimony proved to be so false that later you couldn't believe anything he said." After reciting the psychiatrist's various shortcomings, one Chorus member finally summed up by saying, "He just didn't look right, he had a *plastic* briefcase."

The Chorus members' reaction to the psychiatrist's lack of preparation played into a larger misgiving that they harbored about psychiatry in general. Like most capital jurors, the Chorus members were suspicious that mental health experts were likely to dispense theories of human behavior that were unfounded, a suspicion captured tongue-in-cheek by the New Mexico legislature's proposed law for setting licensing requirements for psychologists and psychiatrists:

When a psychologist or psychiatrist testifies during a defendant's competency hearing, the psychologist or psychiatrist shall wear a cone-shaped hat that is not less than two feet tall. The surface of the hat shall be imprinted with stars and lightning bolts.

Additionally, the psychologist or psychiatrist shall be required to don a white beard that is not less than 18 inches in length, and shall punctuate crucial elements of his testimony by stabbing the air with a wand.

Whenever a psychologist or psychiatrist provides expert testimony regarding the defendant's competency, the bailiff shall dim the
courtroom lights and administer two strikes to a Chinese gong.[11]

Expressing similar sentiments in a more serious vein, the Chorus
members saw the psychiatrist's testimony as a potential Trojan horse
against which they constantly had to be on guard. They viewed the psychiatrist as someone whose explanations were "not believable, there
were things he said that just didn't sound right." Most damaging to the
defense was the perception that the psychiatrist's testimony was an effort
to excuse Lane's actions—rather than to help explain them—a perception that immediately alienated the jury. As one Chorus member stated,
"It seemed like he was just trying to make excuses." This sentiment
echoed that expressed earlier by Ken, when he had described the psychiatrist's testimony as actually "hurt[ing]" the defendant's case in mitigation because, without further context and given his other crimes, "I was
asking myself, you are crazy to blame his past. . . . As a justification for
his lifestyle, just forget it."

The defense also called upon Steven's mother and sister to try and help
the jury understand Steven as someone who was more than a cold-
hearted killer. The Chorus on whole liked these women, seeing them as
"regular people who spoke very lovingly of him." The Chorus members
felt especially sympathetic toward Steven's mom, describing her as a
"typical mom." Another Chorus member elaborated: "The mother reminded me of a stereotypical mother. My heart went out to her. I know
stereotypical sounds very general, but she just reminded me of a 'mom.'
She just really broke my heart. I felt very sorry for her."

In this sense, Steven's mother served a critical role, because she
added an emotional dimension to the Chorus's view of Lane simply by
showing that someone cared about him and believed that he had some
redeeming value. Until she testified, the jury had been exposed to a relentlessly negative view of Lane, and the mother's testimony provided
the first sliver of insight that Lane might have some good in him as
well as evil.[12] Several Chorus members were surprised by their sympathetic reaction to Steven's mother, a reaction that gives credence to

the dark humor saying of capital defense attorneys that just learning that the defendant has a mother reduces the chances of a death sentence by half. For several Chorus members, seeing and feeling Steven's mom's love for him, hearing that she herself felt like a failure for not keeping her son on the straight and narrow, did cause them to pause in their judgment and look at him differently. As they looked at the grown man sitting at the defense table listening to his mother testify, for a moment they glimpsed a boy on the cusp of adulthood trying to cope with the loss of someone he loved dearly and feeling like everyone blamed him.

Ultimately, however, although Steven's mother was able to make the Chorus members suspend their anger and fear for the first time in the trial, her testimony was unable to create a sufficient understanding of Steven's life to entice them away from their concerns weighing in favor of death. Drawing upon their deep-seated belief in the power of the human will to overcome adversity, the Chorus members felt sympathy for Steven, but they simply could not accept that one event explained or excused what had ensued over the following years. As one Chorus member concluded: "The testimony about his brother's death was heartbreaking, it brought tears to my eyes. But, you know, his crime wasn't caused by that blow, he never had a job, he resorted to robbing for a livelihood."

Lane's lawyers did call several witnesses in an effort to help allay the Chorus's fears that a life sentence might not be sufficient to constrain him, and such a strategy made sense. Like Ken, though, the Chorus found that these witnesses actually boomeranged. The Chorus members were quick to recall that while a homeowner had testified that Steven had helped save his home from a fire as part of a prison team fighting fires, the prosecutor had brought out on cross-examination that Steven had "mentioned" to the homeowner that it would help if the homeowner wrote a letter to the prison warden. In the Chorus's eyes, this meant that "Lane had fished for the letter." Although, asking for a reference letter from someone who believes you have performed a good deed might not usually raise eyebrows, by this time the Chorus viewed any evidence put forth by Lane's defense suspiciously. Consequently, the Chorus used the prison warden's letter of commendation in a way that the defense never anticipated: not as an assurance that Steven would be a good prisoner, but as further proof of his manipulative and dangerous personality. The Chorus was silently nodding and saying to themselves 'I knew it' when it also came out that Lane subsequently had been re-moved from the prison firefighting camp because of misconduct.

As the penalty phase concluded, therefore, the jury had listened to a variety of witnesses whom the defense had hoped would quell its con-cerns about Lane's dangerousness while also providing a compelling nar-rative of how Steven's life had ended up hurtling headlong toward a tragic dead end. Through the testimony of Lane's mother and sister, the defense did succeed in striking a spark of feeling in the Chorus that Steven had suffered a tragic moment in his youth, but the other evi-dence and testimony failed to fan the spark any further. The Chorus had seen the psychiatrist as little more than a charlatan hawking a paid-for explanation, and no other witnesses who might have been more credible filled the void. Moreover, far from being mollified about Lane's danger-ousness, the Chorus members found themselves all the more convinced that he would escape if possible and felt that he already had tried to "trick" them once by arguing he was not guilty at the guilt-innocence stage, only to later admit his guilt through the psychiatrist at the penalty phase.

As the Chorus prepared to hear the judge's instructions, all of the pieces appeared in place for them to quickly arrive at a death sentence once they retired to the jury room. Yet even at this point, with all of their concerns pointing toward death, the Chorus members found themselves deeply ambivalent. Unlike Ken, who by this time had become ab-solutely convinced that Lane was the type of person for whom the death penalty was intended, the Chorus members were far from certain that they wanted to vote for Lane to die. Indeed, the five Chorus mem-bers were not even unanimous in leaning toward a death sentence as the penalty phase concluded: Three were inclined toward death, one was undecided, and another was slightly tilting toward a life sentence. Whatever their leanings, however, none of the Chorus members felt completely confident that she knew the right answer to the monumen-tal question of whether Lane should live or die. Viewed through the Chorus's eyes rather than Ken's, the jury's road to unanimity was an ar-duous one marked by personal turmoil and exchanges frayed with ten-sion and anger.

As the judge cleared his throat to begin reading the jury instructions, the Chorus was looking for guidance on how to decide whether to impose the death penalty. They started to sense, however, that the instructions were not going to fulfill their hopes for clear and concise guidance when the judge picked up a very thick packet of papers and turned to face them from the bench. Not only were the instructions extremely long, they sounded like the undecipherable user's manual that comes with a new computer, written by one technician for another. If the Chorus members had been school teachers marking the jury instructions as a writing assignment, they would have given it a stark red "F" accompanied by withering comments. One member, a successful businesswoman who dealt daily with commercial business arrangements, candidly stated, "The judge's instructions were extremely confusing and subject to interpretation, and some people never understood them." The confusion persisted even though "we had copies of them, and we went through them page by page, sentence by sentence. It almost seemed that they contradicted each other in some cases." Another Chorus member remarked, "They were too detailed and wordy for average people. . . . We all felt that way, that they were too, too wordy for twelve people off the street to digest. Understanding them was very, very difficult you know."

Unlike some juries, the *Lane* jury at least had copies of the instructions in the jury room. Although the practice varies, many courts will not provide juries with copies of the jury instructions even in very complicated cases. The *Lane* jury had copies, but only because they had asked for them. Even then the jury members had hesitated to ask because they were worried that the judge might look askance at such a request. The *Lane* jury's apprehension in asking for copies of the instructions reflected a larger concern that plays a dominant role with almost every jury: a *very* strong desire to have the judge and lawyers, but especially the judge, view them as conscientious and hardworking. Consequently, even a simple and eminently reasonable request by the jury, such as being given copies of the thirty-page jury instructions upon which they were to decide whether someone lived or died, was made with some trepidation.

Given the *Lane* jury's hesitation in asking for something as basic as a copy of the jury instructions, it should come as little surprise that they also were reluctant to ask the judge to further explain an instruction's meaning unless they had reached a complete impasse. When the *Lane* jury did decide to ask for further clarification of an instruction, the judge

merely reread the instruction to the jury. As one Chorus member complained: "He didn't clarify at all, and we were still confused." The judge's
refusal to amplify on the instruction's meaning not only left jury members still confused, it also distinctly chilled their willingness to approach
the judge with further questions. A Chorus member explained: "We felt
a bit intimidated because every time we asked a question, we had to file
into the courtroom, they brought in the defendant, they'd call in all the
attorneys, it caused such a big deal, we just tried to resolve any further
disputes on our own. It was really intimidating—not that we'd allow it to
get it in the way, but it became such a tedious process to get additional
data." Although the effect was not intentional, the Chorus members felt
increasingly isolated and on their own as they realized that the court was
not likely to help them resolve any confusion or to figure out how to
make their decision.

Carrying with them only the jury instructions that they found less
than enlightening, the Chorus and other jurors retired to the jury room
to begin deliberations. Like most people faced with an overwhelming decision, they began by making lists. As one Chorus member recalled: "We
tried to come up with what was good with him and what was bad with
him, so we could weigh the two." Making the lists required the members
also to talk about the nature of the evidence and on which side of the
chart ("aggravating" or "mitigating") it should go on: "Anyway, we had
it up so that everybody could see it, that took a lot of time, deciding, you
know, which is aggravating and which is mitigating. There was a lot of
argument about sympathy versus evidence."

For the Chorus members, who were still grappling with whether Lane
should be sentenced to death, the most critical part of the process came
when they began attempting to make chronological sense of the "good"
and "bad" items on their list. By constructing a time line of Lane's life,
the jury undertook what becomes the core effort of almost every jury's effort to finally decide whether they found the defendant's story for life to
be compelling: The jurors were trying to decide if Steven Lane had never
really had a chance to control the life events that had led him to murder
Carlos Castillo. In making this determination, the Chorus members were
working off of their strong assumption that people can exercise free will
even in the face of great adversity. As the jury sifted through the evidence, a Chorus member recalled that they took turns discussing whether
Lane had been "given a chance to do something with his life. One of the

jurors would say, 'This is not as bad as Manson or some of the other serial killers who just kill and kill and kill,' but then someone would counter, '[That's] true, this was his first killing, but is there any hope or effort shown that he could be any kind of citizen?'"

The first day of deliberations was consumed by this roundtable discussion as the jury devised their lists and tried to make cause-and-effect sense of all the evidence. The following morning the foreperson passed out the ballots for the first vote and told everyone to mark their ballot "D" for death and "L" for life. One of the Chorus members, however, insisted that they actually write out "death" or "life," because "I remember thinking if we can't even write out 'death,' how are we going to impose it?" After the ballots were tabulated, nine jurors had written out "death"; three had spelled out "life."

∾

When the vote was announced as nine to three for death, the effect was galvanizing, creating the feeling in the jury room that a strong consensus had coalesced around the conclusion that Steven Lane should be sentenced to death. Yet if one looked into the minds of the jurors as they wrote out their ballots, the appearance of such a strong sentiment for death was misleading. Most of the Chorus members who had voted for death on this initial ballot, for instance, were still very unsure of their vote. This uncertainty and reluctance on the part of individual jurors, however, was completely hidden by what appeared to be almost overwhelming support for death by the jury as a group.

As a result, the three *Lane* jurors who had voted for life—a Chorus member, Peggy, and a juror named Mark—suddenly found themselves in a distinct minority, and the nature of the jury's deliberations underwent a noticeable shift. Psychologists have discovered that when groups deliberate and an initial disagreement exists, group members tend *not* to move toward a "middle" position, but actually become even more extreme in the direction of their original leanings.[13] The *Lane* jury responded in precisely that fashion. Like a chain reaction, the jurors who had voted for death drew on each others' comments and became more adamant in their support of the death penalty. As one of the Chorus members who had only tentatively voted for death discovered, the very process of trying to convince the minority jurors "cemented the rest of our attitudes for death."

Part of this cementing process for the Chorus as they began to feel part of the majority was a growing ability to distance themselves from feeling that they somehow were individually responsible for sentencing Lane to death. As one Chorus member explained, her initial reluctance to impose death was because "I wasn't really ready to give death right off the bat. I questioned whether I really had the right to impose the death penalty." Ultimately, however, she said that she had concluded that "as a citizen in a state that's voted in the death penalty, I couldn't interject my personal thoughts when I was representing the law—set[ting] aside your own personal feelings is what I was trying to do." Another Chorus member more succinctly stated, "I had to go by the law and not my feelings." Listening to the other jurors arguing strongly for death, the Chorus members gradually came to embrace the idea that they were playing a role in a larger scheme and were carrying out a duty that society and the legal system had placed upon them.[14]

Now that even those jurors who initially had been lukewarm in favoring a death sentence had become part of a united and vocal majority, the Chorus recounted that the tenor of the deliberations began to cascade into an avalanche of arguments for death. Especially striking was the emergence of an unshakable fundamental conviction by the majority jurors that any reasonable person would have to agree that a death sentence was the only correct outcome. The Chorus members' descriptions of the passion with which some of the jurors tried to convert the life holdouts conjured up the image of devoutly religious individuals proselytizing to nonbelievers.

Before long, the sole Chorus member who had voted for life announced that she was changing her vote to death, and it became evident that the fervor with which so many of the jurors favored death was itself becoming an argument for death. As the Chorus member explained when asked why she changed her vote from life to death: "Well, I guess in a way it was the strong feelings of the other jurors. I knew I didn't have to change, but I looked at the awful, terrible things they kept pointing out that he had done, and I couldn't argue with what he had done in the past." With ten votes now for death and only Peggy and Mark still holding out for life, the jury broke for the day.

On the following morning, Mark, without explanation to the jury, also joined the majority for death, which meant that the deliberations now focused on convincing Peggy to join the majority. As a Chorus member observed, "That is what we became obsessed about." Although most of the Chorus members themselves originally had been conflicted about sentencing Lane to death, as Peggy continued to hold out, the Chorus began to view her not as someone who was conscientiously clinging to her position but as an unstable personality. The Chorus members had "seen the light," and Peggy's refusal to do so struck them as stubbornly and blindly refusing to face up to the facts. A spiral effect was starting to kick in where the more Peggy resisted the arguments why she should change her vote to death, the more the Chorus believed that "she was getting loonier by the minute—the more we pressed her, the more she was digging in her heels." The quietest Chorus member offered up her assessment of Peggy in soft-spoken tones: "I think she was psychotic."

The Chorus members attributed what they saw as Peggy's irrational refusal to change her vote to several reasons. Some saw her as having deluded herself into thinking that she could impose the death penalty, when in fact "she demonstrated from the very beginning that she would save an ant crawling on her food. She was just one of those caring, loving people that could not ever vote for the death penalty." Another Chorus member thought that Peggy had not understood that the death penalty was a possible sentence when she had been selected as a juror and that she now found herself having to make a decision even though she opposed the death penalty. A third member thought that Peggy knew she would have to decide on death but had lost her nerve, a view with which the Chorus member was not entirely unsympathetic: "You know, it's all good and okay to say you believe in the death penalty, but when you look at somebody across the room and know that you're giving him the death penalty, I'd like to tell you, you can very well think, 'Well, maybe I don't believe in it.' I think that's really the decision she came to—I really think she changed her mind and realized she couldn't impose the death penalty."

In particular, though, the Chorus thought that Peggy had formed a belief that Lane had good in him and that it was her duty to save him from the death chamber. To the Chorus, this viewpoint defied reality:

"She more or less came to feel that she was there to save him. She kind of had a rapport . . . she more or less refused to look at the reality of what he had done." The Chorus members saw Peggy as having become transfixed by the idea that Lane's background had doomed him. One recalled, "She did a lot of crying. . . . She kept saying, 'I understand how he must feel.'" At one point in the deliberations, Peggy said that she thought she saw remorse in Steven's eyes, a comment that some latched on to as proving that her opinion was nothing more than pure emotion and sympathy: "I just remember Peggy had a hard time because she was sitting in front and he was looking at her with sad eyes, so she would feel real sorry for him." Another Chorus member recalled that Peggy's "sad eyes" comment had sparked "a lot of argument, telling her that we couldn't look at his eyes, that we couldn't go by sympathy, we had to go by the evidence."

By this point in the deliberations, Peggy's fellow jurors were variously describing her as "mentally imbalanced," "as having problems herself—it became a whole case about her," "as having trouble dealing with her own life, pulling us all down," and "from the very beginning doing things and saying things for attention." A Chorus member recalled that as the deliberations dragged on, "We were doing all kinds of things to turn her around, because we were eleven to one." As another *Lane* juror put it more bluntly, "it was her against everybody."

As part of their effort to sway Peggy, the Chorus tried to convince her that she needed to do what they, the Chorus members, had done in reconciling themselves to voting for death: She needed to adopt a separate persona—*that of a juror*—as a means of making the decision less daunting and emotional. A Chorus member who had come to feel that "if this is the penalty that this particular crime carries, then it's kind of out of my hands" remembered stressing to Peggy that by insisting on life, she was ignoring the law and allowing her own emotions to overpower her decision making. Another Chorus member recalled that "we had a long discussion as to why we were on the jury in the first place, because most people said, 'This is our civic duty and we'll just go forth,' except for Peggy." After another frustrating day of Peggy refusing to budge, the Chorus and other jurors drafted a series of questions for her to take home and answer before deliberations resumed the next day. Like a student leaving school at the end of the day with her homework under her arm, Peggy left the courthouse that afternoon with a list of questions, including "What would the victim be doing if he were alive today?"

With their arguments seemingly having little effect on Peggy, tempers began to flare. One Chorus member admitted that she found herself "getting pretty angry, I was being pretty forceful. . . . Throughout all of this I was thinking, 'Now, here's a case in black and white and we don't even live in a black-and-white world, but here's a case where we could actually see it [on the videotape]! I was thinking, how can any of these cases ever get through the system?" This Chorus member, whose anger was growing every time Peggy brought up Lane's background as a reason for voting life, finally put a picture of the victim in the middle of the jury table so that "his picture was in the middle of the table the whole day." The Chorus member thought that the picture might help make the "victim real to Peggy, and that was the part I felt all along she was missing that the rest of us internalized—she had lost sight that there was a victim."

With the emotional temperature in the jury room rising and little sign of the face-off ending, the possibility of a hung jury began to be voiced. For one Chorus member whose ardor for securing a death sentence had magnified as the deliberations dragged on, the possibility of a hung jury was appalling and strengthened her resolve to "not give in" to Peggy: "There were a couple of us who were very strong and just wouldn't allow it—I just said, 'no!' Even if we have to go through all the evidence again, we are to come up with a decision, we are not going to cost the taxpayers money." This Chorus member had sensed that Peggy was starting to become nervous about losing her job, and so she took that "opportunity to scare her—I said, 'If it takes us three or four more weeks to go through all the evidence and call all the people back in, we'll do it!' So Peggy was getting pretty anxious."

The prospect of a hung jury not only hardened the resolve of some jurors to secure a death sentence, it actually provided another line of argument for trying to change Peggy's mind. Some jurors began to voice the idea that Peggy's refusal to switch her vote essentially was allowing her to hold the rest of the jury hostage to her own views. A Chorus member remembered that in trying to persuade Peggy, "We would talk about how awful it would be to have this whole thing thrown out and retried because it was eleven to one. We really harped on that." The Chorus member also recounted how the majority at one point interpreted the instructions, which "were extremely confusing," as saying that a hung jury would result in a life sentence: "We made an interpretation on that because we were dealing with [Peggy] . . . [and] we were trying to force the issue." By interpreting the instructions as raising the possibility that a hung jury would result in a life sentence, the jury not only was able to highlight that Peggy stood alone in her beliefs, but also was able to cast her actions as extremely unfair because she could selfishly override the wishes of eleven other jurors and secure a life sentence. Although the *Lane* jurors did not know it, this interpretation was incorrect; a hung jury simply would have resulted in a new sentencing hearing.

By now the frustrations and anger with Peggy had started to boil over. A Chorus member described the "last part" of the deliberations convincing Peggy as "horrendous, people were crying . . . it was so emotional, such a horrible week at the end." The male juror whom Ken had described as a "big burly guy" had become especially vocal in his anger over what he saw as Peggy's intransigence. For the Chorus, a bad situation was becoming worse. Chorus members now found themselves forced to alternate roles between arguing with Peggy and protecting her from the juror who seemed ready to explode out of control. As the jury disbanded after the fourth day of deliberations, the Chorus members described the mood in the jury room as a volatile mix of pessimism, aggravation, and indignation. Each dreaded the next day as one certain to bring more weariness.

A shock awaited them when they gathered the next morning. Peggy walked into the jury room and announced that she had changed her mind. The Chorus had assumed that if Peggy was going to switch her vote to death, it would be a dramatic moment during a heated exchange of views when finally she would realize that she was wrong. As their surprise wore off, the jury room became swept up with emotion. A Chorus member remembered that when Peggy finally announced that she would vote for death, "It was very, very emotional—a lot of sadness—a bunch of grown men just broke down, it was really emotionally hard." In a gesture of reconciliation and to welcome Peggy back into the "family," many of the Lane jurors gathered around her to give her a hug.

As Ken also had recounted, the Chorus told how the jury spent the rest of the morning working to ensure that Peggy would not change her vote once they entered the courtroom. Unlike Ken, however, the Chorus members had been more confident that Peggy had genuinely come to recognize that Steven Lane deserved to be sentenced to death. One attributed Peggy's conversion to the jury having "rehashed everything out" and "reminding her of what happened." She believed that this continual reviewing of "the law" and facts had helped Peggy overcome "having a really hard time" with sentencing someone to death, so that "finally she agreed with everything." Another Chorus member thought that although Peggy had never given up on personally wanting a life sentence, "I think she finally had to admit that he could easily hurt someone else" and, therefore, "somehow she was able to accept the argument" that death was the proper legal sentence according to "our instructions."

In the end, the Chorus believed that the jury had successfully walked the tightrope of carrying out its duty of achieving a unanimous vote for death without browbeating Peggy into changing her vote. This had not been an easy balancing act, and the Chorus had felt acutely the inherent tension that the legal system creates for juries: heralding at every turn the desirability of the jury reaching a unanimous verdict, while simultaneously telling the jury that every juror is entitled to his or her own opinion. These two commands can quickly become at war with each other, which explains how the Chorus members could string together comments that otherwise would seem contradictory: after describing how the jurors had heatedly expressed their frustrations to Peggy so that she was "crying a lot," a Chorus member concluded by stressing that the jury had treated her "with tenderness." Another Chorus member provided a similarly mixed description, at one point describing the process of persuading Peggy as "horrendous and so emotional," but later characterizing the majority's persuasion as "very controlled, I thought."

With the announcement of the death sentence, the Chorus members felt the exhausted relief that comes when an extremely stressful situation finally resolves itself. The Chorus had been five individuals who had been given an awesome responsibility with seemingly little guidance from the legal system, and they had done their best to carry out their duty. It had been, in the words of a Chorus member, "very hard work" and had taken a personal toll. One member, frustrated with trying to capture in words how she came to her decision, had finally uttered with exasperation, "You just don't realize the mental agony of this decision until you've been through it." But while the Chorus members had trouble explaining what finally had changed Peggy's mind and they had not always been comfortable with their roles as jurors and persuaders, they felt in the end that justice had been achieved. They had helped Peggy "accept" that the law required a death sentence and had given her the strength to announce the verdict in open court. With the judge's pounding of his gavel and dismissal of the jury, the curtain formally dropped on the courtroom drama and the Chorus members made their way one last time out to their cars in the courthouse parking lot.

CHAPTER THREE

THE HOLDOUT

NORMAN ROCKWELL'S *SATURDAY EVENING POST* COVERS COMprise a gallery of American institutions depicted at their idyllic best, and for the cover of the February 14, 1959 issue, Rockwell turned his gentle and smiling gaze onto the jury. *The Holdout* shows a woman sitting in a folding wooden chair at the end of a jury table in a room engulfed in a haze of smoke. She is the only woman in the room and appears to be the youngest member of the jury, with her brunette hair neatly pulled back into a pony tail. Littered across the tabletop and the floor are numerous crumpled ballots. As she sits with her back straight and arms crossed, ten male jurors surround her in postures that range from pleading to stern disapproval; the eleventh male juror slumbers outside the circle of persuasion. One juror's hand is inches from her face in an adamant "can't-you-see!" gesture, while an older male juror sits directly at her side with a cigar clenched between his teeth and his eyes boring into her. The woman's isolation seems all the more stark as the observer's eye roams around the room and takes in just how out of place she appears in a room shrouded by cigar smoke, a spittoon beneath the table, surrounded by exasperated and angry men, several with their clothes disarrayed as if they have been engaged in an arduous task.

What could be a most menacing scene is saved by the young woman's look. Her defiant crossing of the arms, cool demeanor, and upright posture leave little doubt that while she may feel harried, it is the beseeching and sermonizing male jurors who are wearing down and

eventually must give way to her will. One is left with the familiar Rock-
wellian glow of knowing that all will be well in the end, because this
juror will have the courage to stand up as an individual for what she
knows is right and not give way in her beliefs.

Rockwell was not alone, of course, in his romantic view of the holdout and how the jury operates. In the 1957 movie *Twelve Angry Men*,
Henry Fonda's character became the icon of the courageous holdout as
he weathered the bombastic comments of his fellow jurors until he ultimately carried the day and persuaded the rest of the jury to vote not
guilty. Most viewers who watch the movie likely will whisper to themselves, "If I were on a jury, I would be the stouthearted juror who carries
the day for justice despite what others might say." But as the interviews
with the jurors quickly made evident, Henry Fonda's role is far more difficult to play when the action is in an actual jury room.

Although it sounds too coincidental to be true, Peggy bore a striking
physical resemblance to the holdout in Rockwell's painting. Slender and
pretty with dark hair, she glanced around with an inquisitive look as she
exited the elevator. She was friendly but slightly reserved in manner, and
over a mug of coffee in a quiet corner she began recounting her view of
the trial of Steven Lane.

With her opening description of the crime scene, Peggy quickly es-
tablished a recall for events and a flair for description rivaled only by
Ken. Including details such as the store's street address, in a clear tenor
Peggy described the night of the murder, recalling precisely how Lane
had entered the store and approached the clerk. Her recollection was
entirely consistent with that of the other jurors, differing from their accounts of the killing only in the greater detail she tended to provide of
where the different witnesses were standing and the sequencing of
events. Peggy's description made it clear that she did not harbor any
doubts that Steven Lane had killed the clerk.

Her certainty about Lane's guilt was a bit surprising. The other jurors
had described how Peggy had prolonged the guilt deliberations by initially refusing to find Lane guilty of capital murder and then had later insisted on a life sentence. Her hesitancy to convict and to sentence Lane
to death had suggested the possibility that she had doubted that he actu-

ally was the killer. Peggy revealed, however, that her reluctance to convict Lane of capital murder had not stemmed from thinking that someone else may have committed the crime. In fact, she had strongly suspected that Lane was guilty even before the trial had begun due to an episode during jury selection.

When Peggy was being questioned as a prospective juror, the prosecutor had asked her a question phrased in a manner that assumed the defendant was guilty. Peggy had replied that she understood from the law that Lane was presumed innocent until proven guilty. Although her comment was the reply of every defense attorney's dream juror and probably made Lane's attorneys especially eager to have her on the jury, they would not have been so pleased if they had known what Peggy was thinking immediately afterward. As Peggy made that comment, she saw Lane, who was sitting across from her, give "kind of a smile and a look," a reaction that Peggy took as an appreciation for her comment to the prosecutor but also as expressing "Yeah, but, well, that's not true [that I'm innocent]." Indeed, Peggy acknowledged that, by the end of *voir dire*, she had concluded exactly what defense attorneys fear is the unstated message being sent when jurors are asked whether they could impose the death penalty even before the trial has occurred: She assumed that Lane was probably guilty if everyone was so concerned whether she could impose a sentence of death. In fact, her sense of Lane's guilt was so strong after seeing the look he gave her and after hearing all the questions about the death penalty, she momentarily wondered if she should tell the court that she should not serve on the jury because she thought that Lane must be guilty.

Peggy's reaction to the prosecutor's question and her awareness of Lane's reaction proved to be a nice introduction to her approach to the world and her attentiveness to the verbal and visual cues around her. Peggy was not one to see the world or people as easily explained or categorized. Consequently, she could understand and even defend a system's rules, telling the prosecutor that she had thought Lane was presumed innocent. At the same time, she recognized that sometimes the system's actions might speak louder than its words: Despite all the talk that Lane was to be presumed innocent, it certainly seemed that she was being asked a great number of questions about the death penalty if the jurors truly were to presume he was innocent. And her awareness of Lane's reaction during her exchange with the district attorney and her interpretation of his expression indicated that she keenly observed people's actions for expressions of meaning.

Peggy's inclination to focus intently on an occurrence, hold it up, turn it around, and examine it from a variety of angles meant that she did not always arrive at the conclusion that most people would immediately draw from an event. The first indication of this surfaced when Peggy's narrative of the crime reached the videotape of Lane shooting the clerk. Like the other jurors, Peggy had been taken aback by the video. But while the other jurors' descriptions had focused on Lane's act of shooting the clerk and had ended once the clerk fell to the floor, Peggy also had been struck by what the camera captured both leading up to the shooting and after it. After watching Lane enter the store, taking his time to get to the counter, and then suddenly firing the gun without warning, Peggy thought, "This does not seem like a classic robbery." She was even more intrigued as she watched Lane's reaction after the shooting: "It seemed to me that when he looked up, it was sort of as if he were in shock, like he didn't quite realize what happened." For Peggy, these actions caught on the film gave her pause over Lane's intentions. She certainly did not think that he had innocently entered the store to buy a bottle of milk. When his gun went off, "the expression on his face before he pulled the trigger was very expressive, evil, angry—I had nightmares about it," but at the same time what she saw on the film did not lead her to conclude immediately that this was an intentional killing. More fundamentally, Peggy's reaction to the video clip—that she could focus on Lane's actions and expressions and not only on the image of the dying clerk collapsing to the floor—was different from that of the other jurors. She had not shared their instinctive response of horror upon seeing the killing: "For some reason when I saw the video, I didn't have the same reaction the other jurors did of 'Oh, my God, that's so senseless'. . . . I didn't have that horror. . . . The first thing I noticed in the video was the expression on his face of stunned shock, not this heart wrenching horror that the other jurors felt."

The trouble that lay ahead for the jury was foreshadowed not only by Peggy's dissimilar reaction to the video clip, but by her deeply questioning mind. Although at one point Peggy declared that "I want to make it clear that I'm not one of those persons who says that every time something happens, something deeper must be going on," she also exhibited a strong belief that events and people's actions often are not as simple as they may first appear. Before Peggy convicted Steven Lane of robbery and an intentional killing, she wanted to make sure that the questions that had arisen in her mind about his intentions as she watched and heard the evidence unfold could be answered. Perhaps ensuring that the deliberations were destined to become difficult, Peggy carried into the jury room the romantic notion of a juror and jury depicted by Henry Fonda: "As a jury aren't we supposed to pick apart every little word?"

Peggy's relentlessly questioning mind would have served well a police detective faced with a baffling murder, a philosopher trying to solve a thorny existential quandary, or a dramatist trying to create a poignant character. But for a jury in possession of a videotape showing someone gunning down a man working the night shift and demanding that someone "open the till," Peggy's questions about Lane's intent seemed only to make simple questions far harder than they needed to be.

Peggy's questions focused primarily on the idea that the evidence had not convinced her that Lane had clearly intended to rob and kill, especially since he had shot the clerk suddenly and without already having obtained access to the cash register. She was willing to convict Lane of some form of homicide based on a reckless killing, but she was not willing to vote guilty on the special circumstance that would make him eligible for the death penalty: that Lane had entered the store intending to rob it and then had intentionally shot Castillo. Peggy soon realized, however, that "from seeing the videotape, the other jurors felt real certain that it was a murder during a robbery from the start." The other jurors believed that Lane shot the clerk before he opened the cash register because he was trying to intimidate everyone into cooperating with the robbery. In an attempt to get the jury beyond the videotape, Peggy went through what she saw as potential holes and inconsistencies in the evidence: "I'd say what about this, what about that? They just focused on the videotape."

At this point, recognizing that the videotape had become the other jurors' Rosetta Stone for understanding what happened in the store, Peggy turned to the video itself and floated her view that the events depicted did not seem like a "normal robbery." Far from her hope of sparking a lively debate about what was depicted, Peggy's comment marked the beginning of the jury publicly casting her into the role of an outsider. Prior to this, Peggy could sense that some jurors were privately becoming frustrated with her questions and refusal to vote guilty on special circumstances. Now for the first time many of the jurors began openly to show impatience with her views: "I was the only one who said 'wait a minute.' I remember them laughing at me because I said it didn't seem like a normal robbery. They didn't like the way I said 'normal,' someone would say,

'*What's a normal robbery?*' I meant not charging in, but they weren't really interested in talking about it, they didn't seem to care." Peggy's recognition of the sarcasm in the other jurors' voices and laughter meant she realized that she stood alone in harboring doubts over Lane's intention and that she was aware that some of the other jurors were dismissing her comments as unworthy of discussion.

Peggy attributed the devaluing of her comments in part to her inability to articulate her reservations about the evidence intelligently: "When they laughed at my comment of a 'normal robbery,' I think it was sort of like the words I used. I mean, if you're talking to someone and they use funny words, you get them put aside, and I was having trouble articulating what I was saying." That Peggy found herself stumbling for words was surprising given that she is extremely well spoken in casual conversation and especially attuned to the meaning of words, carefully drawing a distinction, for instance, between feelings of "sympathy" and "empathy." Peggy, however, attributed her inarticulateness to the very different pressures that come into play in a jury room: "With the group, I felt very, very shy and nervous. I do much better one-on-one; a large group is overwhelming to me. I felt young; half of the jury was old enough to be my parents, so they were these authority figures and I was, 'So who am I?'"

Especially interesting was Peggy's description of how the jury had organized itself as if it was a self-contained society. A rough pecking order had materialized as jurors assumed different roles. Ken and another male juror had staked out the ends of the jury table from the trial's beginning. The other jurors simply had sat down in a chair the first day of the trial and proceeded to keep those seats throughout, "like in school when you choose a seat the first day and keep going to it for the rest of the year." By the time deliberations had started, the jury had gravitated toward Ken as a voice of calm and reason. He was someone whom "everyone liked, articulated well, and had a nice manner about him." The juror at the other end of the table, however, whom Peggy usually referred to as the twelfth juror because he was juror number 12, was not as "polished."

Within the jury, groups had formed that would routinely go to lunch together as the months passed. Peggy was a member of a group of four women who usually ate together, occasionally joined by a male juror. It also was becoming evident that some jurors had more assertive personalities than others. Peggy had grown to particularly like a juror who was a "father figure type," a quiet older man whom she liked and trusted. Peggy also described how several jurors exuded a "superior attitude" because they had been among the first jurors called to the jury box and "felt like they had sat through the elimination of all these [other potential jurors who were struck by peremptories] and so were well liked by the lawyers and judges." As Peggy described how jurors ascribed importance to when they were called to the jury box, it sounded like the creation of a class of nobility based on a rough notion of jury lineage. (Never mind that a potential juror's "lineage" turns purely on a random procedure for picking names from the jury list.)

Now that deliberations had begun, some of the loosely formed social groups began to disassemble under the pressure of disagreement, and other groups formed based on their common views. Peggy started going off by herself more as the deliberations intensified, although she still tried to go to lunch with a group because "I didn't want it to be obvious I'm different, but I was real quiet." Jurors' latent personality traits also emerged in fuller relief with the onset of deliberations. The twelfth juror, who controlled the end of the jury table opposite Ken and whom Peggy described as a "kind of a rough guy," started to vociferously voice impatience with her views.

Although Peggy was not making any headway in persuading the other jurors to rethink their views on guilt, by repeatedly raising her own questions at least she was helping herself reach a resolution. As she asked questions about the evidence, she had begun to sort out in her mind which of her concerns were only "imaginary" doubts rather than "reasonable" ones. As Peggy whittled away at her uncertainties, dismissing those that she could deem "imaginary," her concerns increasingly focused on the testimony of the customer at the counter. This customer had testified about Lane's actions and his demand that someone "open the till," evidence critical to establishing Lane's intent to rob and kill.

Because Peggy strongly believed that pressure and fear can affect people's perceptions, making it possible for them to think in good faith that something had happened in a particular way when it had not, she strongly preferred to experience firsthand what had happened. She felt fortunate, for example, that the jury had the video of the crime, although even then she stated that "the pictures were very clear, but I think when you decide whether someone is guilty or not, you want to have been there, you want to have seen it with your own eyes." When it came to the customer's testimony, therefore, she was wary of just accepting his description of what had occurred, because he "was very nervous. I think he was still traumatized by the whole thing so I think in my mind that made him less credible. It bothered me that the other people in the store didn't testify about what Lane had said to the clerk before firing the shot. I was reluctant to hang the special circumstances on Lane based on that one witness's testimony who was very nervous." Peggy's desire to know firsthand what had happened rather than hearing a version filtered through the lawyers' questions was especially frustrating for her: "It really bothered me that I was unable to speak with the witness."

With the fourth day of guilt deliberations dragging on, the other jurors were growing noticeably impatient and the edge to their comments more sharply honed: "They just kept cutting me off. It wasn't a discussion—discuss is too nice of a word." But with the customer's testimony now the fulcrum of Peggy's concerns, they all agreed that hearing the witness's testimony again might be helpful. To Peggy's amazement, what seemed like a simple request of having a witness's testimony reread to the jury triggered an elaborate process: First the judge had to consult with the prosecutor and defense attorneys, and then court was reconvened with everyone present, including the defendant, the lawyers, and court personnel. The process that Peggy saw unfolding would happen in any courtroom, as trial judges carefully guard against possible reversal on appeal by making sure the defendant and attorneys are present whenever the jury is in the courtroom. To Peggy and the other jurors, however, the process seemed unnecessary and somewhat intimidating.

Finally all of the formalities were completed and the court reporter began to read the customer's transcribed testimony. A few minutes after Peggy had closed her eyes to concentrate, she felt a sharp jab in her ribs. The twelfth juror, the "rough guy," was reaching around the juror sitting next to Peggy and was poking her in the ribs, saying "Did you get that? Did you get that?" In retrospect, Peggy wished that she had stood up and said, "Listen, mister, do you mind?" but instead she "just sat there taking it." Despite being jabbed with a finger at various points of the reading, Peggy did find herself becoming convinced by the witness's testimony, because "when I heard it read without seeing him, it made it more credible, and I was like 'uncle.'" At this point,

Peggy signaled that she had heard enough, and they retired back to the jury room.

With everyone looking at her expectantly, Peggy glanced at the clock and saw that it was fifteen minutes before they usually called it a day, so she said, "Look, can I go home and sleep on it?" Although she expected heavy sighs and an exasperated comment or two, the other jurors said that would be fine, and it dawned on Peggy that "everyone was thinking 'she's so sensitive'" and the jabbing juror was "almost patronizing, like 'we'll wait for you if that's what you need, we'll give you all the time you need.'"

In fact, Peggy had come to the conclusion that Lane had intended the robbery and killing, "but for four days I'd been fighting this and I wasn't real comfortable making that decision right then." As she prepared to go home, Peggy found herself standing next to a group of the jurors that included the twelfth juror, the one who had been jabbing her and had been most caustic in his comments. The man apologized and Peggy started crying, which triggered a further apology from him, saying his actions were "totally uncalled for and you're right, you take all the time you want." As Peggy broke down, she "felt very young-like," but she also knew that the others did not understand why she was sobbing. "I think they thought I was crying because they had picked on me. I didn't like the way I was being treated, but I was more upset because it was dawning on me, 'Oh God, I'm going to be a part of this group that says this man is guilty,' and even though I knew he was guilty, somehow it was catching up with me what all this really was about. . . . I just didn't want to have to convict someone of murder." Peggy "blubbered all the way home," but found that after the release of crying, she had reached an uneasy reconciliation with finding Lane guilty: "I thought it's a shitty thing to have to do, but I didn't make too much more of it."

Although Peggy ultimately had determined that Lane was guilty of a murder committed during a robbery, she remained unsure that what had happened the night of the killing was as simple as everyone else thought. More important for what was to come, the guilt deliberations had laid a groundwork of relationships, personality conflicts, and assumptions that would control the jury's dynamics when they met again to decide if Lane should live or die. Most of the jury believed Peggy was a "problem juror" who was distracted by phantom concerns and required gentle handling lest she become too emotional. The twelfth juror in particular had assumed an antagonistic role toward her. He apparently felt it necessary to act as a brusque ballast to any of Peggy's efforts to untether the jury from the stark image of the shooting. Peggy's nature was inclined toward Hamlet-like questionings, but the jabbing juror was in no mood for Shakespeare; nor were the other jurors. And because these attitudes toward Peggy had been molded during the guilt deliberations, the other jurors were likely to discount future opinions that Peggy might voice.

The other jurors were less likely to realize that the deliberations also had caused tendrils of self-doubt to take root in Peggy's mind. Not only had Peggy, one of the youngest jurors, felt that her views were curtly dismissed by the others as the deliberations went on, she was convinced that she had been inarticulate in voicing her thoughts. She had become emotional by crying in front of the other jurors. Already finely tuned to subtle visual and verbal cues, Peggy had no trouble recognizing that almost all the other jurors had adopted a patronizing stance toward her, approaching her as someone who was flighty and emotionally high strung. Hardest of all, though, was that Peggy herself had concluded that the other jurors had been right all along, that all of her questioning and scrutiny had merely been flights of fancy leading to a dead end: "It was significant that I left [the guilt deliberations] feeling like something is wrong with me because everybody got it, and I made it harder than it was supposed to be." Peggy felt particularly sheepish that her doubts about the customer's testimony had required an elaborate gearing up of the court's machinery—the calling in of the lawyers, the gathering of the court personnel and bailiffs, the formal reconvening in the courtroom—just so that she alone could hear the testimony reread. She felt guilty that they were "doing all this for me," and she burned with the embarrassment of the student who is holding the entire class back.

Although some of the jurors later speculated that Peggy had not understood that the death penalty was a possibility when she was selected as a juror, in fact she was quite aware that finding Steven Lane guilty of murder with special circumstances meant that a penalty trial lay ahead. At this point, she was undecided on whether she favored a life or a death sentence for Lane. Already feeling the emotional weight of having convicted someone of a crime that at a minimum meant he would spend the rest of his life in prison, Peggy did not dwell on what might lay ahead as the court recessed for several weeks. Instead, she took the time to try to catch up with her work and family and to let some of the emotional sting from the guilt deliberations subside.

As the penalty phase began and the prosecutor unveiled for the first time Lane's lengthy list of prior crimes, he no doubt hoped that learning about Lane's extensive criminal past would jump-start the jury after the lull between the penalty and guilt stages. If this was his intention, it worked well, as the testimony elicited angry murmurs in the jury box. As Ken and the Chorus reported, watching Lane's rap sheet come alive through the victims' testimony quickly made them see Lane as an incorrigible individual who sought out criminal activity rather than trying to change his ways. They also came away from the testimony appalled with the revolving door that the prison system had provided for Lane despite numerous convictions, a revolving door that confirmed their inner suspicions that the criminal justice system could never live up to a promise of keeping Steven Lane off the streets.

Peggy also found herself becoming angry as she heard about Lane's history of criminal activity. She was more affected by the assault convictions than the robbery convictions, as the assaults "seemed more violent than holding up a store with a gun," an impression reinforced by vivid testimony on how Lane had "beat the tar" out of one of the victims in a brawl. Even at this juncture, though, Peggy found that her natural inclination to distrust simple explanations tempered her reaction to Lane's priors in a way different from the other jurors. The other jurors, for instance, had been extremely troubled by an incident where Lane had become embroiled in an altercation with several police officers as he was being fingerprinted after an arrest; the fight had heightened many jurors' concerns about how Lane would act in prison. Peggy, on the other hand, felt that "just by listening to it all, I thought, well, I can imagine this police officer ticked him off in some way—not that he has the right not to cooperate under those circumstances—but I just thought there were probably two sides to that story."

As with the guilt phase, Peggy provided a detailed recounting of the prosecution's arguments and evidence for the death penalty that was consistent with the other jurors. Unlike most of the other jurors, however, Peggy did not find that the prosecution's case had her strongly leaning toward the death penalty. She had been alarmed by the violence exhibited by Lane's assaults and had found herself "mad" at him for committing a series of crimes, but still was undecided on the proper punishment. She found herself wondering how Lane had ended up going down such a self-destructive path, suspecting that he had not simply stumbled into such a life. As the defense took control of the witness stand to present their case in mitigation, Peggy was open to hearing, and even curious, about "the other side" of the Steven Lane story.

As Peggy listened to the evidence, she was a receptive audience. Unlike the other jurors who saw individuals' acts as basic free-will choices between good and evil, Peggy saw individuals almost as human supercolliders, their personalities buffeted and shaped in unseen ways by the numerous events, people, and influences that they come into contact with: "People are very complex . . . we have psychological factors, spiritual things going on . . . so that something may appear senseless on a superficial level, but not be on another level." Peggy declined to answer questions about whether certain hypothetical circumstances would make her more or less likely to impose the death penalty, because she saw singling out one factor without knowing how it fit into the intricate weaving of all the factors that cause an event as a hopeless task. Likewise, she objected to a question of whether she thought Lane should "pay for his crime": "I don't know—I guess what I'm trying to say is I'm very much aware that people are complex individuals and there's not just one little spark of a thing that makes a person who he is. His social background, choices he's made—it just sounds so simple to say 'I think he's an individual who needs to pay for causing death'—the wording is too trite."

Perhaps most powerfully, Peggy held on to the hope of redemption for Steven. Peggy had strong religious convictions that included the idea that any individual can redeem himself and become a better person. One of her first comments was "I believe change in a person is possible," and that attitude consistently surfaced when she discussed the evidence. Her faith that people can change also was the source of her belief that someone can do an act that is horrible without being irredeemably evil. Peggy believed that people with good in their hearts can end up in bad situations. Asked if she thought Lane's murder of the clerk was "depraved," she replied, "I thought his conduct was depraved but he wasn't—there's a difference between how you act and who you are."

Although Peggy's worldview made her more receptive to the idea of a life sentence than many capital jurors, she was unwilling to vote for life without first being convinced that Steven Lane had humanity in him worth saving. This meant that she wanted to try to gain some understanding of how he had become trapped in a repeating cycle of robberies and incarceration, culminating in the shooting of the store clerk. Peggy might have faith that even good people can go astray, but she needed to believe that good existed in Steven Lane.

When Peggy heard Steven's mother and sister testify about the loss of his brother and how he felt responsible for his brother's death, Peggy was deeply moved: "I was really distressed after hearing about the brother, I had a pain in my chest, tears surfacing, and then I sobbed." More than any other juror, Peggy stepped into the shoes of the thirteen year-old Steven Lane and imagined the emotional blow of losing a brother, feeling responsible for the death because they had snuck off together to experiment with alcohol, and then shouldering the guilt of watching the brother's death cast his family into despair. In particular, Peggy was affected by a part of the episode that only she mentioned: After the police came to the scene of his brother's death, Steven had desperately wanted to go home, but the police made him stay there as they tried to determine what had happened. This gave rise to a painful image in Peggy's mind: "They painted this picture—I could just see it, here's this kid who's suffered a traumatic blow and then there's these adults around him not seeing the child."

For Peggy, the vision of a bewildered, terrified, and distraught thirteen-year-old whose world has just collapsed around him, having to wait while his brother's body is taken away and the police investigate, poignantly captured the tragedy of the entire episode involving Lane's brother's death: "Here's a kid who was involved in a traumatic experience and I think now that our society today would realize that's a lot for kids to deal with . . . and somehow we would say, 'This kid needs help.'" Peggy had little trouble believing that Steven's loss of his brother and his sense that the family, especially his father, blamed him had started a downward slide that gradually sent his life into a depressing cycle of crime that Steven did not know how to escape. She stressed that before his brother's death, all indications were that Steven was a loving and good kid.

In that traumatized thirteen-year-old kid, Peggy saw the embers of a person still worth saving despite all of the sadness he had since caused. This was especially true because she saw no evidence that anyone had ever attempted to fan those embers of goodness back to life, either through counseling during his long stays in prison or by giving him a second chance when back on the streets. When asked if rehabilitation had been important to her decision, she replied, "It was very much on my mind because we didn't know if he had received any help. It diminished the effects of his priors for me, because I didn't know what had happened to him—I might have felt completely different if I knew someone had tried a lot to help him and he had just resisted." Absent such evidence, though, Peggy was not willing to give up on the chance that Steven Lane still could accomplish some good, even if only in prison.

In arriving at her conclusion that life in prison was the only appropriate sentence for Steven, Peggy embodied almost every attitude that shaped those jurors in other cases who argued most strongly for life. First, she had emerged from the guilt phase after difficult deliberations still harboring questions about Lane's actions. A bruising battle at the guilt phase almost always presages that at least some jurors will enter the penalty phase leaning heavily toward life because they still entertain doubts. These doubts almost always center not on whether the defendant is completely innocent, but on whether he or she had killed intentionally or had been a major participant in the killing. Consequently, like Peggy, these jurors enter the penalty phase with reservations that the defendant is guilty of murder to such an extent that he or she should even be eligible for the death penalty, let alone deserving of a sentence of death.

Peggy also shared the worldview of many jurors who strongly favored life in her belief that one's actions are not entirely a matter of free will, but can be shaped and influenced by external forces. As another juror with this outlook noted: "I was completely different than the others because they stuck with the crime more than I stuck with the crime. I went more with the mitigating circumstances of his background, whereas they went with his crime." This juror described how as she intently listened to the judge's instructions the words "'mitigating circumstances' slapped me in the face," an effect that she was soon to discover had not been shared by many of her fellow jurors. Like Peggy, she found herself in a tug-of-war with the other jurors in her case over whether the penalty decision should focus on the brutality of the murder or on the effects of the defendant's upbringing.

Either of these circumstances alone—doubts about the extent of the defendant's guilt or a particular openness to the idea of mitigation—is likely to forge a juror favoring life. Peggy, however, possessed an additional attribute: As she repeatedly noted, she believed strongly in the power of redemption and embraced an essential hope that people could become better. And jurors who voice such hope—who we might call "Hope jurors"—tend to be particularly strong in favor of a life sentence instead of death. As Cathy, a Hope juror in a different case who largely shared Peggy's beliefs, wrote in a journal that she kept during the trial:

> [T]he big question is still, does the defendant deserve to die for what he did? If he spends the rest of his life in jail, it costs taxpayers a lot of money, but he might be able to be rehabilitated. After all, he's never been in serious trouble before. Maybe it has scared him enough that he could turn his life around . . . I can only hope that he will, while in prison, find himself. I hope that he can somehow be a positive role model for his daughter, and for others; that he can discover a hidden talent or skill and turn it into a way of life. Some may say that's a very naive or "rose colored glasses" opinion, but it's simply one of Hope—which is all he has left.

Cathy's support for a life sentence based on hope was, as with Peggy and many of the other Hope jurors who voiced this view in other cases, underpinned by strong religious beliefs. Cathy noted in the middle of the trial that "I can't tell you how much I've prayed over this, for the wisdom to do the right thing." Unlike Peggy, however, Cathy had others on her jury who believed that the defendant's horrible childhood had largely doomed him to a life of crime, and her jury returned a life sentence. Cathy's final journal entry wonderfully resonates with how her religious beliefs were interwoven with her punishment decision: "One final note—last night I attended choir practice for the first time [since we handed down the life sentence]. Call it coincidence, call it an omen, but I call it the answer to a prayer: the first song we rehearsed was entitled 'We Choose Life.' And we did."

Because this group of jurors saw a glimmer of hope in the defendant, they also frequently felt sympathy for him as an individual. These were the jurors most likely to ask with worried concern how the defendant in their case was faring in jail. One Hope juror who had viewed the defendant in her case as "a lost child" had immediately asked at the start of her interview, "Do you know [the defendant's] situation at this point? I was hoping you did. I just had visions of him either being killed, or of him committing suicide is more of what I suspected. I thought many times about calling the judge." Ironically, the Hope jurors' concern for the defendant sometimes caused these jurors to wonder at first if giving a death sentence might not be the kinder and more humane act. Cathy, for instance, had mused in her journal: "Then there's Death. Which is worse, spending thirty, forty or even fifty years behind bars, or living in Paradise where there is no worry, no fear, only great joy and happiness? I believe with all my heart that there are greater lives for us after we leave this one. Given all the horror stories one hears about prison, I just can't help but wonder if we wouldn't be doing him a favor by choosing death. My own faith in God has certainly been strengthened by this experience." In the end, though, Cathy and the Hope jurors in other cases still thought it better to give the defendant another chance at life.

It will come as little surprise that the members of a jury who did not share a Hope juror's feelings often saw the Hope juror as too emotional and unable to follow the law. They often greeted the Hope juror's expressions of sympathy for the defendant with a coldness bordering on hostility. Even other jurors who had supported a life sentence often described a Hope juror on their jury as having felt an "unnatural attachment" for the defendant. And, of course, in Peggy's case, her fellow jurors came to believe, as one Chorus member put it, that Peggy "more or less came to feel that she was there to save him."

∞

Peggy's attitudes and beliefs had thus made her receptive to the evidence that Lane's lawyers had presented, but she was not oblivious to the likelihood that the other Lane jurors might not respond to Steven's life story in a similar way. Peggy herself found "it a little bit disturbing" that someone could grow up in what appeared to be a fairly normal household and yet end up a murderer: "It would have been easier in a way [to understand his situation] if they had burned him with cigarette butts." Still, she was keenly convinced that the family's failure to respond to the trauma that Steven had experienced as a thirteen-year-old was "very emotionally neglectful, and that's a form of abuse—there may have been love and laughter as well, but his individual needs were not addressed." She sensed, however, that the other jurors were not so certain. Although they, too, had been very moved by the testimony of Lane's mother and sister, afterward, they were "sort of like: What are we to do with that?"

As the defense psychiatrist took the stand, Peggy hoped that he might provide the insight for making sense of what had happened that would swing the other jurors in the direction of life. This was not to happen, though, and Peggy started to feel dismay as she saw her fellow jurors' reactions: "The other jurors thought he was very unprofessional, he didn't have the exact amount of money that he charged the court for his expertise. . . . He said, 'Oh, is that important? All right,' opened his briefcase and got out his calculator and said, 'I'll figure it for you.' So they thought that was very unprofessional . . . and I just thought, well, jeez, probably he has an accountant or a secretary who handles all the billing and makes his appointments." Nor did Peggy share the other jurors' skepticism that the psychiatrist was biased: "[The prosecutor asked the defense psychiatrist] how many times do you testify for the defense and how many times do you testify for the prosecuting attorney. Well, he testified a lot more times for the defense. . . . My thing was maybe that's good. That people commit crimes for good reasons, and he's helping, and it didn't shock me, like 'He's a paid defense expert.'"

The psychiatrist's testimony was also the moment where Peggy fully realized just how differently she was reacting toward all of the different actors in the courtroom drama compared to the rest of the jurors. Peggy thought the district attorney had become overly dramatic in cross-examining the psychiatrist: "and I was watching the prosecution attorney and he was trying to make [the psychiatrist] look so ridiculous, you know, he'd say"—Peggy's tone became incredulous—'And you trusted [Lane], you thought he was sincere?' And the psychiatrist would say"—Peggy softened her voice—'yes, he seemed sincere.'" Peggy found the prosecutor's dramatic style somewhat pompous and even "comical" in dealing with the psychiatrist. More than his style, however, Peggy felt that the prosecutor had crossed a line with his cross-examination of the psychiatrist, becoming "offensive and demeaning." Until then, she thought that the prosecutor had been hard-hitting but generally fair when questioning witnesses. Now, while she still "respected" the prosecutor for doing his job, she no longer "admired" him. The other jurors, however "thought [the prosecutor] was very effective" and that his cross-examination had been necessary to reveal the psychiatrist to be a charlatan.

As Peggy watched the psychiatrist falter before the prosecutor's questioning, she did not hold out much hope that the defense would yet save the day through a closing argument that made clear why Steven Lane's circumstances called out for a sentence of life and not death. In the battle of attorneys, the prosecutor had gained the upper hand from the start. From the jury room discussion, Peggy learned that the lead defense attorney had alienated some jurors as early as *voir dire* by adopting a "gruff" attitude in his questioning: "Quite a few [of the jurors] did not like the way he treated them at *voir dire*." And, Peggy felt, that once the guilt phase had begun, the defense attorney had really started to lose ground: "The defense's strategy seemed to be 'Okay, you've gotta prove it, we're just here, we'll show up.'" Peggy said that one juror remarked that the "defense attorney wouldn't look him in the eye," which that juror took as an unmistakable sign that the attorney knew that the case was a lost cause. The full damage of the defense's strategy of claiming Lane's innocence at the guilt phase was not fully felt, however, until the penalty phase, when the defense attorney argued that Lane was sorry for what had happened and presented his case for life. According to Peggy, for the defense attorney who had "really laid it on" at the guilt phase about how the prosecutor had not proven that Lane was the killer to now argue that Lane was remorseful caused him to "lose extreme credibility."

More generally, the prosecutor was doing a better job "by far" than the lead defense attorney in communicating with the jury and seemed far more committed to trying to win the case. Peggy observed that, "The prosecutor had a very good manner with the jury—he would do things like, after the jury was selected, give us a look like 'I really like this group.'" Although by the end Peggy would conclude that the other jurors were "*overly* impressed with him," she understood why they liked him. During jury selection, for instance, she had felt that the prosecutor had shown a lot more interest in her life than the defense attorneys, an interest that made her like him.

Compared to the district attorney's professional air, the defense attorney was "kind of sloppy," even to the point that the prosecution's charts were nicely made and professional looking and the defense exhibits were not. Even Peggy, who was not inclined to go by outward appearances, noted that the prosecutor's more professional demeanor meant that "he had a confidence, a presence about him." By contrast, the defense seemed to be projecting an attitude of defeat as the penalty phase progressed: "The jury got the feeling the defense was just laying down and dying after the long list of [Lane's] prior crimes came in."

Despite Peggy's wish that the defense counsel had done more to develop how a thirteen-year-old child could suffer long-term effects from the guilt and horror that Steven must have felt from his brother's death, she also expressed an unusual understanding of a defense lawyer's predicament. At the guilt phase, Peggy had not reacted as negatively to the defense's strategy as had the other jurors, although she admitted she was "curious" about some of the tactical decisions that had backfired, such as claiming Lane's complete innocence despite the videotape. When it came to the penalty phase, though, Peggy said that she had "the feeling that the defense attorneys were fighting harder for him than he was himself," an observation that may very well have been true.

Especially in capital cases, defendants often present immense challenges to their lawyers. Sometimes defendants refuse to cooperate in developing their life stories because they want to protect their families from having to air in the courtroom shameful family secrets of sexual molestation and child abuse. Sometimes defendants adamantly resist any suggestion that they suffer from a mental illness, even where the evidence points strongly in that direction. Before he pled guilty to murder in exchange for a life sentence, Ted Kozinski, the "Unabomber," frequently clashed with his defense lawyers because they had wanted to present evidence of mental illness in mitigation. Some defendants—and this happens more frequently than most people would suspect—will even want to ask the jury or judge to sentence them to death, a situation that can present a terrible ethical dilemma for defense attorneys who are supposed to defend a client zealously.

If, as sometimes happens, Lane had given in to a sense of despair after the jury convicted him of capital murder, his lawyers very well may have been fighting harder for Lane than he was himself, a situation that can greatly hamper an attorney's efforts at the penalty phase. For Peggy, the defense had not needed to "connect the dots" to convince her that Steven's life had been ill-fated after the tragedy of his brother's death: "I was able to grasp it and say 'God damn.' To me it was right there. I thought that the crime in this case was that the kid didn't get help." However, after hearing the prosecutor's and defense lawyer's closing arguments, Peggy had an ominous feeling that she alone had connected the dots in a way that argued for life.

As Peggy began to describe the jury's deliberations at the penalty phase, her voice noticeably dropped and her manner became more tense. She recalled thinking as the jury retired to the jury room that all of the jurors were "somewhat in a state of shock." Her pessimism about what was to come was not allayed when the very first topic caused controversy:

"We actually debated whether or not we should ask for a copy of the jury instructions." Peggy found the hesitancy to ask for the very instructions that were to guide how they decided if someone was to live or die almost surreal: "The debate seemed so silly to me. When you look at the instructions and read them, there's so much in there—to even wonder if you should ask for the directions is ridiculous." Some jurors were worried, though, that asking for the directions might cause the judge and lawyers to conclude that they had not been attentive in the courtroom and that "they would think we couldn't be trusted with this [decision]." For Peggy, on the other hand, that the jury even had to ask for the instructions and that some jurors were reluctant to do so "reflected how much we were on our own" and made the jury room feel even more like a world unto itself.

Until the deliberations began, Peggy had been able to push into the background her dread of how the other jurors would react to her after the guilt phase. Now that the moment was upon her, Peggy felt "extremely, extremely uncomfortable. I had a feeling that people judged me as being very sensitive and that they kind of had to walk on eggs around me, that I was kind of a problem juror." Despite her hands shaking under the table from nervousness every time she spoke, Peggy tried to disguise her discomfort and forced herself to participate as the jury began listing the aggravating and mitigating circumstances. Her efforts to become part of the discussion, however, were not keeping her from feeling "very, very young and small."

As the discussion unfolded, Peggy identified eight jurors who were leaning toward the death penalty, some very strongly. She thought that many had made up their minds for the death penalty as far back as the guilt stage and for them "it was going through the motions, you know, 'okay, how do we get this death sentence out, what do we do now?'" The discussion around the table, however, also held out some hope. Although Peggy's foreboding that she alone had been firmly persuaded that life was the proper punishment was confirmed, three other jurors appeared to be undecided, holding out the possibility of as many as four life votes including her own. For a moment, Peggy did not feel quite as isolated. These other three jurors were "very quiet and kept to themselves," but Peggy held out particular hope that Mark, the youngest of the three undecided jurors, might end up as an ally. Mark was about Peggy's age, and even after the turmoil of the guilt deliberations, she was "comfortable" talking with him and felt that he at least would listen to what she said.

Peggy's narrative of the jury's initial discussion of the evidence was consistent with that of the other jurors. The sheets of paper that the jury had taped to the wall for listing aggravating factors soon were full—details of Lane's lengthy history of crime, his failure to reform, his clashes with the police. The list of evidence favoring a life sentence, however, caused much more controversy. The discussion's main focus, naturally, was on the defense's centerpiece of their case for life, Steven's loss of his brother. As Peggy described how the jurors expressed their views, she explained that many simply could not believe that a single episode, even a very tragic one, could shape a thirteen-year-old boy's destiny: "All the other jurors had great empathy for this thirteen-year-old boy who lost his brother, and we had a lot of feeling for it, but we didn't know what to do with it! . . . If we could somehow tie it in, and say it was so damaging psychologically, you know, in some way make us realize that it could permanently affect a person. . . . And then the rest [of the jurors] kind of just disregarded it because, you know, 'so what?' You know, that's real sad, but it wasn't enough to erase this long string of crime, you couldn't make sense of why, why wasn't he able to overcome that? How come he didn't get over it?"

As the jury concluded its first day, Peggy's foreboding resurfaced as she glanced at the charts and thought about the jurors' comments. The discussion increasingly had seemed to "just kind of go through the motions," and Peggy had seen the focus shift almost entirely to a discussion of why a death sentence was necessary: "It got to where we were just going around the table and everybody was saying negative, negative, negative, negative and here I would say, 'but . . . '" Peggy tried to raise the idea that the jury had no idea if Lane had ever received counseling during his prison stays. "I would say, yes, this is an incredibly long list of felonies and, yes, they're horrible, but we don't know whether he ever received help—this part was blank." The other jurors, however, just "assumed that he went through [counseling] and left it at that." At one point, Peggy felt that the deliberations had become "kind of pointless," and she pushed her chair back and began to read a magazine "because most of them weren't open to discussion or talk."

Most frustrating was that the undecided jurors "seemed like they weren't really participating. You know, they weren't going, 'Tell me more about it! Why do you think that?' They were just quiet." Not only was this lack of exchange and debate at odds with Peggy's notion of what a jury was about, but it left her arguments sitting starkly out there as the only comments in favor of life, unable even to spark further inquiry from the undecided jurors. In Peggy-like fashion, though, after expressing her frustration with the lack of any dynamic discussion—"It wasn't like we were arguing, then debating, then bringing up stuff"—she quickly added, "But maybe for the people who were undecided, listening to all that the other people were saying helped them. My gut feeling is that they worked it out on their own."

The morning of the second day saw the jury take its first formal vote, and the results were not promising for the prospects of a life sentence. The announcement that the tally had totaled nine votes for death and three votes for life meant that one of the undecided jurors had quietly switched to death even before the vote. The news quickly got worse from Peggy's perspective. Almost immediately the Chorus member who had voted for life stated that she was changing her mind and would vote for death in the future. Her defection obviously tilted the table even more strongly toward death, but Peggy appreciated that the woman had at least struggled with the decision before deciding for death: "I think deep down she felt the death penalty was appropriate, she was just a little hesitant in making up her mind . . . so it was sort of like writing down life and handing it in made her aware that that's not what she really wanted."

The Chorus member's change of vote, however, meant that only Peggy and Mark, the younger male juror, had not decided in favor of the death penalty. The two had become friends over the course of the trial, and Peggy was grateful that he had not written her off as a "problem juror." She, however, also was troubled by the idea that he might be voting for life to support her rather than because of his conscience. After the second day of deliberations, Peggy approached Mark as they waited for their rides home and "said something to the effect that I was aware he might be voting to support me and that I would hope he didn't feel that he needed to." In saying this, Peggy was trying to do the "right thing" by liberating Mark from any sense of a need to support her if he had actually decided that death was the proper verdict.

Mark did not respond to Peggy at the time, but when a vote was taken early the next day he did switch his vote. Mark's crossing over left Peggy as the lone holdout for a life sentence, and it seemed to her to move the deliberations to a more personal level: "It was like 'Oh, God, now we've got to work with Peggy again.'" And while she had antici-pated that the pressure on her would heighten if Mark changed his vote,

she had failed to foresee just how isolated she was to feel as the deliberations moved into the next stage with her as the only holdout for life. As
Peggy later observed, "To this day, I think, oh, God, what would have
happened if I just hadn't said anything to Mark."

Peggy's perception that Mark switching his vote had left her far more
vulnerable to the majority's pressure has strong support in the psychological literature that explores why individuals conform to the majority
viewpoint. Once Peggy lost her last ally at the jury table, she became
subject to pressures and self-doubts that many of us never would guess
could affect us.

In a brilliantly simple experiment from the 1950s, social psychologist Solomon Asch placed four lines on a board at the front of a room.
The left side of the board had a single line, the "standard" line. The right
side of the board had three "comparison" lines of different lengths, one
of which clearly matched the "standard" line and two of which clearly
did not. The participants in the study were asked to undertake the exceedingly easy task of picking which of the three comparison lines
matched the standard line.

Unsurprisingly, when experiment subjects were in the room alone,
they chose the correct comparison line almost every time. A fascinating
difference occurred, however, when Asch placed a subject in the room
with several other individuals who were not real subjects, but confederates of the experimenter. Asch had these confederates go first, and each
deliberately chose the same incorrect comparison line. Asch then asked
the unwitting subject which comparison line he or she thought matched
the standard one. Although the subjects' physical senses told them that
the other people's answers had to be wrong, an astonishing 75 percent of
the subjects chose the incorrect line identified by the others at least
once. In other words, without any social pressures being exerted other
than hearing other people give a different answer, only 25 percent of
those tested trusted their own judgment every time on a task as simple as
judging the length of a line.

The Asch experiments vividly highlight people's desire to conform
and the fear of being wrong. In interviews after the experiment, the

subjects who went along with the majority said that they did not trust their own judgment because they had believed that the majority must be right, thinking that perhaps their eyesight was failing them or that they had misunderstood the experimenter's instructions and were to judge the line's width rather than length. The certainty with which the confederates chose the incorrect answer also influenced the conforming subjects. One subject, for example, explained, "If they had been doubtful I probably would have changed, but they answered with such confidence."[1] As other researchers have noted from studies like the Asch line study, "The judgments of others are taken to be a more or less trustworthy source of information about the objective reality."[2]

The Asch experiments also give credence to Peggy's sense that both her own attitude and the jury's dynamic changed perceptibly once she was reduced to being the lone holdout. Asch found that the pressure to conform turns more on whether the majority is unanimous in presenting an erroneous choice than on the sheer number in the majority. In a variation on his experiment, for instance, Asch had seven confederates choose the incorrect line, but now also had one confederate choose the correct line before the subject made his or her choice. Although the subject heard far more individuals choose the incorrect line than in the original experiment, the presence of a single supporter of the choice that the subject thought was correct dramatically increased the chances that the subject would resist the majority viewpoint. Asch noted, "It is clear that the presence of . . . one other individual who responded correctly was sufficient to deplete the power of the majority, and in some cases to destroy it." Perhaps even more critically for Peggy's state of mind after Mark switched his vote, Asch discovered that when he further varied the experiment so that the one confederate who initially responded correctly then "deserted" to the majority's incorrect position in the middle of the experiment, the subject's ability to resist the majority collapsed: "The experience of having had and then lost a partner restored the majority effect to its full force." Asch concluded that his results "point[ed] to a fundamental psychological difference between the condition of being alone and having a minimum of human support."[3]

Further research has identified additional situations and factors that increase the likelihood that an individual will adopt the majority's position and may help explain why so many holdouts eventually change their votes. Experiments have found, for instance, that the pressure to conform increases where individuals must announce their positions publicly rather than out of earshot.[4] And while some jurors reported that their juries had used secret ballots and that they had guessed incorrectly for several ballots as to a holdout's identity, the very nature of a jury's decision-making process necessitates that a juror's position ultimately will come into the open. Certainly in Peggy's case, no one was in doubt from the start that she was the juror at odds with the majority's position.

Research also suggests that the conformity pressures which Asch identified at work where the question is one of simple fact become even more powerful when the question to be decided is based on values, especially if frequent and open votes are taken.[5] Few decisions, of course, are more value-based than the death penalty decision, a judgment that requires the jury to make a moral and normative determination of whether someone deserves to live or die. Also relevant to the capital jury's decision, because the jurors can choose only between life and death, are experimental findings that the pressure to conform to the majority's view is further elevated when a group is given only two options from which to choose.

The psychological literature is rich with these types of findings about the human desire to conform, findings that often are counterintuitive. Most of us, for instance, when asked how we would respond if we were the test subject in Asch's line study believe that we would resist the majority's influence and give the correct response; yet research consistently shows that, in reality, most of us would yield to the majority's judgment.[6] This tendency to think that we would courageously act in an independent way, when in fact we often do not, is a phenomenon that researchers call "positive illusions." Psychologists Julie Woodzicka and Marianne LaFrance found an illuminating example of positive illusions when they studied the difference between how women believe they would respond if asked sexually harassing questions during a job interview and how women actually do respond in such situations.[7] When questioned in the abstract about how they would react if asked a harassing question (e.g., "Do you think it is important for women to wear bras to work?"), over two-thirds of the women subjects (68 percent) stated that, at a minimum, they would refuse to answer such a question; over a quarter (28 percent) reported that they would leave the interview or confront the interviewer. Yet when a group of women actually were asked such harassing questions during what they thought was a real job interview, the subjects were not able to achieve even the limited ideal of directly refusing to answer the question. In fact, a majority (52 percent) of the women "ignored the harassment" altogether and answered the question. Even the 48 percent who did not give an answer did not directly refuse to respond to the question; instead, in general, they politely asked why the interviewer had asked the question or requested clarification as a way of trying to refocus the question. Not a single subject directly refused to answer the question, let alone confronted the interviewer or left the interview. As the researchers concluded, the experiment was another example of "the chasm that exists between how people think they will respond to a stressful event and how they actually do."

Asch and a succession of researchers have uncovered a fascinating wealth of information about the psychological dynamics of the pressure to conform. In the end, though, the desire to conform may have a physiological basis, as well. A recent experiment measuring the brain activity of subjects who thought that they were being excluded from a group discovered that a response was triggered in the part of the brain that is associated with physical pain like that felt from a physical blow. As one of the researchers noted, it may be that as part of their evolution, humans developed a physical response of pain to rejection by others as a self-survival technique to "make sure we don't stray too far from the group."[8] Whatever the origins of the response, the powerful pull of conformity can be observed readily, whether on the playground or in the workplace. And, of course, such pressures come into play in the jury room. For those of us who have whispered to ourselves that we would play Henry Fonda's role in the jury room, the sobering reality is that many of us would not live up to our hopes and expectations.

As Peggy sat at the table after the vote shifted to eleven to one, she felt a remarkable mix of emotions. She still was firmly convinced that Steven Lane did not deserve to die, that his life was worth saving. She also had begun to reconcile herself to the idea that she was simply seeing a different Steven Lane from the other jurors. Peggy's realization that a fundamental divide existed between her perception of Lane and that of the other jurors came not only from the discussion of the big issues, such as how to understand his childhood trauma, but also from her different reaction to "little things." For instance, Peggy recalled how some jurors expressed anger that Lane had "casually" picked up a paper and started reading it while the jury was still in the courtroom, an action that they "thought showed he didn't care." Peggy, on the other hand, thought that Lane was feeling "very uncomfortable" and, at that time, and, like many people, tried to "divert his mind" by concentrating on something else, much as Peggy herself had done when she had pushed her chair back and read a magazine when the deliberations had become intolerable to her. Peggy was starting to conclude, "We just saw two different people."

Yet while Peggy was more certain than ever that Steven deserved life and not death, she was uncertain how long her resolve could last. Peggy had started to experience trouble sleeping as the penalty phase began, and her insomnia had grown worse during the deliberations. Her exhaustion was starting to wear her down at the very time when she felt she needed to be her strongest. In describing her reactions and emotions as the deliberations progressed, Peggy used words like "small" and "young" with increasing frequency. The worst part was that she could not easily opt to drop out of the active deliberations as some other jurors had done. Peggy had become the focus of the deliberations, and in some sense every question and every comment was directed at her, asking her to justify how she could still be voting life now that eleven were for the death penalty. Peggy was in a very difficult bind. She already had fruitlessly raised what she saw as the logical arguments for life—his childhood trauma, the lack of any counseling as either a child or an adult, and what she saw as a fairly good prison record. Did she now try to express her more intangible reasons for supporting life, reasons that were in many ways far more personal and emotional and intuitive?

In retrospect, Peggy was not sure whether her next efforts resulted from an uncertainty of how to proceed or a hope that sharing her more personal views might persuade someone to join her, but she did try to explain why she was still in Steven Lane's corner arguing for life. She tried to express how she could "relate" to Steven Lane because she had a sister who was extremely close to her, making it easy for her to imagine the horror that Steven had felt when his brother died and he felt responsible. She also tried to communicate the sense of loss that she knew Steven must have undergone by drawing on an experience she had during the trial. Peggy's young daughter had been having nightmares, so Peggy and her husband allowed the girl to sleep in a sleeping bag next to their bed. One night after hearing about Steven's brother, Peggy looked over at her daughter and had that heart-stopping moment familiar to many parents of young children: She was sure that her daughter was dead. "So I had the same putting myself in his place, here's someone that I love dearly and she's laying there dead! I mean, I had this horror, it was terrible, I felt the horror that he felt when he found his brother dead."

Although Peggy's description of these sentiments exposed her to the criticism of sounding emotional rather than logical, what she was feeling—the closeness to her sister, the horror at thinking her daughter was dead—could not be doubted. She made one other comment in the jury room, however, that she later wished with all her might she never had made. As the jurors arguing for death pressed her about Lane's lack of remorse and humanity, Peggy groped for a way to express her sense that his action was not simply the action of a cold-hearted killer. After cautiously asking "Have you ever looked at something and your brain uses a sense that you normally don't use?" Peggy told how earlier in the trial, when the prosecution had introduced the arrest photos, she had found them "haunting" because she saw "pain and confusion" in his expression and eyes. On some level, Peggy knew that her reaction to the photos ran the risk of sounding like New Age malarkey, but she was running out of ways to explain her position.

The other jurors' reaction was swift and sure: "They made fun of it, they thought it was the most ridiculous thing they ever heard." In particular, the comment rekindled the twelfth juror's antagonism, as he pulled out his driver's license, thrust it in front of her, and sarcastically challenged her to tell what she saw from the picture, as if she were presenting herself as some sort of psychic. With the cool-headed perspective of hindsight, Peggy could think of several things that she wished she had told him that she saw, none flattering, but the other jurors' reactions had sent her spinning, and witty comebacks were the last thing popping into her mind. Instead, she actually found herself looking at the picture on the driver's license, thinking "Well, he's right, I don't see anything—I mean, I looked at this picture and then I sort of doubted myself, well, maybe I *am* kind of far out there." It did occur to her to say that just because she did not see anything in a driver's license photo did not mean a photograph cannot capture a person's emotion, "but I couldn't articulate that, I couldn't say it out loud, I didn't have the power."

The photo incident stands out as a critical turning point in Peggy's ability to continue insisting that her "line" was the correct length despite the majority's choice of another "line." Part of the importance of the episode lay in the reaction of the other jury members to her comments and the sense of hopelessness it engendered in Peggy that they would ever see her point of view. The incident, however, also caused her self-doubts from the guilt deliberations to fully bob back to the surface: "I was feeling extremely small and childish, because here is this guy ridiculing me and I kind of just sit there, instead of saying 'Well, God damn it!' So how did I respond? I just sort of didn't say anything more after that one, so I was feeding into it."

Even prior to this episode Peggy had not been completely immune from moments where it simply seemed easier to give in to a death verdict. "I was feeling very depressed, at moments I was like: Who really cares? Life in prison or death, they're both horrible." But before she had always managed to resist these moments of fatigue by seeking refuge in her certainty that a life sentence was necessary to give Steven a chance to redeem himself. Now her certainty was wavering. She was acutely aware, of course, that she had dragged the deliberations out at the guilt stage only to conclude that she had been wrong. Might not the same process be replaying itself now? "I was very influenced by my thoughts. I was like 'Is there something wrong with me?' They're all so sure, and you know it wasn't that they were undecided for a long time and changed their mind." And while Peggy's fatigue was growing and fissures of doubt were undermining her certainty, she fully sensed that the other jurors' certainty was steadfast: "Basically, they couldn't understand why I didn't have the same answer they did. I think they really felt that they had a responsibility to society to make sure our panel rendered the death verdict. There were so many of them, it was like I was the weak and deformed person that society needs to get rid of. They felt so strongly what they believed, and there were so many of them."

Peggy's temptation to give in to her physical and mental fatigue was accentuated by some majority jurors who were stepping up their expressions of frustration and anger. One juror told how she had gone home the previous night and tried to work out her thoughts and frustrations by writing them down on paper. As she was writing, she started crying because, as Peggy remembered, "she had an overwhelming horror of what would she tell her grandkids if we rendered anything but a death verdict." Peggy was especially struck by the strength of the other jurors' stated convictions compared to her inability to state hers forcefully: "You know when you say something you have to say it with power. If you say it in a small way, people just discredit you."

The prevailing theme of the other jurors' appeals was "get your feelings off the defendant and onto the victim—be sensible, be realistic." To Peggy, the twelfth juror in particular seemed to feel that he needed to be the voice of the victim in the jury room, because "I think he felt a personal connection with the victim." As the penalty deliberations had started to stalemate, Peggy entered the jury room one morning to find that the twelfth juror had taped to the wall a poster that he had made at home saying "something like 'No One Remembers the Victim at the Trial.'" In an interesting parallel to the flash of empathy that Peggy had felt for Lane when she momentarily had thought her daughter was dead, the twelfth juror recounted to the jury how he had received a phone call one night during the trial from a hospital telling him that his son had been involved in a horrible car wreck. Fortunately, the son survived the crash, but for several terrible hours the juror had felt the sickening horror of possibly losing someone unexpectedly and never having the chance to say good bye. After his son's accident, Peggy recalled that the twelfth juror "kept pointing out that the victim's family never got to say good-bye—I think he was really affected by what happened to his son and felt a connection with the family and how their loved ones felt to wake up the next day and the victim is dead. I think that was really influential for him."

Of all the comments directed her way, the statements that stung the most were the ones suggesting that she was forgetting the victim and his survivors. When asked whether she had felt the sense of loss of the victim's family, Peggy emphatically answered yes. She then told how she had been plagued throughout the trial by thoughts of the victim's children and how they would cope without a father. Her troubled thoughts had spurred her to read *Tiger Eyes* by Judy Blume, a book written from the perspective of a young girl who learns to cope after her father is murdered during a holdup of a 7-Eleven store, a plot eerily close to that of Lane's murder victim.

Peggy did not understand, however, why sympathy for the victim and his family precluded the idea that one also could feel sympathy for the defendant. And, she acknowledged, she had a much fuller sense of who the defendant was compared to the victim, a person who appeared only on a grainy video and whose family did not testify. Peggy knew that this balance of sympathies was grating to the other jurors: "They couldn't understand how I had more sympathy for Steven—it's not that I didn't have any feelings for the victim, but that I didn't have as much sympathy for the victim didn't seem right to them." After one such discussion, Peggy turned to the jury instructions, which explicitly say that "each of you are free to assign whatever moral or sympathetic values to each factor as you choose." She read the instruction out loud as if it could cast a protective spell around her and fend off the others' questioning, but it did not work: "I tried to use it, but it just didn't go over," in part, Peggy thought, because she said it in a "small" way.

Peggy barely made it through the third day of the penalty phase deliberations. Weariness overwhelmed her. The short walk to catch her ride home seemed to require a marathoner's stamina. A simple thought demanded reserves of energy that felt as if they had been depleted long ago. Peggy rode home in a daze, knowing that she could not hold out much longer.

Oddly, the realization that she was on the verge of collapse gave Peggy the foothold to find her way out of what was becoming a hopeless situation. As she thought about how thoroughly the jury was deadlocked and how emotional the deliberations had become, a burst of anger and frustration finally hit her. It was almost like stepping into an outsider's shoes and realizing that the whole process had become "ridiculous." She had an honest difference of opinion with the other jurors, and that was that. A personal resolution that "I'm not going through another day of this" began to form, and Peggy felt a sense of relief well up inside her. Suddenly it seemed so simple. She would walk into the jury room the next day, state the obvious point that neither side was about to persuade the other, and the jury would announce it was deadlocked. For the first time in weeks Peggy experienced glimmers of happiness and looked forward "to getting my life back." Crawling into bed, she had the overwhelmingly comforting thought, "I'll be home by ten-thirty tomorrow morning. I can't wait to get this over with."

Peggy woke up the next morning and prayed, both for the strength to make it through the morning and with a sense of thankfulness that the nightmare was about to be over. "All through this time I was praying a lot more than I normally pray, I was writing letters to God saying 'Help me.'" As Peggy looked through her closet for an outfit, she chose to wear her favorite dress, the one that always made her feel good, thinking "I'm going to wear this dress because it will help me to be confident and say it's over." She kept silently repeating to herself, "It's finally going to be over" as she rode to the courthouse. Even the sound of her heels on the courthouse floor as she walked determinedly to the jury room seemed to rap out a reassuring beat: "I could hear my heels clicking and, you know, I felt really good, they're not going to get me now. I felt, I can do this, it's going to be over!"

As Peggy watched the other jurors take their seats and settle in, she prepared to make her announcement. Her nervousness started to return, but she managed to say before any discussion got underway, "We should deadlock, I'm not going through another day of this." Peggy had not been entirely sure what comments to expect, but what happened was totally unexpected: silence. Total silence. Her statement, which was supposed to end the ordeal by acknowledging what Peggy assumed everyone was feeling, just hung in the air: "Their reaction was sort of like bafflement, like this is not right, what do we do?"

Strangely, if someone had started to argue with her or had become angry, it might have given power to her statement's message that they were deadlocked and that to continue would only mean further pointless, hostile comments. Instead, the quiet that engulfed the jury room called out for someone to do something. Feeling responsible for making a suggestion that had paralyzed the jury into a stunned silence, Peggy said, "I wonder what happens now."

Peggy had intended this to be a rhetorical question to break the silence rather than as an actual inquiry, so the response took her by surprise. According to Peggy, one of the jurors picked up the jury instructions and read a paragraph that the juror explained meant that if the jury did not vote for a death sentence, Lane automatically would get a sentence of life without parole. The juror said to Peggy in an accusatory tone, "So it's over, it's going to go your way." At that point, the juror whom Peggy had viewed as something of a father figure walked over behind the other juror, read the paragraph over her shoulder, and concurred, "That's right, that's what it says." The fact that this was inaccurate made no difference because no one realized it.

The belief that Lane would receive a life sentence if they deadlocked infused the other jurors with renewed energy to try to sway Peggy. Peggy recalled one of the Chorus members declaring, "I am prepared to take as long as we need to take to do this right. We have a responsibility to society. I'm prepared to do this because we have a responsibility." Peggy said she had no doubt what that meant: "Whatever it takes to get Peggy to see [that death is the right answer]. We have a responsibility to help her see what the answer is." Even without the belief that a deadlocked jury meant a life sentence, Peggy said, "I think that most of the jurors really felt that we're going to fail if we deadlock." However, the idea that eleven votes for death would be nullified by one dissenter strengthened their resolve to not become a hung jury. And not only was Peggy aware of the voices expressing the unfairness that her lone vote would now dictate the result, she also was painfully conscious that not a single person was suggesting that she might have a right to her opinion. "No one said, 'Well, you are entitled to your opinion, people have different opinions.' Not one person validated my opinion in any positive way."

The effect on Peggy was devastating. "It was like I had been treading water in this pool, and then I just went under." She recalled standing up and saying "God, I don't believe this," feeling the depression and exhaustion encircling her again, even more suffocating than before as the sickening realization sunk in that "this isn't over." Her ability to reenter the jury room that morning had all been built on thinking that declaring a deadlock would release her. She had placed all of her remaining hope and energy into making one statement that she thought would bring everything to an end—"we should deadlock." Not only had the statement utterly failed to resolve the stalemate, it had reinvigorated the others' efforts to convince her to switch her vote. The thought that her vote would now dictate the final result "was just too much for me—I mean, I had enough left in me to say 'Well, I think we should deadlock' but I didn't have enough in me to say 'It's going to be my way.' . . . It didn't seem right. At that point, it wasn't trial by jury, it was trial by juror Peggy. It didn't seem to be right that it was going to be my way when all these people had strong opinions."

Peggy's recollection of the remainder of the day lacked her usual detailed nuance. Although she lasted the full day of deliberations without changing her vote, this was not because she had marshaled her energy for a defiant last stand. Rather, she simply had succumbed to a state of numb passivity. Her answers to the other jurors were perfunctory, lacking any spark of effort to defend her desire for a life sentence.

Her main memory of the day's deliberations was the jury's focus on how she had ever been seated on the jury in the first place. The other jurors began asking "How did you get on the jury? What did you tell them? What did you say in your answers?" The underlying premise of the questions, that Peggy's selection on the jury had been a "mistake," stung all the more because "they were not vicious people and mean, like 'We're going to get this girl.' They really thought I was incapable of having a valid opinion. I remember them saying 'This is clear as day!'"

Peggy had fully known that the death penalty was a possibility when she was chosen for the jury. She understood the prosecutor during *voir dire* to essentially be asking "Do you have the guts to be involved in the case?" Peggy had approached her summons for jury duty almost like a job interview, making sure that she was nicely dressed and, on some level, wanting the approval of the lawyers and the judge: "I didn't want them to think 'She couldn't do it.'" She had found the questions about the death penalty very difficult to answer "on the spot," because she had never really thought about "when" she would impose the death penalty rather than whether she was generally for or against capital punishment. Although she was certain in retrospect that she had not deluded herself when she had told the court she could vote for death under the right circumstances, as the other jurors questioned her in the jury room, she began to wonder if she had been honest with herself.

As the day wore on, the majority's "strong convictions" grew stronger, as did their persistent inquiries about what she had said at *voir dire*. To Peggy, the questions carried a tone of curiosity like someone might adopt toward a person who has done something inexplicable. And although Peggy could not identify a specific moment when her self-doubts finally triumphed, the inquiries' underlying message was rapidly eroding what little self-confidence remained: "I was like 'Maybe I don't believe in the death penalty. . . . Well, maybe you're right, maybe I shouldn't be here. . . . Is there something wrong with me? When people project, 'I don't think she is capable,' you start thinking, 'Why am I here? This must be a mistake.' I really thought that!" By the end of the day, Peggy noted in a defeated tone, "I was acting how they saw me. . . . I got lost in that group—even brainwashed—like I believed their portrayal of me that I shouldn't be there, that I wasn't a valuable juror."

As the day drew to a close, Peggy said, "I thought my brain was going to explode, open up, I was under so much pressure. We ended that day, the day when I thought it was going to be over"—Peggy gave a small, rueful laugh—"with me saying to the others that 'I don't know what to do.'" When Peggy said these words, she was not posing a rhetorical question, she genuinely "was asking, 'can you help me?' I was so overwhelmed." For the first time in the deliberations, Peggy tentatively waved a white flag of surrender, indicating that she no longer felt that she could make the decision by herself. "I was really baffled about what was right." Suffocating from fatigue and depression and knowing that she needed help, Peggy sought help from the only people she could, the other jurors.

In response to her comment, one juror offered, "Well, when I find myself in a situation where I'm the only one, I do some introspecting." To Peggy, the comment was a way of saying "You have made an error and we need to figure it out, you know, rather than saying 'Well, listen, Peggy, this is a life-and-death situation and you're never going to be able to live with yourself if you change your vote, we're deadlocked.' Not one person said that, not even the guy who was my friend." The others jurors then drew up a list of questions that Peggy was to answer that night, questions designed to "get my feelings off of the defendant and onto the victim." Looking back, Peggy now thought the questions were "so stupid! Like, what would the victim be doing if he were alive today? I mean, how can I predict the future?" But she had asked them for help, so she tried to answer them that night. After answering several, she gave up; "I just went this is not right, this is not my way."

As the deliberations had worn on, Peggy increasingly felt the stress taking its toll. Her bouts of sleeplessness were becoming insufferable. She still was working weekends and felt as if she were sleepwalking, becoming forgetful in performing even routine tasks. And although she was not allowed to talk to family members about the deliberations, they knew that she was struggling to keep her head above water, and she felt intense guilt that she was neglecting them. Now, though, after this last day of deliberations, the stress and fatigue had become frightening. That evening Peggy found herself walking around the grocery store in a daze, "kind of waking up 'where am I? oh, yeah I'm at the Safeway.' I was standing in an aisle, my purse was in the car, my keys were in the ignition." Peggy spent the night wrestling the sheets, grappling with what to do, and finally "I just said that I can't have it my way. I had no confidence in myself. I was really full of self-doubt about my ability to make this decision." The decision did not bring the relief of sleep, though, and she crawled out of bed the next morning feeling drained. She went to her closet to choose an outfit. She wore black. The optimism that had greeted yesterday's dawn had been displaced by a gloomy awareness that "something was wrong, I didn't feel good about the decision."

As Peggy described entering the jury room that final morning, her voice became flat and lifeless. She felt as if she were on autopilot as the jury members settled into their chairs, and once again she told the other jurors that she had an announcement. Peggy then told how she had realized that she should not have it all her way and so she was willing to vote for death. By this time she was tired and her emotions extremely brittle. When the other jurors said that they wanted to make sure she was certain of her vote and that they would spend the morning discussing her decision, it only seemed to Peggy to prolong the agony. The morning was a roller coaster of moods. At one point, she started crying and sat at the table crying very hard for a long time. Finally she pushed herself up from her chair and sought refuge in the bathroom: "I was just so overwhelmed by everything. I just felt wasted. I was in a bad way. Then I was in this horrible bathroom trying to be alone when I thought, 'I'm staying in here too long and they don't know what to do.'" So Peggy forced herself to go back.

Peggy thought the discussion was "phony, because they were tired of it, they wanted to go home," but she added, "It was a good idea, it was a great idea to discuss it, but it just didn't do anything." In fact, the discussion only heightened her sense that an unbridgeable divide separated her from the other jurors. And because she had come to her midnight pact of surrender, "I just wanted them to shut up" and render the verdict. The other jurors, however, still thought that it was just a matter of her not getting it: "They talked about, let's go see the video again, maybe if Peggy sees the video again she'll really realize just how horrible this was, that he just walked in and gunned the clerk down." Even through her exhausted mental haze, Peggy thought how she already had told them "over and over . . . I never thought he didn't do evil things; I just never thought he was a evil person." With the willpower that comes with hindsight, Peggy wished she had responded to their pleas for her to step into their shoes and empathize with the victim by saying "I have empathy for Lane and I'm going to stand behind it. I wish you understood. I wish I had been able to help *you* understand how *I* feel, but I've not been able to get you to understand how I feel. I'm sorry you don't understand how I feel, but that's your problem. Period." Peggy's voice had mustered a momentary hint of boldness as she recited this speech, a speech she clearly had given a thousand times in her head after the trial. Her timbre became listless again, though, as her voice trickled off remembering how the episode had actually ended, murmuring "But I didn't have, I didn't have the guts."

Throughout the morning, Peggy said she really had tried to respond to the urgings of the other jurors, "to think that I was having too much compassion for the defendant and I should be thinking more of the victim." Peggy even asked to see a picture of the victim with the hope that it might help her "bond" with him as a counterweight to the empathy she was feeling for Lane, a request that she now thought "bizarre—how can you bond with a picture of a dead person?" Despite all these efforts, though, Peggy's true sentiments never changed; "in my heart I was never there." After her crying spell, however, Peggy assured the other jurors that she still wanted to change her vote. One of the jurors had told her as she emerged from the bathroom, "I'm worried about you," and Peggy had replied, "Don't worry, I'm fine." As Peggy explained, "At that time I'm thinking well, I'll be fine, my mind is made up, these guys are right— I held up the group, something's wrong with me."

By the time the lunch break arrived, Peggy had not so much reached an uneasy detente with her emotions as she simply "had moved past dealing with my feelings." She had convinced herself that "this is okay, this is right, it's not right for it to go my way when all these people feel so strongly," and had vowed simply to accept that this was the way it was to be.

On a deeper level, Peggy knew all was not well. Lunch was a very uneasy affair. Peggy could see the other jurors giving her sideways glances, wondering whether she would waver at the last minute. Now and then a whispered conversation would take place that Peggy knew centered around what the jury needed to do to keep her from cracking. With the forced laughter of someone desperately trying to fit in where they feel they do not belong, Peggy could hear herself "giving this crazed laugh" far out of proportion to the humor of the small jokes that some were telling in an effort to ease the tension. Her contrived laughter seemed only to emphasize that she was an outsider vying for acceptance by the inner group, heightening the others' concerns rather than alleviating them. Most of the other jurors "were kind of quiet," giving the occasional polite laugh of a person who unavoidably finds herself in a bleak situation, like the laughter one hears drifting over from small groups talking after a funeral.

As lunch concluded, the reality hung heavily over the jury that the next step was to summon the bailiff and announce their verdict. Before the jury buzzed the bailiff, however, one of the jurors pointed out that they would be individually polled after announcing their verdict. Peggy was asked, "So are you going to be able to keep—to say death?" But by now Peggy simply wanted it to be over. She had grabbed hold of and clung to the idea that the "right" decision was to do what the majority wanted— "It was sort of brainwashing, not malicious or intentional"—and the last thing she was about to do was reopen the jury discussion. Peggy stated that she could tell the judge yes when asked if she joined the verdict. The jury let the court know that they had finally reached a verdict.

As the jury was going downstairs to the courtroom, Peggy was silently telling herself over and over that she was making the right decision. In retrospect, she remembered that as they were walking across the floor "I was stomping my feet—that was my first clue that 'maybe this isn't right.'" On the passage down, one of the woman jurors who had been quite hard on her during the deliberations leaned over to her and whispered, "I'm worried about you." Peggy replied in a voice that she strove to make sound calm, "Don't worry about me, I'll be okay." Even in her somewhat dazed state, though, Peggy found that "part of me felt like saying"—and here she uncharacteristically displayed a flash of anger— "yeah, *now* you're worried about me, now that I'm on your side. Why weren't you worried about me three days ago? Two days ago? Yesterday???" As she was wont to do, however, Peggy quickly retreated from her anger, adding "But I can see in her own way she might have thought, here I'm giving her a second chance, asking 'are you really sure?'" Even if the woman juror was trying to toss her a lifeline, though, by now Peggy was far too weak to grab it, even to envision the possibility of halting the jury as it was marching into the courtroom by saying 'Wait, I'm having second thoughts.'

Announcing the verdict was, in Peggy's words, "like a dream." She vaguely recalled hearing the judge ask, "And do you join in the jury's verdict of death?" His voice had the low, rumbling benevolent tone she had grown so used to hearing during the trial, but it sounded muffled, as if the soundtrack of a movie was slightly off.

"Yes," she heard herself say. The fine sheen of the polished wood seemed to give way under her fingers as she tightened her grip on the railing in front of her. Any sense of assuredness that she had felt that morning that she was right to change her vote started to flee. Lightheadedness, a sense that the courtroom was going out of focus, made it so that she barely heard the remaining jurors state their acquiescence in the verdict of death. Part of her wanted to shout out right then, "No, no, I want to change my vote," but another part made her feel that she couldn't, that she had told the others that she was sure that switching her vote was the proper thing—they'd expect her to do something like this, go back on her vote, what else would you expect from someone that unstable, who for days was the only one wanting life? She had seen the exchanged glances, heard the tone of their comments behind her back, felt their dislike and anger. She kept quiet as the panic slowly spread through her limbs. She began to ask herself, 'when would it be too late?'

Then, it was too late. Just like that. The judge had smiled his pleasant smile, thanked the jury, and announced that they were discharged from their duty as jurors serving the state of California. Peggy started to cry.

With rivulets of tears running down her cheeks, Peggy sat down in her chair in an unconscious movement as the prosecutor moved forward to thank them. As the prosecutor mouthed his words of appreciation and told them that their decision had been the right one and that he knew how difficult it had been, a sickening regret started to take hold. Someone—Peggy thought it might even have been her—brought up the jury's difficulty in reaching unanimity. As she listened to the prosecutor patiently explain that a deadlock would only have meant that a new sentencing hearing would have been held, Peggy said she "heard this voice inside my head screaming '*What?*'" To Peggy, this was the prosecutor telling them that the jury had gotten it wrong, dead wrong, when they thought a hung jury would result in a life sentence. They had made a mistake, but as she quickly turned to see how the other jurors were reacting to this bombshell, she realized that no one else seemed to recognize the significance of what he was saying. The prosecutor's explanation seemed to "go right past them" and "I was so numb, I just stood there. At this point I knew something was very wrong, but I was in a state of shock."

The relief of closure, or at least numbness, that Peggy had hoped a verdict might bring had vanished. Her "poor husband," who had become extremely worried as he watched the deliberations turn her into an emotional wreck, welcomed her home with flowers, celebrating the end of a trial that had become a curse on the whole family. Peggy threw them away, an act she remembered with immense guilt. That night she was kept awake by a new torment, trying to figure out how to untangle the misunderstanding that had led to someone being sentenced to death. Part of her was optimistic. Surely the legal system cared when a jury had made an innocent mistake and was able to handle misunderstandings like this and allow the jury to start over. Another part of her, however, the part that had watched a lumbering system caught up in formalities and procedures, made her less than sanguine.

Peggy called the judge the next morning to "report the error, to tell him, you know, that we misunderstood the instructions." Peggy said she got out little more than "We did it wrong" before she could feel this "ohhh" on the other end of the phone, and the judge quickly informed her that he could not talk to her and that she should call the lawyers in the case. This started Peggy on an odyssey of phone calls and meetings with lawyers and private investigators. "My big thing was I changed my vote because I confused the directions and it didn't seem to matter. I'm thinking our entire jury misunderstood and you guys aren't worried about it?"

Peggy soon felt like a Don Quixote figure wandering the legal landscape with no one taking her seriously. She tried to make her point whenever she could. The judge sent her a ceremonial letter thanking her for her service as a juror, a standard letter sent to all jurors, and Peggy sent it back with a note along the lines of "well, wait a minute, you can't thank me when there was still a problem to be resolved." Perhaps most frustrating for Peggy was her awareness that she was undermining her own efforts as her frustrations mounted and her despair grew. Her insomnia during the deliberations had now become chronic; she roamed her house during the early-morning hours or lay in bed staring at the ceiling, essentially going "two months without sleeping." The depression that had started during the deliberations now encompassed her entirely.

And on some level, haunted by a sense of responsibility for a terrible injustice and feelings of guilt—in Peggy's mind, if she only had summoned up the courage to insist on deadlocking, all of this would have been avoided—Peggy did feel like "I was literally going crazy." A day would come to a close and it seemed as if she had sleepwalked right through it, with only a vague awareness of her actions. A conscientious employee prior to the trial, Peggy missed meetings at work and failed to keep appointments. More frighteningly, she was doing things that she knew "on some level were strange," especially in trying to get others to pay attention to her story of a jury gone awry. Exhausted, depressed, Peggy had fallen into a trap of trying increasingly desperate measures to get her voice heard, efforts that only seemed to confirm the view of everyone else—the other jurors, the lawyers, the judge—that she was a "crazy lady."

After several months, Peggy sought counseling and began regaining her mental balance. Even after the fog of depression and fatigue had lifted, however, she could not comprehend why the legal system treated her efforts to correct the jury's misunderstanding of their instructions as a mere tilting at windmills. To Peggy, the jury misinterpreting the instructions was a distinctly human mistake—"people get confused and miss things"—especially when under intense pressure. In fact, after hearing the prosecutor say that a hung jury would not have automatically resulted in a life sentence, Peggy was astonished to reread the instructions and find that it was "quite clear when you're not under stress" that the paragraph did not say a life sentence would result. When she had tried to read that same paragraph, however, with eleven jurors staring at her and amid the emotional heat and pressure of deliberations, "I would find myself looking at these words and I was aware my eyes were moving but I was not understanding what I was reading. It was so tense in that room. If I could have brought them home and looked at them, maybe I would have been able to say 'Hey, wait a minute . . . '"

Nor did Peggy think that the other jurors were trying to trick her: "We took the paragraph out of context. It's not that we couldn't read, but people aren't working at their best in that situation. I look at it now, and I think we just couldn't grasp the directions." And because they did not realize that it was possible that they were mistaken, the jury "didn't even think about" asking the judge what the instruction meant.

Peggy also emphasized, however, that by this point the jury viewed asking the judge for any assistance as a last resort. Even simple requests had set in motion a ponderous process, so that, "It was like a stuffy game, even letting them know whether we needed to go to the bathroom or not, you know!" The upshot of the jury's desire to be viewed approvingly ("[the attitude was] we're supposed to be professional, we're all professional people, what will they think if we say we don't understand something?"), coupled with an extremely "pompous and formal" atmosphere, produced a process that Peggy thought "was so serious it became unfunctional" in providing assistance to the jury in making a life-or-death decision.

That a man was sitting in a death row jail cell because she had misapplied a jury instruction not only made Peggy feel guilty, it made her "very angry at [the legal system's] casual 'There's nothing we can do.'" To Peggy, "It didn't make sense to me at all—why did the court want to sweep it under the rug? . . . That just blew my circuits. All that time and money, all the court costs, and you're going to tell me it doesn't matter that the jury didn't understand?" It was not that Peggy saw herself as a whistle-blower trying to expose a scandal—she thought the jury's decision was an honest mistake, not a fraudulent one—but she did think that someone's life should not be taken because a jury got the law wrong: "And if you say, 'Well, you could have asked for clarification,' we didn't even know we were confused." Certainly if the law was to place such a stamp of permanence on the jury's verdict, Peggy thought, "jurors should be tested on the instructions to make sure they understand them."

Although Peggy found the legal system's unresponsiveness bewildering, anyone familiar with the criminal justice system would not be surprised by the lack of response. Almost all judges, for instance, would have refused to speak with Peggy when she called to tell them about the "error," immediately envisioning the numerous grounds for appeal that might result from talking to a juror without the lawyers present.

Likewise, almost all courts would have refused to look into whether the jury had misunderstood the instructions. This great reluctance to pry into the jury's decision-making process stems, in the words of the Supreme Court, from a fear that if courts were allowed to second-guess a jury's verdict, "jurors would be harassed and beset" after the trial by those trying to challenge the verdict.[9] Finality is one of the legal system's most hallowed values, and the prospect of a convicted defendant being able to argue "days, weeks, or months after the verdict" that jurors had misunderstood their instructions or had misbehaved is a prospect guaranteed to send a collective shiver through the legal system.[10]

More fundamentally, the legal system's desire to soundproof the jury room from later prying derives from the belief that a "full and frank discussion" is the lifeblood of jury deliberations.[11] If a jury knew that its deliberations were subject to second-guessing by judges and lawyers after a verdict was rendered, the courts fear that the "destruction of all frankness and freedom of discussion and conference" might result.[12] In a moment of candor, the Supreme Court has acknowledged that "there is little doubt that post-verdict investigation into juror misconduct [or misunderstanding] would in some instances lead to the invalidation of verdicts reached after irresponsible or improper juror behavior." Yet, the Court went on, it worried that the cure of allowing postverdict inquiries might kill the jury system itself: "It is not at all clear . . . that the jury system could survive such efforts to perfect it."[13]

This strong inclination to insulate jury decisions from scrutiny is dramatically highlighted in a trial that resulted in two defendants being convicted of fraud. Although jurors frequently complain that jury service poses a hardship, a juror on this jury described the trial as "one big party." Seven of the jurors regularly drank during their lunch break, with four male jurors often sharing "one to three pitchers of beer" as they ate, and the foreperson drinking a liter of wine by herself. (The other two jurors who drank were of a more temperate nature, limiting themselves to one or two highballs with their lunch.) More astonishingly, the four beer-swigging jurors smoked marijuana "just about every day" over the course of the lengthy trial, and two of those jurors also snorted cocaine during the trial. The biggest drug user, John, who had described himself to another juror as "flying" during the trial, turned the jury room into his own little drug den, bringing pot, coke, and drug paraphernalia into the courthouse. Apparently the drug use did not sap John of his entrepreneurial ambition, however, as he sold a quarter-pound of marijuana to another juror during the trial.[14]

The Supreme Court, however, refused even to order a hearing to explore the allegations of juror misconduct and incompetence. Citing the desire for finality and the need to protect "full and frank discussion in the jury room," the Court reiterated the law's aversion to allowing jurors to cast doubt on their own verdict once it has been rendered. Absent "external" influences such as an attempt to bribe a juror, therefore, the Court would not allow parties to a legal proceeding to challenge a verdict, even a finding of criminal guilt, by exploring "the internal processes of the jury."[15]

If the Court is so protective of the jury's deliberation process that it has been unwilling to allow jurors' own admissions of substance abuse to be a basis for inquiring if they were too drunk or stoned to be competent jurors, it is easy to see just how difficult a task Peggy faced. She was asking the courts to go directly to the "internal processes of the jury" and determine whether the jurors had in fact misunderstood the jury instructions. Even a sympathetic judge would likely blanch at the difficulty of trying to unravel how a jury had reached its decision, especially if jurors had different recollections of how they had reached their decision or interpreted the jury instructions. In Lane's case, for instance, although Peggy undoubtedly had become convinced that a jury deadlock meant her lone vote would result in a life sentence, not all of the jurors re-called misinterpreting the jury instruction in such a way. Moreover, courts are ever fearful of what they call slippery slopes: a situation where a ruling in one case might trigger an avalanche of similar claims requiring the courts to make all sorts of further inquiries and rulings in future cases. Consequently, when a juror like Peggy comes knocking on the courthouse door to say that her jury had misunderstood the instructions, courts will be especially afraid that if they investigate her claim, soon they will be in the position of testing every jury on whether it had properly applied the law.

Although Peggy felt isolated and abandoned by the legal system, she was not alone in her plight as a juror who felt that her jury had wrong-fully sentenced someone to death. Because the courts are so unresponsive to such claims, however, jurors in Peggy's position are left with few options besides petitioning the governor for clemency, an option that seldom succeeds. Two Virginia jurors, for instance, who had voted to sentence Bobby Lee Ramdass to death after the trial judge refused to answer their question of whether Ramdass would ever be eligible for parole, later petitioned Governor James Gilmore upon learning that Ramdass in fact would have been ineligible for parole. Because the jurors believed that "the outcome of the verdict would have been very different" if the judge had answered their question, they did not think it fair that their verdict should be the justification for executing Ramdass.[16] Governor Gilmore denied the jurors' petition and Ramdass was executed.

In rare instances, however, a governor will take heed, as Arkansas governor Mike Huckabee did when he commuted Bobby Ray Fretwell's death sentence to life after receiving a letter from an elderly juror who wrote that his conscience was bothering him. The juror explained that he had been the lone vote for life and had switched his vote only because he feared being shunned by the small community in which he lived. As Fretwell's execution date approached, the juror's conscience increasingly haunted him, and he pleaded with the governor to show mercy. Despite strong opposition from the victim's family, Governor Huckabee "prayed and sought God's help with this decision" and ordered the sentence commuted.

In a misery-loves-company kind of way, Peggy was somewhat con-soled to hear that hers was not the lone case of a juror believing that an injustice had occurred only to discover, in Peggy's words, that the court-house "door was very much shut" once the verdict was rendered. Learning that others had found themselves in the same predicament, however, did little to ease her angry frustration that the legal system would declare itself content so long as all the formalities had been observed. Even though she understood on a rational level why courts might be reluctant to reopen a verdict, Peggy simply could not square her basic notion of justice with the idea that a jury could mistakenly impose a death sentence and the courts would not do anything to correct it. She had not asked to be called to jury duty, but once the summons had come she had done her best, only to find that she had voted to sentence someone to death based on a mistaken understanding.

Her desire to rectify the mistake had come close to consuming her. A counselor she saw after the trial told Peggy that she "thinks too hard about life." Whether she thought "too hard" about life or not, Peggy certainly did not simply accept the easy answer. This quality had made her an ideal juror for Steven Lane's defense lawyers as they tried to tell a story for life that did not offer up an easy answer. Unfortunately for Peggy, however, it also was a trait that made it impossible for her to quietly accept a verdict that she believed was unjust. The courts and lawyers told her that it was an outcome that she had to live with, but even long after the trial was over, Peggy said, "I think about the whole thing every day."

CHAPTER FOUR

THE TWELFTH JUROR

PEGGY'S INTERVIEW ADDED YET ANOTHER LAYER TO THE *LANE* jury's story plot. The other jurors had been aware that she was finding the decision emotionally difficult, but they had not completely fathomed the depths of her struggles. The problem was not so much that they did not care, but that the jury room is not an especially conducive atmosphere for stepping back and patiently understanding what each juror is feeling. A jury's overriding mission is to forge a unanimous verdict, a charge that by its nature forces individual stories and feelings to retreat into the background. In a jury room bubbling with heated opinions and bristling with strong personalities, the other jurors at most gained glimpses of Peggy's full reasoning and reactions. With any comment greeted by two or three replies, a sustained explanation that interweaves emotions and reasoning becomes very difficult. As the sole holdout, Peggy commanded the jury's attention more than anyone else, but it was the type of intense and critical attention more apt to produce stutters and misfires than persuasive Darrow-like soliloquies. As a forum for self-expression, the jury room is more the pandemonium of a daytime talk show than the soothing comfort of a support group.

Outside the jury room, Peggy came across as highly likable, intelligent, and articulate. Given an opportunity to discuss the case calmly, her explanations of how she had approached the decision were easily understood as reflecting a constantly questioning mind that was not content to settle for simple answers. One could not help but admire the strength of personal conviction that she had exhibited as she clung to her life vote in the face of intense pressure. These traits, when coupled with her innate optimism about human nature, would make her an appealing friend.

Yet these same qualities help explain why Ken and the Chorus had become so frustrated with her as a holdout. Her optimism seemed to them hopelessly Pollyannish given Lane's long history of violent crime, his seeming inability to be rehabilitated, and the absence of any tangible signs of remorse. Likewise, her belief that Lane's background explained his life of crime struck them as naively accepting of any excuse that the defense might peddle. For Ken and the Chorus, a verdict of death seemed not only a remarkably straightforward proposition but one that their sense of justice obligated them to pursue. Consequently, in the jury room, Peggy's continual questioning of the evidence and her strength of personal conviction were interpreted as meaning either that she was incapable of understanding what the evidence meant or that she simply could not bring herself to do what the law required.

Despite her experience in the jury room, Peggy did not show signs of resentment or hostility toward the majority jurors based on what had occurred. She had been convinced that they were sincere in their beliefs, and she had attributed the strength of their comments, even the more acidic ones, to their overwhelming sense that death was the only just verdict. The majority jurors had not relished their task of arguing for death, but had genuinely believed that, under the circumstances, they had a duty to return a death sentence. To achieve what they thought was the proper outcome, however, they had to reach unanimity despite one juror insisting on life, a quandary none of them enjoyed. With no rule book or training on how to reach unanimity, they had done their best as strangers thrown into a small room and told that they needed to reach a verdict.

One juror, however, the man whom Peggy had referred to as the "twelfth juror," had engaged in behavior that seemed out of bounds even in the rough-and-tumble context of jury deliberations. If a jury becomes a society in miniature as it deliberates, the twelfth juror appeared to assume the role of jury room bully. Although reticent in their comments about the twelfth juror, Ken and the Chorus members stated that they had found it necessary to keep him in check lest he become overbearing in his comments to Peggy. And while Peggy had not borne a grudge toward Ken and the Chorus members, she did find herself disliking the twelfth juror. For reasons she did not understand, he had cast himself as her direct antagonist, poking her, ridiculing her, and sarcastically confronting her.

None of the jurors had described this juror's physical appearance in detail, but had referred to him at various points as "rough" and a "Harley-Davidson" type of guy. These descriptions, coupled with his harshly judgmental attitude toward Peggy, invited the image of a loud and overbearing personality housed inside a somewhat menacing exterior. Frank, however, turned out to be a man in his mid-forties dressed in a crisp button-down blue shirt and blue jeans who spoke in a low, steady cadence that carried the gentle trace of a country accent. He was solidly built, but not in an intimidating way that would cause you to surreptitiously move down a couple of stools if he seated himself next to you at a bar. His face was anything but menacing, tending toward the handsome. Although his smile was not wide open, neither did it project any repressed hostility. His manner was polite, direct, and businesslike.

Frank showed none of Peggy's inclination to ponder the questions. Although Peggy had mulled over most questions before giving an answer, often offering different understandings that a person might have of the question, Frank sped through them. He gave firm and definitive answers to a series of questions about whether he agreed or disagreed with various characterizations of the crime, victim, and defendant. Any questions that required him to utilize his own words elicited short, to-the-point responses. For Frank, Lane's occupation simply was that of "criminal," adding "he was a pro, prison was all he had ever done, just about."

Frank had not seen the killing as especially bloody or gory in a physical sense, but he had found it "vicious" and "repulsive." Frank's voice rose a notch in intensity as he summarized the killing as "senseless and stupid, it was so stupid!" Not only was the crime pointless ("There was no need for the killing, he was mad and taking out his anger"), but it also was literally stupid, because "anyone with a lick of sense knows that all of these stores have video cameras—I mean, I can't picture what he was thinking."

The videotape in particular emerged as a touchstone to which Frank returned whenever explaining pivotal points in his decision-making process. Practically his first words were, "We *saw* it happen," and soon after he identified watching the videotape, which the jury saw very early in the trial, as the moment he began strongly leaning toward the death penalty: "Just seeing the way he walked into the store and shooting that guy." Frank paused, then softly said, "I can still see it right now, him walking in and shooting the guy."

Given the other jurors' descriptions of Frank's role in the deliberations, his emphasis on the killing, especially his intense anger at Lane as he watched the murder unfold, was far from surprising. Nor were any surprises to be found in his succinct but strongly voiced view of Lane as someone who had acted out of his own free will and had to bear responsibility for his actions. Frank quickly dismissed any suggestion that Lane had anyone or anything to blame other than himself. He believed that Lane had been raised in a loving family and that any characterization of Lane as having suffered abuse was completely off base. When asked if Lane had received a "raw deal in life," Frank replied, "He thinks he did, but I don't." Frank repeatedly emphasized that Lane had chosen to take the low road: "He knows what he should do, he just didn't want to—he just kept doing what he wanted to do," adding later "[Lane] had a good decent background and chose to go the wrong way." The most that Frank attempted to offer in the way of speculation was that he thought some of Lane's troubles could be attributed to Lane "wanting to come off as a macho man all the time."

As Frank clipped along, his brief answers started to become predictable in expressing the strength of his outrage over the killing and his condemnation of Lane as someone acting from his own free will. Unsurprisingly, Frank answered "not at all" to a series of questions about whether any mitigating factors had existed that might have argued for a life sentence. The predictability ended, however, when Frank was asked whether Lane reminded him of anyone.

His reply of "*yeah, me,*" took a moment to register. Frank's face did not have the wry look of someone who had just sprung a Hitchcock plot twist, but wore a matter-of-fact expression, as if he had stated nothing more dramatic than that a year consists of 365 days. Frank then added, "I kept comparing his life to my life—I mixed my background with his a lot, because I had the same choices he had, but I knew which ones to make to keep out of those situations."

Frank related how the defense had "tried to place emphasis on what Lane's father was like and an incident that happened in his childhood." Frank had found Lane's family life very familiar—"I knew what the family was like"—because it reminded him of his own family. Frank's father had been an alcoholic, and "He would backhand us or beat us with anything he could pick up. It didn't make any difference what he could get a hold of, if he decided we needed it, we got it."

Frank also had identified strongly with Lane's mother, "who kind of sounded a lot like my mother, tried to get us to church you know, teach us right from wrong." In fact, Frank, who had great admiration for the prosecutor overall, recalled that he had become quite angry with the prosecutor during his cross-examination of Lane's mother: "Lane's mother reminded me of mine, and that's the only time I really got mad at the prosecutor, the way he was talking to her, the way he was asking her questions and stuff. I mean, the woman was up there pleading for her son's life." Although on one level Frank was willing to excuse the prosecutor because "of course he was only doing his job," he returned to the topic later, noting "During the mom's testifying, that's where I felt that the prosecuting attorney was browbeating the mother. It was more like a sneering-like attitude towards her. She was there trying to defend her son from the gas chamber, and I don't think she was lying about his background. But he tried to make us believe that she was piling it on."

Frank's identification with Lane's family situation of a harsh father and loving mother was interesting, but hardly seemed to justify his saying that he saw himself in Lane's background. He then revealed that he had felt a similarity to the teenage Steven when he learned of Lane's loss of his brother, because Frank also had lost a very close friend to tragic circumstances when he was around thirteen: "My friend was murdered and they never found out why or who did it, and back then they didn't have all this counseling that you can get now, you know?" The connection between Frank's and Steven's lives seemed to make more sense, given that they both had suffered a tragic loss at a vulnerable age. It still seemed a stretch, though, for Frank to say that he had "mixed" his life's story in with Steven's.

Frank hesitated before continuing. He prefaced his next revelation by stating "I don't want to come off like a—" and then stopped before he actually said the word "victim." Frank, though, had indeed gone through an experience that qualifies as traumatic by anyone's definition. He quietly added, "And it was when they didn't handle things like they handle stuff now. So I had to bite the bullet . . . and it took a long time to work through that." Not sounding moralistic or embittered, Frank concluded, "So I know you can come from a rough start and you don't have to do what Lane did. I mean, I didn't come out to be an Albert Schweitzer, but at least I kind of turned things around."

With this revelation, Frank no longer fit the easy caricature of a jury room bully with a simplistic sense of right and wrong. The twelfth juror had turned out to be an individual acting in response to experiences with which he had struggled. And there was even more in Frank's past that was essential to understanding his stern judgment of Steven Lane.

Many capital jurors, as we have seen, bring to the jury box a strong sense that individuals act as agents of free will. Even after hearing about a heartbreaking childhood that has them in tears, jurors often scrutinize defendants' lives for a perceived fork in the road where defendants had a chance to choose the high road rather than continue on the low road. Frank, as it turned out, had little trouble understanding how Steven's experiences had led him into trouble, because Frank, too, had started down the low road.

As a teenager, Frank started getting into trouble with the law. He was placed on probation instead of serving jail time, but, Frank explained, "I was really going nuts with my mom and dad. At that point they couldn't control me, even though even at seventeen if my dad caught me, I'd get the hell beat out of me." Still shy of eighteen years of age, Frank ran away from home to a brother who was living in another state. His brother, however, sent him back home, and "my mother went to this judge who had me on probation and said that I was just out of control." With a sense of lingering guilt Frank added, "At the time I didn't realize what I was putting her through." The judge told Frank, "Son, you've got two choices—you either go in the service or you go to jail."

Frank enlisted in the military, but even then the high road was still a distance away. He did not step straight into a Hollywood script of coming under the command of a demanding but good-hearted drill sergeant who turned his life around. Rather, he continued to get into serious trouble, saying: "It took three years into the service before I really changed, I mean military jail time; I got thrown in for fighting." Frank identified his time in the jail as the moment that he finally made the choice to turn his life around: "I just said, 'You can't go on like this.' I mean, when I got out that time, I just buckled down, I said, 'Try to do something better.'" In part, Frank's resolve to change resulted from "wanting to show my parents I could do better in my life," and he went on to a career in the military, including a stint as a military policeman.

When Frank looked at Steven Lane's life, then, he saw his own life as empirical proof that Lane could have made the choice to turn his life around. Frank "felt sorry" for Lane at various points during the trial, not so much because of what Lane had been through, but more because he had not been able to make the right choices: "I felt sorry for him, but I just wondered why a person would keep letting his life go on like that. . . . I mean, you come to where you got to sit down and take charge, don't let anybody else, everybody can't rule your life for you—you've got to take control of it somewhere." For Frank, that moment of taking charge came as he sat alone in a military jail after six years of heading in the direction of serious trouble despite efforts by his parents and other authority figures to turn him around. As he watched Steven's story unfold in the courtroom, at times he felt as if he were watching a retrospective of his own life, and occasionally he found himself feeling sorry for Steven and becoming protective of Steven's mother. Unfortunately for Lane, however, Frank also felt that he knew Lane had a choice as to how the story would end, because Frank himself had chosen a different ending. Frank absolutely would not accept the idea that Lane was in some sense a helpless victim of circumstances. Frank looked at his own life and knew otherwise, and with that intense identification with Lane's life, Frank become Lane's harshest critic.

Frank's close identification with Steven because of his sense that he had been through similar experiences growing up is far from unique. A distressing number of jurors from a number of cases had suffered through difficult pasts. Not infrequently, jurors would stop abruptly in the middle of describing the defendant's case for life, their voices often becoming thick and throaty, and explain that they had been subjected to circumstances that they perceived to be similar to those in the defendant's life. The number of jurors who did not grow up in Leave It to Beaver families, having to fight as adults the after-effects of tragedies like child abuse, sexual molestation, and drug addiction, provided a sobering perspective on how people bring their own experiences and views of themselves to the judgment of others. As they heard the defendant's family members testify about the defendant's upbringing, these jurors tended to find themselves nodding in painful recognition at what they were hearing.

Like Frank, though, the nod of recognition usually presaged an unforgiving view of the defendant. One juror, for instance, who like Frank had answered "myself" when asked if the defendant reminded him of anyone, first detailed how he and the defendant had both grown up in rough neighborhoods riddled with gang and drug activity and were raised by single mothers who struggled to put food on the table. His response to the defendant's case for life closely tracked Frank's reactions, expressing on one level sympathy for the defendant, but ultimately feeling "mad because of the choices [the defendant] made," reiterating with emotion that "he *did* have a choice to do the things he did." Indeed, one of the hallmarks of this group of jurors was the adamance with which they rejected the defendant's arguments for mitigation; one juror practically shouted "NOT AT ALL" when asked if the defendant had "gotten a raw deal in life."

This reaction of initial sympathy yielding to strong condemnation might be surprising at first. Indeed, defense attorneys searching for potential jurors who will be sympathetic to their case for life initially might be drawn to those who can identify with the defendant. As these jurors' reactions made clear, however, identifying with a defendant's experiences often led them to become the most vocal advocates of a death sentence precisely because in their minds they *knew* that the defendant had a choice. As one juror summarized his response to a case for life that reminded him of his own upbringing: "In my opinion a lot of people come from dysfunctional families, but you don't have to stay there. You get out and do something. You don't blame someone else. I came from a dysfunctional family, and I left a long time ago."

Frank's reaction upon identifying with Lane was unusual only in that he did not share with the jury the reasons why he was so convinced that Steven Lane had acted out of free will. Frank explained that while he had been tempted at several points to tell the other jurors why he felt so strongly that Lane was accountable for his actions, he had not "because I didn't know if it was really right or proper to, because that was something in my own mind, and the way the instructions were handed down, I really didn't know if I could even legally say anything about that." Consequently, Frank said, "I was just trying to stay with what we were presented with in court, not my own experiences." Although his parallel experiences inevitably influenced his own decision making "because it was there," he also found that "he couldn't speak it out" in the jury room.

Jurors in Frank's position are not always so reticent in sharing why they think the jury should reject the defendant's case for life. One juror, for example, told how in her case she had convinced other jurors not to excuse the defendant because, like the defendant, she had "been through the drug thing" and had been raised by an alcoholic father. She knew, therefore, that those factors were no excuse. Similarly, a juror in another case where the defendant had been abused by his father had "presented during deliberations" that he, too, had been abused by his father and that he had not spoken "150 words" to the man since childhood. This juror had dismissed the defendant's case for life by sarcastically telling his fellow jurors that "my father never took me to a baseball game or played catch with me, but I did not go and do what the defendant did."

This group of jurors poses a particular challenge to defense attorneys because they are especially inclined to dismiss the opinions of expert witnesses for the defense as being unconnected to reality. Frank had been particularly unreceptive to the psychiatrist's testimony that had suggested that Lane's childhood had led him into a life of crime from which he could not escape, because the testimony simply did not resonate with his own experiences. And most jurors in Frank's situation responded similarly as they listened to an expert tell about the defendant's hardships, thinking 'Yeah, well, I went through that and didn't end up a killer.'

The jurors themselves thus sometimes became self-appointed experts, offering themselves as Exhibit A as to why the other jurors should not give weight to the expert's testimony. One juror, for instance, explained why she had found the testimony of a defense expert on drug abuse to be unbelievable: "[The expert talked about how] prolonged use of methamphetamine can make you not aware of your doings and such. . . . I thought it was a crock, because when I was in college I did this stuff . . . so when I was sitting there listening to this drug expert I was thinking, 'Have you ever done this stuff?' Do you actually know what was, I mean, is this all just textbook knowledge? Because he knew nothing. . . . I had done this stuff, I know everything he was saying was just so far-fetched. I wondered where he got all this from." This juror was eager to share her insights with the other jurors and was joined by another juror in "debunking" the expert's testimony: "There was another girl in there, too, who was a former addict and . . . a recovering alcoholic, and she told the jury, too, 'I've done this stuff.' We both told the jury, 'I've used it, I've done it, and I would no more go out and say, 'Let's go kill somebody today and let's get cash and get more drugs.' I never was up for four or five or six days as he apparently was. Even so, when you do the drugs you know it's illegal, you know it's wrong, so I just believe you're responsible for your actions." This juror also reported that she had openly discussed her prior drug use when asked during jury selection. Upon hearing the juror's responses, the defense attorney may have hoped he was getting a juror who would empathize with the defendant's drug problem; instead, he ended up with the defendant's severest critic during deliberations.

If a juror identifies strongly with the defendant's situation, therefore, the implications often are ominous for the defense. Intriguingly, though, a juror's sense of déjà vu upon hearing the defense's case for life does not always bode ill for the defendant. If the juror identifies not with the defendant, but primarily with someone in the defendant's family, such as the mother or the father, the juror's identification sometimes swings them toward sympathizing with the defendant's case for life. For this group of jurors, the reaction often is a shared sense of helplessness with the defendant's family members who had tried so hard to keep the defendant from slipping into a life of crime. These jurors often express the sense of how easy it is for a teenager to go astray in today's world despite a parent's best efforts.

Sometimes the connection with the defendant's family comes not from specific parallels to the defendant's life but simply from a general empathy with a parent who had struggled to insulate a child from life's perils and temptations. One such juror remarked how the defendant had strongly reminded him of his youngest son. The defendant and his son were similar in appearance and age and, although they had not known each other, had attended the same high school. These parallels had caused the juror to "just keep sitting there thinking 'but for the grace of God' type of thing." While the juror felt fortunate that "I got a good kid," as he "watched the defendant's mother up there, I just thought about myself and my ex-wife and my own mother going through the same type of a thing, how it was tearing the mother all apart." This sense of identification with the defendant's mother's situation led the juror in that case to argue for a life sentence.

As would be expected, the jurors in this situation who are most affected are those who have had personal experiences underlying their sense of connection to the defendant's family member.[1] A juror in one case, for example, described how hearing testimony detailing the defendant's father's severe alcoholism and his abuse of the defendant was "very, very difficult" because "there was too much connection between, too much similarity to my history, it was almost like Scrooge and the

Ghost of the Christmas Future." This juror had been married to an abusive alcoholic, which made her identify strongly with the defendant's mother as the woman testified about her husband's destructive influence on her son. The juror stated, "I certainly know the damage it did to me" and "I could identify with it so strongly having seen a sort of minor-scale version of it through my own living with an alcoholic." In particular, she took great offense that some of the other jurors downplayed the mother's testimony about the damaging effects of the father's alcoholism: "I felt like I was going to get near to tears. . . . I said 'None of you seem to have any sympathy for that woman—I have a lot of sympathy for her, and I have a lot of empathy for her. I know what it's like, I know what it's like, and I know in my guts.'" This juror's identification with the defendant's mother was particularly strong because the juror also had a son about the defendant's age. In many ways, the juror became the voice of the defendant's mother in the jury room, pleading for her son's life and explaining how her son ended up so far adrift.

In Lane's case, however, none of the jurors had felt a particularly strong connection with Steven's family members. They expressed sympathy for his mother and sister, but not a connection that kindled a desire to speak up for them in the jury room. Indeed, the juror who felt most protective of Steven's mother was Frank himself, seeing in her the heartache he had caused his own mother. Unfortunately for Steven, though, Frank also believed that Steven's mother had provided him the basic lessons on right and wrong, just as Frank's own mother had, and that Lane now had to bear the consequences for choosing to ignore them.

As Frank recounted how his own experiences had strongly shaped his view of Steven's case for life, his antagonism toward Peggy became more comprehensible, if not excusable. Of course it did not help that Frank and Peggy had dramatically different views of the world. Peggy saw people's lives as if they were Impressionist paintings, comprised of a multitude of experiences that could be understood only by peering at them from a variety of angles and distances. Frank, by contrast, saw the world as painted in fairly broad brush strokes. As you looked on, you either liked what you saw or you did not, and if you were not happy with what was on life's canvas, you did not stroke your chin and discuss what you saw or what it all meant. You grabbed the brush and changed the painting.

More fundamentally, Frank thought that Peggy simply did not know what she was talking about when she argued that the jury had never been shown that Lane had an opportunity to change the course of his life. As Frank sat there in the jury room rather than rotting in a jail cell because he had chosen to turn his life around years earlier, Peggy's argument that Steven had become inescapably ensnared in a downward spiral struck him as saying that it was raining outside when he could look out the courthouse windows and see the sun reflecting off the leaves. Hearing Peggy argue otherwise was infuriating.

Most fascinating, however, were not Frank and Peggy's differences, but their striking similarities. Indeed, their deep antipathy appeared to emanate in part from a strongly shared tendency to heavily personalize their interpretation of the evidence. This inclination to intently relate the evidence to their own lives and beliefs was far more marked in Frank and Peggy than in the other *Lane* jurors, who had tended to view Steven's life more from a disinterested observer's viewpoint. The other jurors were not immune from reacting emotionally to the evidence, but they did not tend to relate events from the trial to their own personal lives as they described the evidence or their reasoning.

Frank and Peggy had reacted strongly to Lane as an individual and had directly related his life to their own. Peggy had actively tried to see the world through Steven Lane's eyes. Personal experiences with her sister and other family members allowed her to understand what the young Steven must have felt when his brother died. She saw a person in front of her whom she was trying to comprehend both from his life events and from nonverbal cues, such as facial expressions. And perhaps most important, she could not distance herself from feeling personally responsible for passing judgment on another person, a responsibility that became a tremendous burden.

Frank, of course, had related Steven's life directly to his own based on their similarities. Even more generally, though, Frank's overall approach for evaluating any circumstances was to turn first to his own experiences. For example, asked hypothetically whether his choice of life or death would have been affected by various factors, Frank often answered by referring to people he knew. Mental retardation would have affected Frank's penalty decision, because if a defendant "was really mentally retarded like a cousin of mine, I could not give the death penalty." Mental illness would affect his decision because "my mother-in-law has Alzheimer's, and if she killed my father-in-law I could never hold her responsible." Unlike most jurors, Frank even stated that he would be much less likely to impose death on a defendant under the influence of drugs because "I know what drugs can do to people, and they can make you totally do stuff you'd otherwise never do."

Frank and Peggy also had shared a strong inclination to search the evidence for clues to puzzle out what they thought had really happened "behind the scenes" rather than simply to accept the explanation that they were given. In one instance, the jury had been shown a picture of a gun that Lane had used in a prior robbery, a gun that caught Frank's attention because it was a unique gun that "I'd like to get." Although the prosecution had not made anything of it to the jury, what really captured Frank's attention was that a bandanna was shown with the gun and Frank could tell from the photo that the bandanna was "caught between the firing pin and the cartridge." This observation led Frank to conclude that Lane had tried to fire the gun only to have it jam on him. Frank tried to tell the other jurors that the gun had jammed and this was proof that Lane had tried to kill before, but he reported that they "said that's your assumption and you can't prove it, and I said, 'Whether I can prove it or not that's what happened.'" With a tone of frustrated bafflement, Frank recalled, "I couldn't figure out how the other jurors couldn't figure it out! They wouldn't consider it, though, because they said it hadn't been proven."

The arrest photographs, which had led Peggy to focus on what she perceived as signs that Lane was more than a mere cold-blooded killer, also had provided clues to Frank. Peggy had focused on the look in Lane's eyes; Frank's attention had been drawn to his tattoos. After seeing the photos, Frank noticed that Lane tugged on his shirt sleeves during the trial as if consciously trying to conceal his tattoos. Frank came to believe that the tattoos must show that Lane was a member of the Aryan Brotherhood. As Frank told the other jurors, "I've got tattoos and I am not ashamed of them—there's tattoos and there are tattoos that show you are a member of a gang, and he might not want us to know that he was a member of the gang." As with his gun hypothesis and to his great frustration, the other jurors were not open to Frank's deduction about the tattoos, saying that it went beyond what they were allowed to consider.

Both Frank and Peggy, therefore, had a way of interpreting what they were hearing and then voicing their views in a manner that made them outsiders within the jury. In a different case, Peggy and Frank's mutual propensity to personalize what they were hearing at trial might have made them powerful allies. In Steven Lane's case, though, it cast them as the "emotional" jurors on opposite ends of the spectrum. The conflict was further aggravated because while Peggy had found herself placed in the role of Lane's champion in the jury room, Frank had come to view himself as the juror who needed to speak up for the victim.

More than any other Lane juror, Frank had been angered by how little the jury had heard about the victim. He repeatedly brought up what he perceived as the unfairness that "we heard so much about Lane and how he was affected and everything" and yet heard so little about the victim that "you would have thought it was a drug trial rather than a murder trial." Frank found it particularly offensive that the evidence was "so one-sided" in developing Lane's life because the victim had done absolutely nothing other than show up for work so he could earn a paycheck to support his family.

Although Frank's anger had been simmering throughout the trial over what he saw as the legal system's exiling of the victim to anonymity, it was a personal incident that galvanized his resolve to become the victim's advocate in the jury room. The incident was strikingly reminiscent of how Peggy's fleeting belief that her young daughter had died one night during the penalty phase had cemented her conviction that Lane's loss of his brother had shaped his future. For Frank, the epiphany came during the penalty phase in the form of a phone call at two in the morning from the hospital telling him that his teenage son had been in a terrible car accident. The hospital would not tell Frank his son's condition; "All the nurse wanted to know was our insurance number." Any parent would be in agony during the drive to the hospital, not knowing if their son was alive or dead, but Frank's distress was made all the worse by a sense of self-recrimination. At the time of the accident, Frank and his son "were going through some very rough times" and "there were a lot of things that had been said." As Frank and his wife drove to the hospital in the stillness of the early-morning hours, Frank "got to thinking there were a lot of things we should have been saying to each other," and he prayed over and over to himself that they would still have the chance.

Frank's son survived after a touch-and-go night, but, as Frank stated, the ordeal had "made me so mad at Lane, even though he had nothing to do with it." Thinking of everything that he might never have been able to tell his son if he had died had caused Frank to think of how Lane "just walked in and shot the guy and he has no chance to talk to his family, his kids or wife or anybody"; the wife just gets "a phone call one night."

Frank had watched Lane end the victim's life on the videotape and then had witnessed the legal system coldly treat the victim as if he had never been a person beyond a crime statistic. Yet Frank knew from his son's accident the sickening feeling that the victim's wife must have felt after she picked up the phone and heard of her husband's murder; he had little trouble imagining the many things she would have wanted to tell him but now would be unable to. His son's accident had made Frank "do a lot of thinking about" how the victim and his family seemed to have been lost in the process; he emerged thankful that his son was alive and angrily resolved to make sure that the victim and his family were not forgotten in the jury room.

Frank's use of his son's accident as an epiphany, much like Peggy's reaction upon momentarily believing her daughter was dead, is the type of serendipitous event that gives attorneys nightmares. On one level, lawyers know, of course, that it is unavoidable that jurors will interpret the evidence through their life experiences. An attorney would not be surprised, for instance, to learn, as happened in various cases, that a juror who was a doctor served as an ombudsman for the other jurors in understanding testimony regarding drug use or that a highway patrolman was critical in convincing his fellow jurors to accept ballistics testimony as a valid basis for conviction. In a case that will give heart to English teachers everywhere, a juror who taught high school English played a key role throughout the deliberations in clarifying definitions of words like "heinous" or by explaining the subtle difference in meaning between "pity" and "compassion."

Although lawyers might not like that jurors will be influenced by their occupations, even more unsettling for a lawyer are occurrences and events that cannot be anticipated. Even the most experienced trial lawyer, for example, could not have anticipated that Frank and Peggy would seize on events involving their children as a way of understanding

Lane's case. Nor were Frank and Peggy the only jurors who described events during their trials that lawyers simply could not have foreseen as having strongly shaped their deliberations

In one case, for example, a juror agonizing over the punishment decision had a dream during the penalty phase in which he shot his son for having committed the same crime as the defendant. The dream made the juror realize that if he could shoot his own son for committing such a crime, he also could sentence the defendant to death: "That's when I really came to my decision." The following day the juror returned to the deliberations and became a vocal voice in persuading the jury to return a death sentence.

A juror in another case became an outspoken advocate for a life sentence for a reason that the prosecutor never could have envisioned when choosing the jury. She actually had agreed with all of the prosecutor's penalty phase case, including the district attorney's closing flourish arguing that the defendant deserved the harshest punishment that the law allowed. For this juror, however, that argument led her to argue strenuously for a life sentence, because "I thought life was the harsher punishment than death, being in a six-by-six cell for the rest of your life." But unlike other jurors who sometimes had tried to make this argument, this juror had the force of personal experience to make her persuasive. She had undergone a medical treatment that had required her to be isolated in a small space for three months: "It was just me, there was no getting in or out." Consequently, this juror who had found the three months of cramped isolation to be a horrible experience had opposed a death sentence because "it was the easiest way out; I think he needs to suffer for a while."

Among the more dramatic examples of serendipity affecting jurors' perceptions were unanticipated events that occurred in the courtroom. In one case, the lights suddenly went out in the middle of the trial, the silence and darkness broken only by the sound of the judge ducking behind the bench and the deputies unholstering their guns and telling everyone to stay still. When the lights flickered back on moments later, the judge peered over the bench, the deputies nervously glanced around with their guns drawn, and the defendant sat at the defense table as usual. The jurors found that they had been surprisingly calm and unalarmed during the power outage, because, as one juror put it, "Nobody would try to spring that boy." A judge would never allow the lawyers in a case to unexpectedly shroud the courtroom in darkness as a way of allowing the jury to test out whether they feared the defendant. In this case, however, fortuity had accomplished precisely that, and the results helped convince the jury to return a sentence of life because they realized that they did not think the defendant posed a future danger to others.

A courtroom incident in a different case also helped the defendant win a life sentence. The defendant's mother had been testifying at the penalty phase, and the jurors' distinct impression was that she did not really love her son, an impression consistent with how she had treated him when he was growing up. Then, with no warning, the mother fainted on the witness stand. As everyone stood frozen, unsure of what to do, the defendant bolted out of his chair, clambering over the defense table in an attempt to help her. As the jury watched with mouths agape, six sheriffs tackled the defendant and held him down as he continued to struggle to reach his mother. Although the episode inspired a moment of "sheer fear" as the defendant climbed over the table, one juror who prior to the episode was leaning toward a death sentence found himself impressed that despite the way she had treated him, "This boy's going to help his mother." The defendant's love for his mother moved this juror away from favoring death. A defense attorney would have difficulty imagining a more persuasive way to convince the jury that the defendant was more than an emotionless killer without any sense of humanity.

Of all the strange happenings that jurors described as influencing their decision, perhaps the oddest was the juror who was favoring death in a case where an infant had been killed. Part of the defense's argument for a life sentence had been that the infant's crying and wailing had caused the defendant to "snap." This juror was not particularly sympathetic to that version of events at first, but one night during the penalty phase he watched the movie *Three Men and a Baby* and became "convinced that the constant crying of a baby could have led the defendant to 'snap.'" The juror who had been pushing hard for a death sentence relented and accepted a sentence of life; the defense attorney never knew that it was not her eloquence but the acting of Tom Selleck, Steve Guttenberg, and Ted Danson that had clinched a life sentence.

Although Frank had not been a wallflower in the jury room prior to his son's accident, after the incident he became even more blunt and challenging. In his now-familiar candid manner, Frank openly admitted that he had been confrontational, saying "A couple of ladies told me I was browbeating Peggy and I wasn't really—well, actually I guess I was, I mean, I can get pretty vocal." Frank had sensed that Peggy had not liked him "from the get-go." They had first clashed at the guilt phase, when Frank had been "ready to go in there and do everything within an hour." Not surprisingly, he found her hesitation to convict Lane of capital murder extremely aggravating. His frustration finally had manifested itself during the guilt phase in his jabbing of Peggy while the witness's testimony was being reread.

Now that they had arrived at the penalty phase, Frank's patience had worn exceedingly thin. Even before the penalty deliberations had formally begun, Frank "had a feeling, and as it turned out everybody else did, too, about Peggy, that she was going to be a stumbling block." And once deliberations began, Frank quickly concluded that Peggy "just didn't have it in her to vote for death." Frank did not hesitate to respond with sarcasm to what he saw as her emotional appeals in arguing for life. He recalled that at one point Peggy had described how as a social worker "she sees sorrow too much" and how she recently had felt the heartbreaking grief of holding in her arms a baby who had just died. Peggy had concluded her story of the baby's death by saying that Lane's case was now a chance for her "to give life." Frank had responded: "If you couldn't hold an innocent baby that died and that never took a life, how could you want this guy who has taken lives to live?" Peggy became upset and started crying, and several of the jurors told Frank that "I wasn't being fair to her," but Frank plaintively explained, "She was the one who brought it up first."

As he described additional exchanges that had ended with Peggy in tears and with him apologizing, it became clear that Frank had seen himself as playing a particular role on the jury. He sensed that the others expected him to be brusque, to raise the arguments that they were too polite to make or were not worldly enough to fully comprehend. In particular, Frank saw himself as the person who needed to make sure that Peggy did not sidetrack the deliberations away from the unshakable fact that an innocent victim had been killed in cold blood.

Frank had come on strong in fulfilling what he saw as his role of keeping the deliberations focused on the killing, in part because he knew that other jurors would keep the deliberations from getting out of hand: "There were several jurors who were the balancing point, they deliberately tried to keep everybody calm." Frank's sense was that the majority jurors were acting something as a team in trying to persuade Peggy, with each person bringing certain strengths to the process. At several points, Frank found himself playing out an unspoken good cop–bad cop routine with one of the Chorus members who "was very articulate." Frank would voice his opinion, often with a tone suffused with anger, but then "when I would get stuck in what I was going to say, she could fill in the words for me, what I was saying." At bottom, Frank believed that in his own way he simply was helping to push hard for a death sentence that his fellow jurors also adamantly desired: "[Most of the jury] was set on the gas chamber from the word go, and I don't think they would have deadlocked unless the judge forced us to."

Perhaps because Frank had seen himself as serving a purpose in his "browbeating" of Peggy and therefore felt no unconscious need to soft-pedal his actions, his no-nonsense narrative of the jury's deliberations closely matched Peggy's description of the tenor of the exchanges and the pressures brought to bear on her. At one point Frank said the deliberations became so loud and angry that the judge, whose chambers were below the jury room, had sent the bailiff up to make sure that everything was okay. As Frank succinctly summarized the deliberations, it was "Peggy against everybody."

Like Peggy, Frank had found the jury instructions to be unnecessarily long and confusing: "The judge sat there and read so many instructions that they were twisting in and out." He readily acknowledged difficulty in following the instructions, attributing the confusion in part to "the way they were worded—they could be put in more common words." Moreover, Frank identified the instructions as a major source of disagreement within the jury. In particular, he had shared Peggy's understanding of the jury instructions as saying that, in Frank's words, "if twelve people couldn't unanimously condemn Lane to the gas chamber, it would automatically be life without parole." It was, of course, this misunderstanding of what would happen if the jury deadlocked on the penalty that Peggy had identified as leading her to change her vote to death.

Although Frank did not purport to understand what in particular had triggered Peggy's change in vote, he was the one juror who correctly sensed that she had never really abandoned her belief that Lane should not receive the death penalty. Unlike Ken and the Chorus members who thought that Peggy had finally, albeit reluctantly, realized that a death sentence was necessary, Frank attributed her vote for death to "pressure, yeah, I think it was pressure because nobody had budged—I think she caved in, that's what happened." Frank had been especially alarmed when she had suddenly announced, "Okay, you guys win," because "I didn't trust the way she turned so fast after three or four days, because she was dead set for life and it was getting hot in that jury room." Still, Frank did not know what the jury could have done at that point other than what it did, giving Peggy more time to think about whether she really wanted to vote for death. Frank noted that while Peggy "had plenty of chances" to change her vote back to life, he personally remained nervous that she would not be able to follow through in announcing the death sentence in the courtroom. And although he felt a sense of relief when Peggy stuck with her vote when the verdict was announced, Frank recalled, "I never did feel that she changed her mind."

Frank turned out to be an intriguing mix of the traditional and the unconventional. Asked Gallup Poll–type questions about his attitude on law and order issues, his responses tended strongly toward a traditional conservative viewpoint, reflecting sentiments that judges are too soft on crime, that criminal defendants are favored at the expense of the victims of crime, and that a greater use of the death penalty would decrease crime. But then, just as Frank's answers seemed to be becoming predictable, he would stray from the traditional viewpoint because of his own personal experiences and a realization that people have ghosts in their backgrounds with which they must deal. When asked, for instance, if a defendant who does not testify is probably guilty, Frank replied, "Oh, that doesn't mean he's guilty—I mean, there's stuff *I* wouldn't want to answer on the stand."

One episode during the trial particularly captured how elusive Frank could be to figure out as a person. Frank noted that during *voir dire* he had been fully candid that he was "for law and order." When asked the critical question of whether he could impose a death sentence if the jury convicted Lane of capital murder, Frank had unhesitatingly replied, "Yes, in a minute." To Frank's amazement, the defense attorney did not strike him from the jury and he sensed that the prosecutor was pleased to have a strong law-and-order juror sitting on the jury. Then one morning as court was convening, Frank strode through the jury room door and into the courtroom wearing earrings in both ears. The prosecutor's shock was evident as his eyes caught the gleam from the earrings as Frank eased himself into his seat in the jury box. At the time, Frank had figured that the prosecutor simply had been startled to learn that his law-and-order juror occasionally wore earrings. After the trial, though, the prosecutor told Frank that he had feared that Frank had worn the earrings as a sign of solidarity with Steven Lane, who also wore earrings. Frank had been amused at the idea, saying with a smile "I don't know why he would think that."

In the end, though, Frank's recognition that life is not a Disney movie did not detract from his fundamental belief in taking personal responsibility for one's choices. Wearing earrings to express individuality is fine, youthful missteps are forgivable, but a lifetime of blaming others for your mistakes is inexcusable. Frank had been outraged to see Lane as he sat at the defense table "looking bored and belligerent at the same time," refusing to take responsibility for the killing or to at least show remorse. For Frank, certain acts and choices demand justice. It was as simple as that. Out of the many, many weeks of evidence and argument, Frank had seen all that he really had needed to know within the first days of trial. He repeatedly found himself returning to the image of the killing on the videotape: "I've seen a lot of stuff, but I never—movies, that's make-believe—this wasn't make-believe, watching him shoot that guy. The videotape was very powerful. I own a handgun, and I don't handle it anymore. To me, there's only one reason you pull out a handgun, and that's because you're going to use it. Just the thought of him pulling out a handgun and deliberately shooting another person! It irritates the heck out of me. . . . It's hard, I can't really describe how—but the videotape made my decision."

Frank's overarching focus on the victim and crime was an outlook that was central to a certain type of juror, a type that might be called fundamentalists—not in the religious sense, but in their fundamental belief that certain types of murder morally require a sentence of death. This group of jurors typically exhibit not only Frank's laserlike focus on the victim and the crime almost to the exclusion of all other factors, but also his impatience for any view that the death penalty is not the appropriate punishment. As a fundamentalist juror in another case captured the sentiment: "At one point I got so sick of this one juror's bullshit arguing for life—I shouldn't say that, but in my mind we were dealing with there is right and there is wrong, enough said."

The fundamentalist's vote for death went far beyond a fear that the defendant someday would be back in society.[2] As one such juror explained, "While life without the possibility of parole would remove him from society, it was not really a just verdict and did not really satisfy the need to punish him for such a violent crime." In describing their punishment decision, the fundamentalist juror placed great emphasis on the viciousness of the crime. Frank had identified watching the videotape and its depiction of what he saw as Lane's cold-blooded actions in taking the clerk's life as the moment that he knew Lane deserved death. In similar fashion, other fundamentalist jurors stated that their minds were made up for death once they focused on the act of the killing and the victim's defenselessness, making comments such as: "How did I decide? I put myself in the victim's position."

Because fundamentalist jurors emphasize the nature of the crime, their decision-making process differs somewhat from other jurors. Fundamentalist jurors, for example, are far more likely than other jurors to say that they made the guilt and punishment decisions "on the basis of similar considerations" than "on the basis of different considerations."[3] Their focus on the killing essentially creates a presumption for death in many cases. As one juror explained: "As we talked, we kept coming up with he's guilty as sin, it's up to them to convince us he should get life." Like Frank, who had emerged from the guilt phase "pretty sure" that Lane deserved death, other fundamentalist jurors also tend to lean strongly toward death coming out of the guilt phase before hearing any evidence at the penalty phase.[4]

Fundamentalists as a whole also tend to be strongly unreceptive to any explanation of a defendant's actions based on his or her life's events. Although a defendant may have called a number of witnesses, taking days and sometimes weeks to put on a case in mitigation, many fundamentalists had great difficulty even remembering what the defense had argued in favor of a life sentence, providing only cursory summaries like: "There really wasn't anything against the death penalty, except who he was, a person with a screwed-up background." One such juror explained his spotty recollection by saying how he had been almost completely focused on the murder itself: "All I was trying to figure out was whether it was a vicious killing or whether he had simply made a mistake. All this other stuff I didn't even think about. I guess I just have a one-track mind." Another juror who had very good recall of the guilt phase but little memory of the penalty phase explained somewhat sheepishly that he had been so convinced that the defendant deserved the death penalty after the guilt phase, "I wasn't paying much attention at this point [the penalty phase]."

It may be tempting to reduce the fundamentalist jurors' viewpoint to a simple expression of a desire for vengeance, a wish to retaliate angrily against a defendant for the horror he or she has caused. A few jurors did use the language of revenge; one even said that he had envisioned himself "as a sort of knight on a white horse avenging the senseless death of these innocent victims." By and large, though, this group of jurors rejected the idea of revenge as a basis for their decision. One juror lost his temper when asked whether he had voted for the death penalty because the defendant "deserved" to die, snapping "I hate that word 'deserved.' It makes it sound like we voted for the sentence for some crazy vengeful reason."[5]

Instead, jurors like Frank expressed a belief that by taking the victim's life the defendant had created a moral imbalance, and the only way to right the balance was to impose a sentence of death. Especially important from this viewpoint was the sentiment that a sentence of life was not a sufficiently severe punishment to right the imbalance. As one juror explained her vote for death: "I guess I was trying to find a balance. If you take something, something should be put in it's place to even it out. . . . I found his crime to be abhorrent, and I don't perceive prison as being the worst thing in the world that can happen to someone. It just didn't seem like an equal. It didn't seem to balance out that he was going to go on living." Another juror tried to articulate how her motivation was not vengeance but an effort to impose the punishment that in her mind fit the crime: "Not that he deserved [death] as vengeance against him, but it was the punishment that suited the crime—they were heinous crimes, super-heinous crimes, world-heinous crimes." Jurors who vote for a death sentence are noticeably more comfortable in agreeing that "the principle of an eye for an eye" rather than "vengeance" is important to their punishment decision.[6]

These jurors' belief that a life sentence could not restore the balance stemmed in part from a perception that prison life was too easy.[7] More basically, though, these jurors consistently conveyed the impression that even if they were convinced that a life sentence meant swinging a sledgehammer in a rock pile for the remainder of the defendant's life, any punishment shy of death would not restore the moral balance.[8] And it was this conviction—that only a death sentence would "fit the crime"—that the fundamentalist jurors who shared Frank's general outlook expressed repeatedly; making comments such as "I just didn't believe that a murderer who killed in the fashion that he did should be allowed to live" or "This is not the type of person you want around—he didn't deserve life without parole, he deserved capital punishment." At bottom, these jurors saw the defendant's killing as having put the moral ledger gravely out of balance and now wanted the defendant to pay what one juror termed "the full penalty" to restore the balance. These jurors would have agreed with the nineteenth-century commentator who said, "[An] execution is a way of saying, 'You are not fit for this world, take your chance elsewhere.'"[9]

Once we understand the fundamentalists' certainty that justice requires a death sentence for the defendant, their conduct in the jury room, like Frank's actions toward Peggy, become more comprehensible. The certainty of belief creates an inclination to dismiss any other viewpoint as representing a lack of understanding or the absence of a moral backbone. As one fundamentalist juror stated, "A lot of the jurors wanting life had to search their souls and that type of baloney. . . . I mean, you can either do it or you can't. It either applies or it doesn't. . . . It was pretty clear-cut to me." Indeed, fundamentalist jurors occasionally spoke so emphatically of the need for a death sentence based on the fact of the killing alone and were so dismissive of any arguments for life that concerns arose that some jurors were being seated who could not, as the Constitution requires, consider the possibility of a life sentence once they determined that a deliberate murder had occurred.[10]

The fundamentalist jurors, however, tend not only to be certain in their beliefs, but also to passionately share Frank's belief that it is up to them personally to act as the victim's voice in the jury room and to ensure that the jury carries out its obligation to protect society. As one fundamentalist juror put it: "Death was the only just punishment. . . . We had a responsibility to remove him from society. . . . This related to my military experience, that at some point you have to remove someone who is AWOL—get rid of the 'dead wood'. . . . I had a duty to stay in that jury to see that fairness was implemented. That was a responsibility, not a choice. . . . I was the one carrying the jury, steering them, that was my job."

Not surprisingly, when the fundamentalist jurors' unwavering belief that the defendant deserves death is coupled with their sense of personal responsibility to obtain a death sentence, often they become a particularly powerful presence in the jury room in arguing for death. As one juror described the fundamentalist juror on her jury, "He was so adamant he had the strength of four or five." Their manner of argument often resembles Frank's self-described "browbeating" of Peggy. Their combativeness and intolerance of other views often places them on the periphery of the jury as a social group, as Frank had ended up with the *Lane* jury. Indeed, it was not unusual for other jurors to describe fundamentalist jurors in less than flattering terms, like the juror who said: "This Archie Bunker type sat down, declared himself foreperson, and said, 'You're more or less an idiot if you don't do this or that.'"

Lack of social acceptance by the other jurors, however, does not necessarily mean that the fundamentalist jurors are not on some level appreciated. Frank sensed that the other jurors had with unspoken approval looked to him to pressure Peggy in ways that they were unwilling to do themselves, and jurors sometimes expressly acknowledged that they had let the fundamentalist juror play such a role. One juror, for instance, reported how in her case, "[T]he dynamics got to be just horrible" with one fundamentalist juror in particular trying to "coerce" a life holdout. This same juror, however, then added with a touch of guilt that "I wouldn't have allowed him to browbeat her to that extent if I didn't think that [the holdout] really felt he should receive the death penalty. . . . I just think it would have taken longer without the. . . . guy."

Although not all fundamentalist jurors are table bangers (nor by any means are all table bangers fundamentalists), jurors with Frank's viewpoint are determined to make sure that the nature of the crime and victim is a major part of the jury's discussions. A juror on a life jury explained how even when it became clear that ten of the jurors wanted a life sentence, the two jurors strongly for death kept returning to their concern that "they didn't want to run into the victim's parents and feel like they didn't do the right thing by the victim and parents." Although these two fundamentalist jurors did not prevail, their arguments were not completely without effect. One of the jurors who had argued strongly for a life sentence had a recurring nightmare after the trial that resonated with the words of the death holdouts: She kept dreaming that she ran into the victim's parents at a grocery store and they began pursuing her up and down the aisles because she had not voted for a death sentence. (She always woke up before they caught her.)

The fundamentalist jurors were adamant in expressing their sentiments for a death sentence, but few communicated any sense of satisfaction in carrying out what they perceived as their duty to restore the moral order. Although Frank stated that serving on the jury actually had made him more supportive of capital punishment "because I saw what he had done and I saw the background," he also volunteered that "it really bothered me, even though I voted for the death penalty, it bothered me to have to sentence him to death." Fundamentalist jurors sometimes broke down in tears, and many voices cracked with emotion as they described having to make the decision for death.

Frank also expressed a feeling of anger that was shared by many of the other jurors over being put into the position of having to make such a difficult decision. Frank directed his anger at Lane himself, remarking "I was mad at him for putting me in a position of having to impose the death penalty—does that make sense?" Or as a juror in another case stated, "At some point in the trial I became angry at the defendant—he comes in from another state, creates a terrible situation killing people and dragging others, such as myself and the other jurors, into the mess; it was so unfair that I had to deal with and be affected by his actions." Other jurors directed their ire at the "system" or the lawyers. One juror who was extremely strong in her fundamentalist approach to the death penalty unleashed her anger in the judge's direction: "And so here we're sitting in this room trying to eat your lunch and to look at this crap and it was tough, it was just tough for everybody to get together and say 'death.' You know, because I said, 'God damn it, what does that judge do? What do they pay him for?' And to me he was nothing more than a— I'm not sure what he is—I'm not sure why they pay him. He was leaving this guy's life in our hands, and I didn't think that was fair. I thought, he makes big money, let him decide if this guy lives or dies! And that's what we were all really bothered by was having to just say 'death.'" This juror, who had exuded a tough, almost challenging we-did-what-we-had-to-do attitude throughout her answers, then started quietly crying, concluding "We were in there being God, and we didn't like it—but death just seemed the fairest of the two choices—it was really hard."

Frank had proven to be a far more likable and complex person than any of the other *Lane* jurors had ever suspected as they witnessed his bursts of anger. Ironically, after hearing Frank's story, Peggy almost certainly would have been the most understanding of his actions in the jury room. Her worldview of each individual as a complex collage of experiences would have recognized how Frank's own background had shaped his view of Steven Lane, his punishment decision, and even of her. In fact, Peggy might have been relieved to learn that an explanation existed for why Frank had adopted such a harsh view of both her and Steven Lane.

Although Frank's treatment of Peggy is still troubling, his candor about his actions was disarming. He had not gloated about his "browbeating" nor had he communicated any sense of delight that Peggy ultimately had changed her vote. Rather, Frank had viewed himself as having a personal duty to be the victim's champion in the jury room, and he had carried out that duty in the best way he knew how. And although Frank had formed an unshakeable judgment of Steven Lane as someone who was responsible for his actions, he had not come to that judgment from the sheltered perspective of someone who had never known what it was like to stray from the straight and narrow. Frank had traveled the low road, he knew its temptations and how hard it can be to find your way back to the high road. In his mind, however, he also knew with utter certainty that it could be done, and he had brought the force of that certainty to his decision that Steven Lane should die. Peggy might be wandering the hallways of the criminal justice system trying to find the right judicial door to knock on and explain how a case had gone terribly awry, but Frank had no doubts that justice had been done.

CHAPTER FIVE

LOOKING INTO THE KALEIDOSCOPE

TO BEGIN MAKING SENSE OF WHAT HAPPENED IN THE TRIAL OF
Steven Lane, it is helpful to understand that the *Lane* deliberations were
both typical and unique at the same time. The concerns and worries that
the *Lane* jurors argued about were largely the same as those that other
capital juries focus on in their deliberations. The facts might vary from
crime to crime and defendant to defendant, but a jury's deliberations invariably gravitate back to debates over the defendant's continued dangerousness and what punishment would fit the crime. Likewise, the
process by which the majority jurors eventually convinced Peggy to
change her vote, the arguments that they made and the powerful influence of the majority's will, were strikingly similar to how most juries
reached unanimity. Viewed through a long-range descriptive lens, the
Lane jury's deliberations were fairly representative of how capital juries
work their way through the maze of legal questions and rules to reach a
verdict.

If the long-range lens gives the impression, however, that any two
randomly chosen juries when presented with the same facts invariably
will work their way to the same conclusion, such an impression would ignore the uniqueness of each jury. Juries may tend to focus on the same
critical questions as they try to make the life-and-death decision, but certainly the *Lane* jury's experience underscores how individual jurors can
react differently to the very same evidence based on their experiences

and beliefs. After describing Peggy's insistence on a life sentence, a Chorus member paused and marveled that Peggy had "heard the exact same things we did" and yet had formed a completely different response. In numerous other cases, jurors were similarly startled to learn that not all had shared their view of the evidence. One juror, for example, walked into the jury room thinking that his jury would reach a verdict within an hour only to discover, "but *noooo*, some people went to a different trial than I did." Another juror had hated the prosecution's argument for death because "the prosecution appealed to revenge and some really baser kinds of human impulses," only to have her anger turn to shock when she learned that "the effect on some other jurors was the opposite. Things that really put me off really convinced some people. They loved it, they wanted to applaud. I was just surprised that people actually thought that way, and I was thinking 'God, I would never say that.' Some of those people really appalled me."

Because different jurors bring distinct perspectives, the very nature of any one jury's deliberations will be unique, creating the possibility that a different mix of jurors might decide the case differently. One can ask, for example, whether the *Lane* verdict might have been different if the clerk of the court's spin of the jury wheel had turned up the name of another Hope juror like Peggy instead of Frank's name. In several cases, for instance, an alliance consisting of only a handful of jurors favoring a life sentence withstood the pressures of a majority that favored death. As a juror in one such case described it: "The [three jurors favoring life] saw eye to eye, stuck up for each other, and made it hard to have a one-on-one discussion." To the great frustration of the majority jurors who had favored death in that case, the alliance proved unshakable and eventually swung the jury all the way to life because the other jurors wanted to avoid a hung jury.

The point, however, is not to engage in a game of what-if scenarios, but to recognize that a capital case will involve the collision of a variety of personalities and facts that escapes any one theoretical model. Perhaps the best that can be done is to offer the metaphor of a kaleidoscope and how it offers up distinctive patterns when its different colored pieces come together. As distinctive as any one pattern may be at first glance, however, a single twist of the kaleidoscope will cause the very same pieces to tumble into a completely different image. A capital trial might be thought of in much the same way: Different pieces of evidence and information will have been placed inside the evidentiary kaleidoscope, and the twelve members of the jury then will have to look into the kaleidoscope and decide whether the image they see is one of a life sentence or that of a death sentence. And, of course, jurors can try to change the pattern that the other jurors are seeing by arguing that the kaleidoscope should be twisted again and the evidentiary pieces allowed to tumble into a different image.

With capital juries, what pattern the jury ultimately is likely to agree on—whether it is one that projects a death sentence or a life sentence—depends in part on what pieces of evidence and information are added into the mix. As the *Lane* jury deliberations demonstrate, a jury is more likely to see a death sentence if the pieces that comprise the pattern include doubts about the meaning of life without parole, a defendant who has a prior history of violent crime, a trial strategy that denies any responsibility for the killing, and a victim who was randomly chosen off the streets. A defense attorney, on the other hand, would be wise to try to add pieces that assure the jury that the defendant functions well in prison, that he or she poses little threat of future violence, and that he or she did not intend the killing of the victim or, at least, was not the main instigator. Most important, the defense must place into the mix the pieces of the defendant's life story that will help convince the jury that the defendant's acts were influenced by the pull of events and circumstances beyond his control.

Once the jury takes the evidentiary kaleidoscope into the jury room, the twelve jurors will turn and tumble the pieces, with each juror telling what pattern he or she sees. In the end, how many turns of the kaleidoscope and what pattern the jury finally agrees on will hinge on a host of factors, such as the different jurors' views of the death penalty, who in the jury room dominates the discussion, how the deliberations are conducted, and the level of contentiousness carrying over from the guilt phase decision. Nor are these the only factors; research continues to uncover additional influences that affect what patterns the jury sees, such as the racial composition of the jury and each juror's religious beliefs.[1]

Even if the myriad of patterns that the evidentiary kaleidoscope can produce cannot be described fully, jurors like Ken, the Chorus, Peggy, and Frank provide a close-up look of how a jury can look into the kaleidoscope and keep tumbling the pieces until a unanimous verdict for death is reached. Perhaps then it is worthwhile to try to see how a jury in another case eventually reached a verdict of life. By looking at the case of *People v. Brown* through the jurors' eyes, we can gain some insight into how the *Brown* jury, unlike the *Lane* jury, looked into the kaleidoscope and eventually saw a life sentence.

The *Brown* case is particularly illuminating because it highlights the critical role that capital defense attorneys play in shaping whether a jury will see a pattern of life or death. The media recently has highlighted some of the more egregious cases of attorneys who have made a mockery of justice. The "sleeping lawyer" cases in particular have tended to catch the public's imagination, like the Texas lawyer who dozed during a capital trial and unabashedly told the court, "I'm seventy-two years old. I customarily take a nap in the afternoon."[2] Unfortunately, no shortage exists of similarly disturbing cases. A brief sampler might include the lawyer who was so drunk during the capital trial that the judge sent him to jail for contempt of court, but then allowed him to resume representing the defendant after spending the night in jail.[3] Or the lawyer who presented not a single piece of mitigating evidence at the penalty phase and whose only argument for life consisted of this closing argument:

> DEFENSE COUNSEL: "Ladies and Gentlemen, I appreciate the time you took deliberating and the thought you put into this. I'm going to be extremely brief. I have a reputation for not being brief. Jesse, stand up. Jesse?
> THE DEFENDANT: Sir?
> DEFENSE COUNSEL: Stand up. You are an extremely intelligent jury. You've got that man's life in your hands. You can take it or not. That's all I have to say.[4]

That lawyer waxed eloquent compared to the lawyer who represented James Fisher in a capital prosecution alleging that Fisher had murdered his homosexual lover. At the penalty phase Fisher's lawyer, a former state senator, waived his opening statement, presented not a shred of evidence in mitigation, and when asked to give his closing argument as to why the defendant should be allowed to live, replied, "We waive." (The lawyer later admitted, "At that time I thought homosexuals were among the worst people in the world, and I did not like that aspect of this case.

I believe my personal feelings towards James Fisher affected my representation of him.")[5]

Commentators and some judges have for a long time strenuously argued that cases like these demonstrate that the courts do not adequately guarantee that capital defendants are receiving the effective assistance of counsel guaranteed by the Constitution. Certainly the fact that some of these outrageous lawyering cases were found to pass constitutional muster lends powerful support to the argument that the standard of what constitutes effective assistance of counsel amounts to little more than the "foggy mirror" test: "If you place a mirror in front of defense counsel during trial and it fogs, counsel is in fact effective."[6]

Lately, it appears that the Supreme Court finally may be starting to pay closer attention to some of the more egregious cases of representation, creating a glimmer of hope that the courts will no longer tolerate flagrant cases of ineffective assistance. The Court's greater sensitivity to the problem of bad lawyering may be a result of studies showing that the appointment of ill-prepared and inexperienced defense lawyers is a prime reason why so many innocent people are ending up on death row.

It is, of course, a step forward if the courts finally crack down on lawyers who miserably fail their clients. No one should be deluded into thinking, however, that disciplining sleeping lawyers now means that individuals who are accused of capital crimes will always have adequate representation. The jurors' stories make it unmistakably clear that a lawyer can do some investigation but still utterly fail to provide adequate representation for a defendant whose life is on the line. In many of the life cases studied, the margin between a life or a death verdict was razor-thin and the jury voted for life only because it was provided with a compelling story for life. In those cases if the lawyer had done even a little less, had not painstakingly pieced together a picture of the defendant's life history, the jury likely would have returned a death sentence instead. Yet under current legal standards, the lawyer who did a little less and whose client as a result is sentenced to death would still be found to have been "effective" under the Constitution. We ironically end up with the lawyer who does just enough to get his client executed: Because the lawyer presented some mitigation evidence the courts will say that the lawyer was "effective" and allow the death sentence to stand, but the attorney, by having failed to engage in the intensely thorough construction of a case for life that is required in a capital trial, never gave his client a true chance.

The case of *People v. Brown* is certainly one where the defendant's only hope for a life sentence rested with defense attorneys who meticulously worked to enhance the chances that the jury would see a pattern of life. As described by the jurors, the killings in the *Brown* case would appear to be the archetypal case for loathing. One juror aptly summarized the case when she said, "These killings were up there in the top five of the most horrible, gruesome things you can ever imagine one human being doing to another." Jurors had little trouble recalling the grisly details of the crime:

> They took the victim out to this secluded point and then the series of events unfolded. To summarize, it was basically torture, rape, and murder. The details are rather gruesome. . . . They were sitting around the tent talking, and I can't remember who hit him first but the beating kind of began. He was handcuffed and leg-cuffed and they beat him with sawed-off mop handles, beat him with fists. At this point, [Brown and his accomplices] are sitting around and drinking, joking, telling the victim that they would let him go. Then they pulled out a B.B. gun and kept shooting him at close range, eighteen or twenty rounds were fired, and both [the defendant in his confession and the accomplice's testimony] described the victim as writhing in pain. At that time he was still begging.
>
> The next torture, the victim was injected in his temple three times with lice poison. As the accomplice described it, the victim was woozy and his eyes rolled back and at that point Brown said, "If you suck my cock, I'll let you go," which the guy refused to do. I think the victim was in shock from the many cruelties, but this cruelty was especially hard—the cruelty of leading someone on as if you're going to let them go. At this point [Brown said in his confession] that the kid was beaten so bad that he needed hospitalization, but if they were to take him to the hospital they knew they'd have to file a police report. At this point the intent to end his life probably came to their minds if it hadn't already. The two accomplices left the tent while Brown forcibly had anal intercourse with him and then the accomplices came back into the tent. During all this torture, they all reported sitting around laughing. There is some doubt of whether he was stabbed first or had his throat slit, but most of us believed that Brown slit his throat first. The second murder, the vic-

tim was stabbed also. Back to the first murder—he was stabbed eight times, four in the front and four in the back and had his throat slit from ear to ear.

It gets worse after this. They realized the guy was dead or dying and they decided to dispose of the body. The first thing they tried to do was decapitate him, and they were unsuccessful in their attempts. . . . [After a number of failed attempts,] finally they stood and wrenched his head off. Then they went for, I believe, the arms went first, so then they keep working on the arms, then working on the legs. They put the body parts in different bags and the head in a Safeway grocery bag. To this day, every time I see a Safeway bag I think of a head. They buried the body somewhere else. Then they went and saw a movie in town, and life went on. Six months transpire, and he does the second murder.

Another juror on the case was particularly taken aback by the dismemberment of the first victim's body:

[Brown and his accomplices] actually talked about how they dismembered the body and how difficult it was and how many different tools they used in cutting the head off—they couldn't do it with the machete, they couldn't do it with a hatchet, and he finally had to take what he called a bow saw, what you would saw a log with, one of those with a rough serrated edge. That's how they finally got the head off. The accomplice [who testified against Brown] was happy to tell about it. Oh, God. The forensic person backed it up because of the marks on the bones. It was like these people wanted his head off and they were going to get it off, you know. You could see the gash marks from the pictures, and the marks left on the vertebrae where they tried with the machete.

And just in case the verbal testimony was not sufficient to drive home the horror of the crime, the jury was surrounded by constant visual reminders:

We saw a number of pictures that were horrible. They were decomposed shots. These were the worst pictures. We had to look at a decomposed anus and a decapitated head for six months. Actually the pictures that stuck more in my mind were of the first victim. They showed the pictures because it had to do with the evidence—the slit throat, and all the stab wounds. But the one where they tilted his head back, you could see his spinal cord, you could see everything. I will never forget that. They are all really in my mind forever, seeing stab wounds. I've never seen that before.

Unless cannibalism was added in, it is hard to imagine a more grisly constellation of facts likely to inspire a visceral reaction of saying "this person deserves the ultimate penalty." Not only were the physical aspects of the crime terrible because they involved torture and extreme brutality, but George Brown displayed the type of callous behavior most likely to anger jurors: toying with a pleading victim, treating the victim's body as a worthless object, acting as if nothing unusual happened after the killing as he went off to the movies.

Nor did Brown project any type of remorse as he sat through the trial "aloof and unemotional." One juror said, "Most of the time he sat there like a lump on a log." Several jurors described how they had watched Brown intently and tried to catch his eye to see if he would look at them, but he always ignored their efforts. One juror felt intense anger at what he perceived to be Brown's "smugness" as the defendant listened to witnesses describe his terrible crimes. Like the other jurors, this juror concluded that Brown "showed absolutely no remorse at all."

Compared to Lane's crime, Brown's actions were far more grotesque, and he appeared to be every bit as remorseless as most jurors had perceived Lane to have been. This inevitably raises the question: Why were the *Lane* jurors swayed by their loathing and why were the *Brown* jurors not? The *Brown* jurors left no doubt that they were horrified by what he did. One juror started weeping just recounting the facts, and most of the jurors were leaning strongly toward the death penalty after hearing the gruesome testimony. When asked how strongly he favored a death sentence for Brown after the guilt phase, one juror replied, "100 percent positively. I would have dropped the cyanide tablets myself, said, 'bye, bye' and waved at him. I wanted him dead."

❦

What becomes immediately apparent when comparing the *Lane* and *Brown* cases is that Brown's attorneys were able to place into the evidentiary kaleidoscope a number of striking pieces that help to project an image of life. In Steven Lane's case, of course, the defense was unable to convince anyone but Peggy to fully put aside their anger and distrust of Lane. The jury had viewed the psychiatrist who testified for Lane as little more than a con man, and his mother and sister had not been able to paint a picture of Steven's life that convinced the jury that he had not chosen to take the low road. Lane's life story had invoked sympathy within the hearts of the *Lane* jurors, but a majority of them had remained unmoved by the defense's argument that Lane was not fully responsible for the events leading up to the killing of Carlos Castillo. And, of course, many of the jurors still feared the violence that Lane might commit in the future in prison, or even more frighteningly, if he ever got back into society.

The Brown defense's first task then was to try to convince the jurors to put aside the horror of two gruesome murders and "look at the human factor." Skilled capital lawyers know that just as the *Lane* jury had done, most juries will at least figuratively draw a time line to puzzle out at what point the defendant got caught up in his life's events. In fact, so many juries actually do draw out a time line of the defendant's life that it gives rise to what might be called the "butcher paper phenomenon": the tendency for a jury to request from the bailiff a roll of paper that the jurors then tape to the wall and use to chart out the defendant's time line with a Magic Marker. After sketching out the time line, the jurors attempt to decipher chronologically how a defendant's life's events unfolded and determine if he ever was presented an opportunity to turn his life around and escape a life of crime.

Given that jurors tend to strongly embrace a free-will view of human behavior, a skilled defense attorney will want to be very involved at the penalty phase in helping the jury draw the time line.[7] In one case, for example, a defense attorney in his closing argument commanded the butcher paper himself and drew out a time line for both the defendant and himself, visually depicting for the jury how different the defendant's life was from someone like the lawyer who had experienced a normal upbringing. The lawyer's objective was to encourage the jury to think in terms of contrast: how if one could go back in time and sample simultaneous moments in people's lives, the split screen would show moments such as the nine-year-old defendant tearfully pleading with his mother to not shoot the hypodermic loaded with heroin into her tied-up vein at the same time that the lawyer as a third grader was piling into the back of the family station wagon and popping a wad of Bazooka bubble gum into his mouth as he set off to play a game with his Ace Hardware Little League team.

In an effort to diagram the time line for the jury, Brown's lawyers presented a wide variety of witnesses who testified in vivid detail to events that helped explain how George Brown found himself wielding a machete dismembering his victim late one night. Critical to telling their story of how George could ever come to do such acts to another human being were George's sisters, who had witnessed firsthand the incredible abuse George had suffered at the hands of his father. Fortunately for George, they were able to re-create the atmosphere of terror for the jury through powerfully eloquent stories that stuck with the jurors. One juror prefaced her descriptions of the stories with the statement: "His father was like an animal, like a literal animal." She then recounted how George had suffered:

> Severe, acute child abuse, child neglect, child torture. The child abuse stories were from his sisters and neighbors. [The father] raped all the daughters, and we heard graphically about the daughters' experience with their father. He would be at the kids mercilessly. He would tie George up for a day, two days at a time. He would have his girlfriend over. He would make the daughters wait on him while he was having sex with his girlfriend, with the mother downstairs. . . . He was drunk all the time. Whatever food there was he'd take and give the kids nothing but chicken feet. He would beat the mother up and got into fights at bars, was antagonistic, was hateful. He hated George because he was the darkest skin. In those days, dark black skin was considered less desirable, and the father was light skin. He always told him he wasn't his kid. One time he locked them all in a bureau for over twenty-four hours, all five kids hunched up, while he was drunk. He beat them with razor straps. He poured alcohol on them. He had them tied up and was beating them with straps. He then poured alcohol on them to see them writhe with more pain. He chased the girls, they would run to the car. He had sex with them continuously from when they were four to about sixteen. One of the times when they went [on a car trip], he made them sit with their legs spread open with a mirror on the floor of the car so he could look up their dresses.

Another juror similarly recounted how

> His dad made George feel inferior because George had darker skin than the others and made him feel he wasn't really a part of the family, that he was somebody else's kid. His dad was good with a knife.

One time George was getting into his teens, I guess it was right before he was sent off to prison or just when he got back from his first go around at a reform school, George was going to confront his father about the abuse of his mother and the fact that he was sexually molesting his sisters. The father took a knife to his mom's throat as George was coming down the stairs and said, "Boy, if you give me any trouble I'll slit her throat." . . . And it was the whole family, it wasn't just one person coming in and saying how bad a family life this kid had, I mean, it was over and over again. There wasn't any wavering.

As if the accounts of relentless daily abuse were not poignant enough, all of the jurors recalled a particular incident that seemed to capture the horrors of George Brown's childhood in one episode. Stuck in a life that seemed to hold only emotional and physical pain when people were involved, the sisters recalled for the jury how as a young child George had a pet dog and rabbit. Between beatings and watching his father do horrible things to his sisters and mother, George would escape to the comfort of his pets. Playing with them became his one oasis of love and comfort in a terrifying world. He fed and cared for them, and in what must have seemed a miracle to the young boy, they would give him the sense that he was loved and that they wanted to be with him and depended on him.

One day the father came home in a drunken rage, as usual. Almost as if to make certain that any flickering sparks of love or trust that George might still hold in his heart were fully smothered, his father stormed out to the backyard with his gun, shot George's pet rabbit, and cooked it for dinner. The horrified children would not eat the rabbit, so the father took it out to George's dog and tried to make the dog eat it. As the dog turned away from the rabbit, refusing to eat it, the father threatened to kill the dog. With George pleading for the dog's life, the father shot the dog as the boy looked on. One of George's sisters poignantly summarized the depths of hatred they came to feel toward their father with her simple statement that the only reason she went to her father's funeral was "to make sure the son of a bitch was dead."

Stories such as those that the sisters told, stories that made the jurors visualize the defendant as a small child watching his pets, his only sources of love in a hate-filled home, killed in front of him by a monstrous father, are the verbal pictures that are worth a thousand clinical words. With such a narrative background, the jury can look at a picture of the defendant "in his little sailor suit when he was only four or five years old" and glimpse, for at least a moment, the defendant as someone other than the adult sitting twenty feet away on trial for two repulsive torture murders.

The one potential weakness of such testimony, of course, is that it is subject to the suspicion that it is being exaggerated out of familial love. In George's case, the defense muted such concerns by fortifying the sisters' emotionally compelling stories with testimony from other witnesses. These witnesses bolstered the theme that forces beyond George's control had left indelible marks on him and molded a personality that would later lead him to commit two brutal murders. One of these forces was George's wrongful incarceration in an adult prison for stealing a bike when he was a juvenile. The defense presented this event to the jury in part through the testimony of a judge who had helped secure the defendant's release from the wrongful detention. A juror recalled this witness as

> a very flamboyant, articulate judge who literally, while she was on the stand, took over [the] courtroom. She was one of the judges that upon hearing what had happened to George being incarcerated for stealing a bicycle at fourteen, was instrumental in getting him released from prison. . . . He spent [seven] years in prison for stealing a bicycle and doing a childish prank at some girl's house that he had this infatuation with. And she literally took over the courtroom. . . . She was presenting the fact that black, [rural] working-class families, they were basically screwed by society. These were the outcast people. She did a lot to bring that to life. . . . And if his next-door neighbor had been a white boy, would he have gotten [seven] years for stealing a bicycle? No . . . [Seven years for stealing a bike] in the full-blown penitentiary. You just can't comprehend that such a thing would happen. But this judge actually was there and was explaining it.

Asked if he would have been disinclined to believe what had happened without the witness's testimony, the juror replied, "Not that I would have doubted it, but she added such, such—what's the word when something is so positive it's so undeniable—it's such reality."

The final piece provided by the defense to complete the picture of George's life story came from an expert witness on child abuse. In contrast to the *Lane* jury, which had viewed the psychiatrist's testimony with distrust and sometimes disdain, the *Brown* defense used the professional expert in the one way that makes juries most receptive to expert testimony: as an accompanist who is there to help the jury understand the other evidence that they have heard during the trial rather than simply holding herself out as "The Expert" telling them to rely on her opinion.

Against the backdrop of the heart-wrenching stories about George's terribly abusive father, the defense expert explained the effects of child abuse to the jury. Because the expert's testimony was firmly grounded in the other testimony that they had heard, most of the jurors found themselves receptive when she "said that this is one of the worst cases of child abuse and neglect she had ever seen, and he never had a chance. . . . Her testimony just helped us so much . . . to understand what caused him to do what he did." Tellingly, although the government's expert stated that Brown still had control over his choices despite the abuse he suffered, most jurors found the defense expert more persuasive because they felt that her testimony made more sense based on everything they had heard. As one juror explained, "We had all the other witnesses *plus her.*" The defense expert's credibility, already heightened because her explanation fit best with the other evidence, was further enhanced because, as several jurors noted, she often testified for the prosecution and was an advocate of the death penalty. As a result, although most of the *Lane* jurors viewed the expert as a hired gun, the *Brown* jurors placed greater confidence in this witness's narrative because they knew it was one that she did not often tell.

Brown's lawyers were aware, however, that convincing the jury that Brown's life story was a tragic culmination of events largely beyond his control would not be enough. George's horrible childhood might be sufficient to at least muffle the jury's loathing reaction, but it still would leave the dangerousness factor.

Like the *Lane* jury, the *Brown* jurors learned at the penalty phase that George Brown had a long history of violent criminal acts and heard very disturbing testimony from several of his prior victims. As with Steven Lane, therefore, the distinct possibility existed that the *Brown* jurors would view Brown as someone whom the criminal justice system simply could not control. As jurors in any case always made clear in explaining their punishment decision, even the most compelling life story would not overcome their sense of duty to keep a defendant from causing further harm. One *Brown* juror, for example, had been extremely affected by the abuse that George had suffered, saying that "hearing about his childhood was the worst thing I've ever been through," but, she immediately added, "I could have put out of my mind what happened to him as a child and say 'the guy goes to the gas chamber' if I thought there was any chance he could harm someone [else]."

To address the grave question of whether Brown would cause future harm if not given a death sentence, the defense called witnesses from his prior stays in prison to establish that Brown functioned fairly well in prison. A prison nurse in particular was highly persuasive for a number of the jurors. Her persuasiveness was derived, in part, because she came across as a hard-as-nails type of person who was accustomed to prisoners trying to deceive her, and yet she had always found George to be trustworthy and cooperative. One juror stated: "She is a strong, strong proponent of the death penalty, but she did not think the death penalty was appropriate based on her relationship, interviews, knowledge over the last seven years of what he was like, and that weighed, you know. Here was a professional who deals with these types of people all the time, who is a proponent of the death penalty, and who doesn't think he's a good candidate for the death penalty. That weighed in my mind."

The prison nurse's statements dovetailed nicely with other testimony that presented a picture of the defendant as someone who could not handle life outside the prison walls but adapted positively within the structured life of a prisoner. One juror said he came away with the impression that "George was generally a very helpful person. He was a good influence in the prison, and that was one of the defense's biggest points, was to show that he would be a contributor to prison. . . . He was seen as a bridge between the races, and I can perceive that he was helpful to the guards. He was helpful in keeping order in the prison, and I think he squealed on someone who had weapons. . . . I think he was in ways a giving person." And unlike the witnesses on Lane's behalf, these witnesses did not have any startling revelations that undermined their basic message: George Brown was a good prisoner who might even make a positive contribution if serving the rest of his life behind bars.

The jury also heard "extensive testimony to convince us that . . . no one has gotten out," and the testimony did reassure the jurors about prison security. The testimony, however, was less successful on another score. The jury had been shown photographs of the prison and given descriptions of being a "lifer" that were intended to dispel any concern that Brown's life in prison would be a "country club existence." The evidence, however, did not really come across to the jurors as particularly bleak, with one juror recalling that while "they did not present a pleasant picture, it was not an exceptionally depressing picture either." The defense, however, received an unexpected assist in convincing the jury of the harshness of prison life from an inmate who had been called as a witness during the guilt phase. After being sworn in, the inmate was warned by the prosecutor that if he did not tell the truth, he could be sent back to a "supermax" prison where he previously had served time. What caught the jury's attention was the witness's clear dread of such a prospect: "You should have seen that guy react when they said, 'If you don't tell the truth we're going to send you back up to [the supermax prison].' That was the only time he ever showed any emotion—and this was a guy who could like handle almost any prisoner around. So to me that type of prison is more of a punishment—that kind of isolation—than the death penalty. He would have done anything to avoid that prison." More than the prison expert's testimony, the spontaneous crumbling of the inmate's macho manner at the mention of the prison helped convince the jury that prison in fact would be a severe punishment for Brown's barbarous crimes.[8]

One possible stumbling block still lay in the defense's path of trying to convince the jurors that life without parole was a choice that they could consider with a clear conscience that George Brown would never kill again. If sentenced to prison, Brown might be surrounded by rows of razor-sharp barbed wire and always be in sight of armed guards, but might not a lawyer or bleeding-heart judge find a way to unlock the prison door and release him back into society? Certainly the Chorus members in deciding Steven Lane's fate had been affected by the possibility that life without parole might not guarantee that Lane would never find a way back onto the streets.

Although the *Lane* jury had not asked the judge about whether life without parole meant that Steven would never get back on the streets, a number of jurors from other cases did ask their judge, including some of the *Brown* jurors. If a jury sends a note from the jury room asking the judge about the meaning of life without parole, it often means that the jury's deliberations have reached a logjam, and the jury will scrutinize the judge's answer like a cryptologist looking for hidden code. Ultimately which way the logjam breaks—toward life or death—largely depends upon the judge's answer.

If the judge answers in unambiguous terms that life without parole means that the defendant will remain in prison for the rest of his or her natural life, the jury is very likely to come back with a life verdict, often within minutes after receiving the judge's reply. As a juror explained in one such case: "If we had thought that life without parole meant he would ever get out, we wanted death, but we were assured that life without parole meant he would never be released."

On the other hand, if the judge is seen as equivocating in some way—telling the jury that "the governor has the power to commute sentences but you should not speculate about that possibility" or, in some cases, declining to answer the question all together—jurors are likely to draw on their underlying skepticism and interpret the judge's answer or refusal to answer as a judicial wink and a nod that the defendant might indeed be released someday. One juror, for instance, placed great emphasis on the judge's use of the word "assume" when the judge instructed that the jury was to "*assume* that life without parole meant that the defendant would never be released." The juror instead assumed that the judge's answer meant that no guarantees could be made. Predictably, juries that understand the judge as saying life without parole might allow release someday also are usually quick to return a verdict after the judge's reply to their question, but theirs is a verdict for death: "We didn't want to see him out in the mainstream of life, we didn't want to take that chance, because if we gave him any lighter of a sentence than the death sentence, we were afraid that he would someday be released and do it all over again. This man is a bad man."[9]

While the *Brown* jurors did not send out a note to the judge, during jury selection several of the jurors had "asked the judge if [life without parole] meant what it said it meant." Fortunately for George Brown, the jurors recalled the judge as saying "Yes, that's exactly what it meant . . . that it really meant he was never going to get out. That's what we wanted to know, and we were told that he would be spending the rest of his life in prison or on death row until he would be executed. The judge said he would never get out." Consequently, as they deliberated, the *Brown* jurors, unlike some of the *Lane* jurors, did not find themselves worrying that Brown someday would be back on the streets; instead, their focus was almost entirely on what punishment fit two torture murders by a man with his own tortured past.

As the *Brown* jurors retired to begin their punishment deliberations, they had before them a kaleidoscope with pieces that, depending on the viewer's perspective, could project a strong image of either death or life. And as the jurors took turns describing what image they saw as they tumbled the pieces, their different descriptions were not unexpected. Some jurors were so aghast and infuriated by the horrors of the crimes that they believed that no punishment other than death could begin to balance the moral scales: "Those who felt the death penalty was more appropriate kept saying 'Look at the viciousness of the crime, the decapitation, the torture, his prior crimes. I mean, this is a really bad person.'" As one of the jurors for life noted, "The jurors for death made some very convincing statements about how he dragged the body up, he left it there, he picked him up by the hair, slit his throat, sawed off his head—you know, it's not too hard for them to conjure up real horrible images that would sway people." The jurors for death also looked at the time line and argued that "okay, maybe he was abused, maybe he was bad when he got out of a prison for stealing the bike, but he should have been able to turn his life around over time."

Other jurors, however, looked into the kaleidoscope and saw a life sentence. As one juror described the arguments of those who wanted a life sentence: "They kept insisting that we look at the childhood, that there were two bad things—the child abuse since he was five and then he was in prison for seven years for the theft of a bicycle. If it was just one of those, you know, we might decide to give him the death penalty, but he had a double curse—first he was at home not getting any protection, not getting any love, *and then* you put him in adult prison for seven years as a young teenager. You think you're getting away from the hell of his home, but you're entering another hell-type situation." The jurors favoring life made no attempt to argue that the crimes were not repulsive but concentrated on "compassionate speeches" emphasizing that Brown himself had been a victim and that he had never had a chance to choose a normal life.

This group of jurors in favor of a life sentence responded with equal fervor to every argument made by the jurors favoring death. Simon, one of the jurors who argued most vehemently for life, shared much of Peggy's outlook on life and human behavior. Drawing on his background as a "social work major and having studied a lot on the social sciences about the way society impacts an individual," Simon had quickly concluded that George Brown had been indelibly shaped by his horrific childhood. He also shared Peggy's view of the power of redemption: "I just thought if society was to do anything, it certainly couldn't do anything by killing the guy, and I'm the type of person that looks for what can we get out of this, what's the plus we can get out of this even though it's a bad situation. I guess that I felt if he had a chance to live he might be of some plus to people that already were in prison, he might be able to help them." Simon, however, differed in a critical way from Peggy: He was not alone on the jury in arguing for life, and thus he did not hesitate to argue vocally that the jurors favoring death were failing to understand what had happened to George Brown.

The jury did not vote until the fourth day, although the discussions leading up to the first vote left no doubt that the jury was seriously divided. Once the jury did start voting, each ballot brought considerable suspense when the foreperson announced the total. At various points, the ballot totals ranged from eight to four for life all the way to eight to four for death, with some six to six splits thrown in to underline just how divided the jury was over the decision. It would take seven days of deliberations before the jury returned a unanimous verdict.

As would become apparent as the deliberations continued, the inability of the *Brown* jurors wanting the death penalty to gain a strong majority at the very outset meant that they would never gain the momentum necessary to obtain a verdict of death. Their arguments were strongly and passionately made as they tried to persuade the others to favor death. Even several of the jurors who consistently voted for life felt the pull of the death jurors' arguments; one remarked, "I could see where if enough people had been adamant about him being executed it probably would have persuaded me." Unlike in *Lane's* case, however, the *Brown* jury room never was filled with the sense that an overwhelming sentiment existed within the jury for the death penalty. Instead, a middle block of four jurors moved back and forth between the groups favoring life and death, allowing neither to gain a clear upper hand for the first four days of deliberation.

As usually happens, though, a jury that is not controlled from the outset by a strong majority for a death sentence eventually will gravitate toward a life sentence.[10] And this is what began to happen as the middle block of jurors slowly started to drift into the group of life jurors. As these jurors shifted, they stated that the more they thought about George Brown's life, the "more comfortable" they became with "finding mercy." This had not been the case in the very beginning, because while every juror had been sickened by what Brown had suffered through as a child, not all of them had been convinced that it had doomed him to a life of violence. Some had argued, for instance, that he had periods in "his life that he didn't do any crimes, therefore he must be a normal person. The child abuse didn't affect him that much in the end."

As the jury spent hour after hour going over the time line of George Brown's life, however, the vacillating jurors gradually became convinced that, in fact, he "never had a chance." The only two black jurors on the jury were critical to helping the undecided jurors arrive at this view. The important role that these two jurors played is consistent with a recent groundbreaking study that has found that not only do black jurors often see evidence differently, but the racial composition of the jury can affect what the jury as a whole sees. Among a number of important findings, the study made an explosive discovery when it looked at how a jury's racial composition affected cases like that of George Brown, where a black defendant is accused of killing a white victim: If even one black male juror served on the jury in such a case, the chances of a death sentence were "substantially reduced."[11]

The study found that the dramatic difference in the rate of death sentences based on the presence of black male jurors reflects a difference in view between black and white male jurors about almost every factor that is pivotal in tipping jurors toward death or life. On the whole, black male jurors are more likely to see the defendant as remorseful, are more receptive to the defendant's evidence that his background had adversely influenced his life, are more inclined to have lingering doubts about the defendant's role in the crime, and are less likely to believe that the defendant poses a future danger if given a life sentence.[12] And although these differences in perception exist in all categories of cases, they are especially pronounced when the case involves a black defendant accused of killing a white victim, the type of case that has raised the most troubling concerns about racial discrimination in the death penalty.[13]

In George Brown's case, not only were the two black jurors convinced that Brown's horrible upbringing had damned him to a life of crime, but they also provided crucial context for the other jurors. As a white juror explained, the black jurors helped the other jury members make sense of life events that some might not otherwise have fully understood or appreciated:

We had two blacks, just two blacks on the jury, and there were points where the [discussion] geared more towards race, more towards blacks. . . . They would say you all may not realize that for a black person . . . this is how we as a culture might look upon this event, or, you know, help explain the home situation and the dominant father and matronly, passive mother. A lot of people had anger towards the mother, saying how could she know of [the father's terrible abuse] and never do anything, you know, how could that happen, and [the black jurors] helped explain. I mean, a lot of the whole flavor of deliberations was trying to get an understanding, trying to make sense, of these bizarre events . . . and for some people who were brought up in a more traditional or normal, for lack of a better word, environment, it's just beyond their comprehension. They can't get an appreciation when everything has been normal for you, they just may not be able to appreciate how abnormal or dysfunctional things are for others and how it affects the capacity to love, the capacity to trust. There are some people who could not see that, because they just assume that [criminality] is an inherited trait. . . . I mean, it was truly a dynamic case. . . . It was, again, a black person's help [in explaining], and we were looking for understanding.

By the middle of the fifth day of deliberations, the middle block of jurors was now voting consistently for life and the tally was a firm nine to three vote for life. In an effort to dynamite the death holdouts off their position, some of the jurors in favor of a life sentence began to craft arguments that were interesting mirror images of those that had been directed at Peggy. Although Peggy had been told that she needed to get her attention off of her emotions and instead to focus on "the law," the majority jurors in *Brown* found themselves making "some very human appeals" to the death holdouts "on the ability to show mercy." One juror for life recalled that "guilt to an extent was used—it's like, 'Are you that hard of a person that you can't find mercy in your heart?' Things like that." In another mirror-image argument to that which was made to Peggy, the life majority jurors in *Brown* used the jury selection questions to try to plant doubts in the death holdouts' minds. The life jurors reminded the holdouts that they had promised during *voir dire* that they would not automatically impose a death sentence, leading one of the life jurors to raise his voice and say, "God damn it, if you told them that you could decide for life, what more mitigating circumstances do you need to hear, how much worse could someone's life be that you can't even consider life as a possibility?"

One of the jurors still for death, Jerry, identified most strongly with the two young victims. The victims had been runaway teenagers who hustled for sex as a way of making ends meet. Although Jerry had not been a runaway, he was gay and was familiar with the hustling scene. He saw Brown's horrible killings as a brutal assault upon the gay community. He also was distressed by the idea that sentencing Brown to life in prison might give him access to young male prisoners. Jerry worried that this access would expose these prisoners to assaults by Brown or, alternatively, allow Brown to find willing partners, which would mean that Brown was not really being punished for his horrible crimes.

Ultimately, though, Jerry found his anger and insistence on a death sentence lessening. He had become good friends with several of the jurors who now were firmly in the life camp, and he began to listen with a more open mind to their arguments. Finally, although he already felt himself inching his way toward a vote for a life sentence, it was the direct appeal of one of the black jurors that made him fully agree that the defendant had been "victimized" by his upbringing:

> [And I was convinced by a] black juror. . . . Oh boy, this is going to sound really terrible when it comes out of my mouth—it was his manner and charisma, his compassion and his articulation did move me so much in regards to the black race, in terms that George was victimized. Here's a black man who was almost in the same situation as George, without the atrocities and the abuse and everything, but black, poor, lower middle class from the South. [He] led a very compassionate life in the Army. . . . Finally, I guess after nothing more than a benefit of the doubt and compassion, I agreed it would be life without parole. He's a wonderful guy, have you met him? He's wonderful. He's a wonderful, wonderful soul, such a person.

Jerry had looked at the time line, listened to the other jurors, and ultimately compared his life with Brown's and realized that "while I was a teenager worrying about getting new clothes, he was already in prison being raped and abused. He never had much of a chance."

Despite Jerry's defection, though, the other two jurors still favoring death—Michael and Karen—remained adamant in their insistence that Brown deserved to be executed for such ghastly crimes and that he should be held responsible despite his past. Now well into their sixth day of deliberations, the jury members did not know what else to do. They had looked into the kaleidoscope countless times, argued about what image was shown from every conceivable angle, held out hope as the jury moved to ten jurors favoring life, but now they had stalled. Stalemated, the jury had to concede that they were on the verge of becoming what every jury feared, a hung jury. With great reluctance, they sent out a note to the judge telling him that they were unable to reach a decision.

A note telling a judge that the jury is hung is guaranteed to hit a sharp judicial nerve. Just as nature abhors a vacuum, the justice system abhors indecision. In the fourteenth century, juries routinely were locked up "without meat, drink, fire, or candle, or conversation with others, until they were agreed."[14] If a jury became deadlocked, a judge would put the jurors in an oxcart and release them only once they reached a verdict.[15] Even well into the twentieth century, cases arose where judges would try to force a verdict by requiring the jury to deliberate throughout the night, threatening to deprive jurors of food from Saturday to Monday, or suggesting to a jury deliberating in the dead of winter that cutting off water and heat would help them reach a verdict.[16]

Although judges no longer have oxcarts waiting for jurors if they became deadlocked, they do have instructions that are intended to keep a jury from becoming hung if at all possible. The instructions essentially tell the jury to go back and continue deliberations, urging the jurors to abide by the somewhat conflicting advice of respecting each other's opinion while also asking every juror to rethink his or her own view and to keep in mind that if they cannot decide, another jury no smarter than they are may have to hear the case again. This type of instruction has been referred to by such colorful labels as a shotgun charge, hammer charge, the third-degree charge, dynamite charge, and nitroglycerine charge. As the nomenclature suggests, the idea of the instruction is that "It can blast a verdict out of a jury otherwise unable to agree."[17]

Although jurors from cases that had received a dynamite charge did not remember the instruction's precise wording, they certainly recalled its essence, often in their own colorful way: "The judge said . . . you'll be here until the cows come home." Juries that received a dynamite charge thus returned to the jury room with the unmistakable understanding that the judicial system expected them to reach a decision, or, as one juror explained, "the judge wouldn't let us *not* reach a decision." A juror in another case reported that the jurors told the judge several times that they were deadlocked, but the judge patiently replied each time that "he had confidence in us" and "he'd send us back in to try again."

When the *Brown* jury informed their judge that they were deadlocked, he did not outwardly show frustration. He did, however, tell them "to keep on trying," and they understood him as saying that a hung jury would be a failure for both him and the jury after a trial that had lasted months. As one juror said, "He was like, 'please don't do this.'" The judge told the jurors to continue deliberations and "asked if there was anything we needed that would help us." Unsure of what to do or what would help them, the jury returned to the jury room and, in one juror's words, "simply went through more of it." Although emotions had flared at various points, now "people were getting more impatient," in part because everyone had "run out of speeches to make" and it seemed as if nothing would change. The jury adjourned for the evening with everyone worn down and devoid of any sense that a light waited at the end of the tunnel. On some level, it seemed senseless to have to return the next day with such dim prospects for the vote changing.

As the seventh morning of deliberations got under way, however, some of the life jurors sensed that Michael's comments were signaling the possibility of movement. The judge had offered to provide any materials that might help jump-start the deliberations, so the jury agreed that it might be helpful to hear again the testimony of the defense's expert on child abuse and the prison nurse who had come to know Brown well as a prisoner. The judge provided the jury with transcripts of the testimony to take back to the jury room. Like a drama group reading from a script, the jurors took turns reading from the transcripts, a process that by necessity drew everyone back into the deliberations. By going back over the testimony of these two witnesses, the jury also found the deliberations focusing intently once again on the time line of George Brown's life, because these were the witnesses who "were able to give us the best indicator of his thought processes . . . rationales for some of his behaviors." Their testimony also gave the majority jurors another opportunity to argue that Michael and Karen were stubbornly and irrationally refusing to acknowledge the effects of Brown's horrific childhood. As the jury worked their way through the testimony, the majority would pause after each of the experts' observations and say to Michael and Karen, "See, here is . . . another explanation for his behaviors."

The process eventually eroded what remained of Michael's insistence on a death sentence, or, as another juror said, "It wasn't as if he all of a sudden saw the light . . . we had to drag it out of him." Michael still was far from convinced that Brown's background had overcome his ability to make the choices that led to the horrible killings, but he found enough of an explanation in the expert's testimony that "he could sleep with himself" and let go of feeling that only the death penalty could serve as punishment for what Brown had done. Moreover, Michael had found it increasingly difficult to be one of only two people arguing that someone should die as ten other people argued for "mercy." A number of jurors in other cases who found themselves in Michael's position also noted that they felt as if they were being portrayed as heartless and as lacking compassion, a portrayal that grew with uncomfortable intensity as the number of jurors supporting death dwindled to two or one.

With Michael ready to change his vote, Karen quickly and quietly decided to make the verdict for life unanimous. Her reason, quite simply, was that she did not want to deadlock the jury. Unlike Michael, she never embraced the idea, even reluctantly, that a life sentence was the "right decision." Rather, her change in vote was a pragmatic conclusion that it simply was not worth deadlocking the jury, especially since the jury was confident that George Brown would never leave prison.

In making this decision, Karen exhibited the single biggest difference between death and life holdouts who changed their votes. A holdout favoring life rarely changes her vote and sends someone to the death chamber if she simply sees the majority's favoring of death as an honest but understandable difference in opinion.[18] To change a life holdout's vote, therefore, the majority jurors have to actively convince the holdout that a death sentence is *the only right answer* and that to cling to a life vote is to defy the law and violate his or her oath as a juror. Even Peggy, although she later became convinced that she had made a terrible mistake in voting for death, had concluded at the time she changed her vote that the other jurors must be right in insisting that a death sentence was the only correct verdict.

By comparison, many death holdouts who ultimately switch their vote never accept the idea, even as they change their vote, that a life verdict is the most just outcome. These are jurors, often fundamentalist jurors like Frank, who strongly believe that death is the only just verdict and have trouble accepting that the other jurors do not agree. Generally they attribute their change in vote to wanting to avoid forcing taxpayers to foot the bill for another trial or because they are uncertain about the consequences of a hung jury and want to make certain that the defendant at least will be in prison for life. Not surprisingly, this group of holdouts often continues to express great dissatisfaction after the trial with the life verdict, lamenting that their juries did not have the "guts" to impose death or had "wimped out when it came to the penalty phase." Indeed, a few death holdouts had such strong feelings that they took consolation in speculating about the defendant's life in prison, like the juror in one case who calmly revealed that he was able to "give up a death sentence" because with AIDS running rampant in prisons, the defendant was certain to contract the disease and die a slow, painful death.

Fortunately for the *Brown* jury, Karen did not express such strong feelings or show any regret over changing her vote to life. Instead, she quietly acquiesced to a life sentence, and the jury room, which for the past seven days had echoed with strong opinions, became uncharacteristically silent. And, then, as often happened after the jury had successfully struggled its way to unanimity, the majority jurors brought the holdouts back into the fold, joining hands and letting out a cheer.

George Brown's case stands as a remarkable piece of capital litigation. On a scale of one to ten in aggravation, the double-torture murder stands as a "ten" compared to other cases. The defense did have some factors that work in favor of a life sentence: Brown's accomplice had received a sentence of less than death in exchange for his testimony (a factor that makes juries lean toward life if the accomplice is equally culpable); the victims were individuals who had run away from home and were living a high-risk lifestyle; and Brown had not denied the crimes at the guilt phase (which makes juries more receptive at the penalty phase to a defendant's case in mitigation). Still, given the horrendous nature of the crimes, the defense had to reach a "ten" in mitigation to have any realistic hope of avoiding a death sentence for George Brown. His attorneys, through their meticulous development of the defendant's life story with a Shakespearean eye for detail and how to bring out the "human factor," succeeded.

The *Brown* case, however, also highlights the importance of who is taking turns looking into the kaleidoscope and interpreting the pattern. The *Brown* jury, like the *Lane* jury, had some jurors who from the beginning pushed extremely hard for a death sentence as the only way to achieve justice. But unlike the *Lane* jury, where Peggy stood alone in strongly insisting that the image was one of life, the *Brown* jury had a critical mass of jurors who strenuously favored life and acted as a counterweight in the deliberations and stopped the jurors favoring death from building up any significant momentum. These life jurors were vocal in their insistence that the other jurors keep looking at the pattern until they agreed that the pattern was one of "life" and not "death"; indeed, Simon had argued so passionately that Brown deserved a life sentence that he confessed after the trial to "a certain amount of guilt, wondering if I worked too hard to change people's minds or pushed too hard for life—it can sound like personal assaults on people in the deliberations." And, of course, the two black jurors provided invaluable context to the evidence that the jury heard about a black defendant's upbringing, context that helped shape what the other jurors saw when they peered into the kaleidoscope and that directly led to at least one of the three death holdouts changing his mind.

The final lesson on how each twist of the kaleidoscope can cast a different image, however, was not to take place until several months after the jury returned its verdict of life. Under the laws of most states, a jury's verdict of life or death must be formally confirmed at a later sentencing hearing before the judge. Although not required to do so, jurors often attend the hearing, as did a number of the *Brown* jurors.

At the hearing, the elderly, handicapped father of one of the victims took the stand and talked movingly about the loss of his son and how, while he respected the jury, he thought that they had acted out of misguided compassion and that he wished Brown had been sentenced to death. The father's gentle chastising made the jurors feel sympathy for him, but they still felt that they had done the right thing. Then, however, they watched in horror as the victim's father slowly made his way back down the aisle past where Brown was sitting and Brown said, "I don't have to take this shit." This triggered an angry exchange between the father and Brown, with the elderly father challenging Brown to a fight, while the victim's mother sobbed uncontrollably. Jerry, who had been one of the last death holdouts, recalled looking on with a sickening feeling that maybe they had made a mistake: "Here's an old crippled man upset at the loss of his son. If you're Brown, you sit there with your mouth shut and you take what the man has to say. You don't in court start yelling at the father, 'Fuck you, old man, fuck you, shut up, fuck you. It was terrible, terrible."

The jurors were deeply shaken by what they had witnessed. Jerry said that he and the other jurors who had been present at the sentencing hearing had talked afterward and agreed that the defense had been extremely wise to not let Brown testify at the trial, because "if we had seen this type of hatred and viciousness on the stand, we probably would have executed him." For Jerry, the exchange had caused the kaleidoscope's pieces to tumble once more into a different pattern. He did not know how the other jurors felt, but after seeing "the absolute hatred" that Brown had directed toward the father, Jerry said, "It made me just want to kill him, to ask the judge, 'Can we reconvene? Can the jury go out again?'" Luckily for George Brown, they could not.[19]

CHAPTER SIX

THE UTOPIAN JURY
MEETS REALITY

The jury contributes most powerfully to form the judgment and to increase the natural intelligence of a people, and this is, in my opinion, its greatest advantage. It may be regarded as a gratuitous public school ever open, in which every juror learns to exercise his rights, enters into daily communication with the most learned and enlightened members of the upper classes, and becomes practically acquainted with the laws of his country, which are brought within the reach of his capacity by the efforts of the bar, the advice of the judge, and even by the passions of the parties.

—Alexis de Tocqueville, *Democracy in America* (1835)

I can remember thinking, "Gee, this decision is ours, the twelve lousy people in here that's been together for a while."

—Juror describing his thoughts as the jury deliberated
over whether to impose a sentence of life or death

AS MUCH AS LAWYERS AND JUDGES OBSESS ABOUT JURIES, THE legal system often appears to pay scant attention to what actually is being asked of the individuals called to jury duty. Attorneys will fight tooth and nail over whether the wording of a jury instruction properly incorporates prior legal precedent, but hardly anyone asks whether the final wording is comprehensible to the folks who must apply it. The legal system will claim legitimacy because juries are the community's conscience, but then appears to turn a blind eye when the jury does not

reflect the community's makeup. The criminal justice system feels free
to sternly lecture jurors on the necessity of taking personal responsibility for their decision, but then comes across as indifferent or even hostile when jurors try to find out information that they believe they need
to fulfill their sense of responsibility. Sometimes it seems as if the justice
system is enraptured with the idea of the jury but would rather not have
to deal with the realities of actual jurors.

Indeed, the tales of all jurors, not just the *Lane* jurors, of what had
happened in their jury rooms made clear that the creators of reality television shows like *Survivor* and *Big Brother* did not have to travel to the
jungles of the Amazon or build special sets. They simply could have
turned to the local courthouse on Main Street, U.S.A. The plot concept
would be astonishingly simple: Throw twelve strangers together, provide
them with no training whatsoever for what they are about to do, have
them hear two adversaries present weeks or months of conflicting evidence, have professional advocates argue that the other side is wrong or
lying, lock the twelve strangers into a small room, and then ask them to
decide whether a human being should live or die. And, oh yes, any decision must be unanimous, so if the jurors disagree with each other, only
one group's views can emerge as the survivor.

And luckily for the budget-minded producer, the set need not be
particularly lavish. Props are minimal as jurors discover that the evidence itself creates the jury room's atmosphere: "Sitting in the jury room
we were surrounded by evidence—particularly sobering were the styro-
foam heads with wooden dowels though them, representing the gunshot
entry and exit wounds. . . . Against the wall were boards with photos of
the bloody, bloated corpses . . . [and] autopsy photos . . . graphically
showing the bullet wounds. And set between these were pictures of a
smiling [defendant as a] five-year-old along with photos of his two-year-
old daughter."

Some jurors were forced to deliberate the defendant's fate in conditions that seemed almost apocalyptic. One jury deliberated after an
earthquake during which "the courthouse took a beating and we were in
there with no windows and Saran Wrap over the holes and stuff." A
juror in another case described her jury room as set up in a way that
might have caused even reality television producers to draw the line:
"You know, even the fashion in which the jurors are kept is a crock.
You're in this little hallway where you can come out and smoke, and
then right there you have a door with a little screen on it with prisoners

waiting to go to the other courtrooms. So you're sitting there having a cigarette and talking among yourselves and these guys are talking to you, I mean filthy crap! . . . especially to the women. And they would stand there and they urinate in the hallways, you know. And we'd have to walk through these halls, and I'd say, 'This is gross!' I don't know, they treat jurors like we're the criminals, for Christ's sakes."

Producers also will find that the jury room, usually small and self-contained, helps foster a sense of isolation, the better to foment heated discussions. Jurors repeatedly talked about how the jury room's cramped quarters created an emotional pressure cooker: "It was hard sitting in that little room, it was a cramped little room with really no room to move around—it was intense, it was really intense sometimes." Especially hard for some jurors was the inability to leave the room when emotions started to flare: "The worst thing in the world is being stuck in a room and you can't get up and walk out when you're pissed off." Another juror in describing the tensions in the jury room noted, "We knew we were locked up; we actually were locked up." In one case, the pressure was so great that a juror had a "breakdown" after one day of deliberations and had to be replaced.

More than once, the jury room's bathroom, the only place of relative privacy, became a sanctuary for a juror seeking a moment of peace as the pressures grew. A juror in one case recalled how the emotional temperature in the jury room had approached boiling as the eleven jurors tried to persuade the lone holdout for life: "She cried, we all cried." Finally, "the holdout went into the bathroom, and she was gone for quite a while, and we couldn't talk about any of it while she was gone. And I remember, because when she left she said that when she walked back into the room she will give her decision one way or the other. She was gone for maybe twenty to twenty-five minutes, it seemed like an eternity. She returned crying. She said, 'Death.'" One can only try to imagine what it must have been like to be a holdout trapped inside a bathroom for close to half an hour, trying to sort out one's thoughts about whether a person should live or die as the eleven other jurors wait on the other side of the door.

And, of course, a camera in the jury room would capture plenty of verbal fireworks. Jurors not infrequently described their jury as "like family," and the description may be apt if, like most families, this includes heated disagreements and black sheep as well as affection for each other. A juror in one case fondly recalled the jury that he served on: "We were all friendly, we'd go play cards, have doughnuts every morning . . . had coffee. We had a good time. We'd go out for walks together. Some of us would go out to eat together—very loving, warm, friendly group." Later in the interview, however, the same juror recalled, "We got some pretty hot stuff going there a few times—that's where you're going to find a murder or two, in the jury room."

A juror described a similar interaction within a jury that sat on a case for five months: "We really became a family. We knew everything there was to know about each other—homes, family, kids, businesses, personal time, refinancing mortgages, the kid took the car . . . everything, boyfriends, girlfriends, sexual encounters. I mean everything, because we could . . . spend so much time together." There was a "black sheep" in the family: "She didn't fit . . . she was a psychopath, she was psychotic, she was deranged . . . she drove me nuts," but the rest of the jury tolerated her like the proverbial crazy aunt. And when it came time for the penalty deliberations, the jury was split evenly with strong feelings on each side, which erupted into very emotional discussions: "We were loud, vociferous; several times [the bailiffs] had to come in and say, 'Would you calm down!'—they got complaints from another jury from another courtroom that we were too loud." But according to the juror who had described the jury as being like a family: "Personal animosity never, never entered into it. We could argue heatedly, completely. It was like a work situation, it's like 'You stupid son of a bitch, can't you see? Okay, let's go get something to eat.' Personal attacks never got into it." A number of the jurors from this jury continued to get together on a social basis after the trial had concluded, a not uncommon practice; over a third of the jurors reported keeping in touch with other jury members after the trial.

If juries are like families, though, a number of juries ended with estranged and bitter family members. A juror on one case merrily described how she and five other jurors had gone on a picnic after the trial. Another juror on the same jury who had been extremely troubled because he felt that "an injustice had been waged" against the defendant described in a disaffected tone how, after the jury was dismissed, he left without speaking to anyone. Needless to say, he did not attend the picnic.

Nor as tempers flared were all juries able to keep their arguments "like a work situation." Granted, no jurors leapt off jury buses to avoid deliberations and no chairs were hurled out windows—as court officers have witnessed in some cases[1]—but yelling matches, table banging, in-

sult trading, and jurors being reduced to tears were very common occurrences. Several juries even verged on erupting into fistfights, with jurors
stating that they had to restrain others from punching each other. One
juror candidly admitted that she was so frustrated with a juror holding
out for life whom she felt "was an absolute nitwit" that "I came closer to
slapping her than I have anyone in my adult life." In at least one case,
the verbal confrontations did escalate into a physical fight during the
jury's debate over life and death. After first saying "We all worked well
together," a juror continued, "but the death penalty stage of the trial was
real tense for us in there. Fights broke out, and once these two girls went
at it, they started hitting each other."

Discovering that jury deliberations are not models of decorum is not
to suggest that juries are incapable of living up to their role, in Tocqueville's words, of being "made judge of what is allowed and of what it is
forbidden to do against society."[2] In many ways the human emotions
that flared up in the jury room may indicate that jurors are bringing the
type of emotional commitment to their task that we would want from
people to whom we are entrusting such a momentous decision. If we are
to have a death penalty, placing the decision with twelve citizens to act
as the community's conscience may be the best of imperfect options.

At the same time, it is important that the legal system not fashion
its rules based on an unrealistic conception of juries. Tocqueville may
have been correct that jury service is a lesson on democracy in action,
but certainly part of the lesson is that democracy is messy. If we are to
burden individuals with the weight of so momentous a decision, then
the criminal justice system has an obligation to respond to the realities of the jurors rather than to a romanticized version. The jurors'
stories highlight certain basic problems within the jury system that
need attention.

Although most jurors stated that they still supported the death
penalty after seeing the process at work,[3] jurors often expressed a less
than rosy view of the overall criminal justice system. Typical comments
of dissatisfaction noted: "I was disappointed with the criminal justice
system in general. It may be the best in the world, but it still was generally lacking both in defense and prosecution." A juror who strongly supported the death penalty in her case found that overall she was now
more opposed to capital punishment: "I feel more strongly now how
careful you have to be, so I'm more opposed than before. It's just that our
system doesn't work very well. . . . I'm more concerned that people get

fairer trials, that they have equal access to good representation. I have more concerns about the problems in our legal system than I did before."

Sometimes the criticisms were directed at specific aspects of the system that struck jurors as counterproductive. One juror, for instance, marveled that after months of trial aimed at uncovering facts, the attorneys were allowed to make closing arguments that were no more than "sales pitches—they were based loosely on the facts but also had a great deal of embellishment on each side, and it seemed totally inappropriate and unnecessary." Particular frustration was directed at a judge's denial of what the jurors viewed as commonsense requests, such as receiving copies of the jury instructions or transcripts of a witness's testimony. Not only did these denials strike the jurors as "silly" or "stupid," but they seemed to treat the jurors like children who could not be trusted with basic information while at the same time they were entrusted with the decision of whether someone should live or die.

And like the *Lane* jurors, many jurors were disillusioned once they heard the jury instructions. Jurors would enter the jury box after hearing days and weeks of penalty phase evidence wondering: How do I do this? What is important? What exactly am I to be deciding here? To their dismay, the instructions they were given were what one juror summarized as "just gobbly gook, mumbo jumbo." Jurors understandably were bewildered and often angry that the instructions would be so impenetrable for such an important decision. Said one: "Everything the judge reads is very confusing. The jury instructions are very confusing; they should be in plain English. They really should! These are really important things the jury is deciding, deliberating. Somebody would raise part of the instructions and nobody could understand what they meant, and somebody said, 'Oh, I think it means this,' and we had to try and interpret them. It just is not clear cut at all." Even for the terms "aggravating" and "mitigating" circumstances, the two primary axes upon which the entire death penalty decision turns, jurors would say, "That confused me, all that aggravating and mitigating stuff," or candidly admit that "aggravating and mitigating factors were used, but I still don't know what they mean."

At the end of her interview, Peggy suggested that juries should be tested on their understanding of the instructions before being allowed to make a life-or-death decision. Although administering comprehension exams to actual jurors might not be a feasible reform, it is not asking too much to require that instructions be drafted and tested among potential jurors to ensure that they are comprehensible before being given to actual juries to implement. This is especially true given the fact that juries in real cases will have to apply the instructions during the heat of deliberations when misunderstandings are most likely to occur. The legal system's need to guard against endless inquiries after a trial into whether a jury understood the instructions may be sound policy, but only if we have confidence that the everyday citizens called to jury duty readily understand those instructions. The jurors' comments left no doubt about the desirability of current efforts to craft more understandable jury instructions and to adopt reforms such as instructing jury members on what they will be deciding *before* they hear the evidence.[4]

Adding insult to injury from the jurors' perspective, judges sometimes would appear to turn a cold shoulder when the jury asked them to clarify instructions or define terms such as "mitigating."[5] The judges' responses ranged from telling the jury essentially "to do the best you can" to simply re-reading the instructions. As a result, jurors often would complain that "some of us just couldn't get it straight." A juror in one case said their judge was "very irritated" when they asked a question and, "He basically scolded the jury for it and said, 'You can read it! It means exactly what it says!'" The juror not only thought that the scolding tone was "pretty crappy of the judge," but "We were scared to death to call down and ask anything again, you know, fear of . . . get[ting] chewed out in front of the courtroom." A juror in another case similarly recalled with a glint of anger: "I got the impression the judge didn't want to answer our question—why the hell didn't he tell us what it meant?"

The legal system needs to reconsider how to respond to jurors' questions that bear on legitimate topics, such as the meaning of a jury instruction, if it wants to ensure that juries are applying the same rules consistently. Proposing that a judge be responsive to a jury's question or request will make many trial judges nervous as they contemplate appellate courts looking critically over their shoulders. The proposal also will likely cause considerable discomfort to many prosecutors and defense attorneys who will fear that a judge's attempt at clarification will favor the other side. Although such nervousness is understandable and helps explain why the legal system currently refrains from answering many jurors' questions, this reaction engenders little sympathy when viewed from a juror's perspective. Jurors are being asked to determine a person's fate based upon legal rules, yet when they find one of the legal rules unclear and ask the judge about it, essentially they are told that the rule is too hard to clarify in a way that makes the legal system comfortable. Consequently, the task is left to the very people being asked to abide by the rules, the jurors, to figure out what the legal system cannot adequately express.

Not all jurors, of course, came away disillusioned with the criminal justice system or their service as a juror. Slightly more than a third of the jurors (35 percent) stated that they would "welcome the opportunity" to serve as capital jurors again, although rarely with the eagerness of the juror who enthused, "I would do it twice a year if I could. I'd be a professional juror, I thought it was fascinating." Approximately another third (35 percent) stated that they would serve again "reluctantly," usually explaining how emotionally difficult the decision had been, but then also expressing the view that a sense of civic obligation would lead them to serve again if told that they were needed. Slightly less than a third (30 percent) replied that if summoned again for capital jury duty, they would actively try to get out of it or simply refuse to serve, offering succinct answers like "I'd tell them to stick it," "I would move," or "I wouldn't wish it upon anyone, I'd never, ever do it again." Interestingly, jurors who served on juries that returned life sentences were slightly more likely to say that they would refuse to serve again or would do so only reluctantly.

The fact that not all jurors ended up disillusioned, however, should not discount the tremendous personal sacrifice that was asked of them. A significant majority (60 percent) stated that they found the "experience emotionally upsetting," occasionally adding comments like "It was the most agonizing situation of my life" or "It was devastating." Over a third (35 percent) reported that they had trouble sleeping or lost their appetite during the trial. Even when they slept, jurors often reported that they had terrifying dreams that sometimes continued well after the trial. One juror explained that for months afterward, "All I dreamed of was murder and bullets." Most of the nightmares that were described centered on visions of the defendant escaping and coming after the juror or dreams of grisly autopsy photos that woke the juror up in a cold sweat "dreaming of slit throats." Some of the nightmares, however, would be especially intriguing to a dream analyst, such as the juror who, after being selected for the jury, dreamed that he was standing in a narrow hallway outside the courtroom without any shoes on as some people dragged the defendant by him. Not wanting to enter the courtroom, the defendant reached out and grabbed the juror by his bare ankles, at which point the juror woke up startled. As they ponder the dream's meaning, amateur psychoanalysts may want to scribble on their notepad that, in the jury room, the juror later became a strong advocate for a life sentence.

Jurors frequently noted that the stress they felt was heightened because they were not allowed to talk with anyone about the proceedings while the trial was under way. Given that some trials lasted months, family relationships sometimes were placed under great strain. Unable to talk to their spouses about what had become an emotional cyclone within their lives, the jurors felt as if they were consumed by a secret that their mate resented. One juror told how her "home life was ruined" because her husband wanted to know what was happening, and when she explained that she was not allowed to talk about the trial, he accused her of not trusting him. Another juror recalled, "I'd be screaming at my husband at night, all these things bubbling out, getting very emotional. You keep picturing all these things, it was terrible, and not being able to talk about it is the most difficult thing." A few jurors even reported developing drinking problems or resuming smoking as a way of coping with the stress.

This sense of isolation extended beyond the family and often was the aspect of jury service that jurors identified as the most frustrating. Jurors frequently were taken aback after toiling in relative anonymity during the trial to discover a very different courtroom once they reached a verdict. The courtroom that had been practically deserted during the day-to-day trial now was packed full of reporters and observers. While the presence of an audience added to the sense of "electricity" in the air, some jurors were appalled: "Where the hell were all these people through the whole trial? . . . I just looked at these people and I was disgusted with them. You know, it was like people who go to races to see wrecks, that's how I felt. God, like they wanted blood; it was sickening."

A juror in one case described how, after announcing the death verdict to a courtroom that had gone from empty to overflowing, it became "a circus." The jury members retired to the jury room to collect their belongings and then stepped onto the elevator as a group one last time to go down to the parking garage, the somber ride punctuated by several jurors crying. Before the elevator reached the basement garage, though, the elevator doors opened on the ground floor and revealed a "madhouse" of reporters standing outside shouting, "There's the jury!" Trapped on the elevator, the jurors looked out paralyzed when suddenly a "little voice" in the back of the elevator broke through saying in a wavering voice "*Shut the fucking doors.*" The speaker was a woman who hardly had spoken at all during deliberations, "a petite, quiet lady, you wouldn't expect something like that coming out of her mouth." As the juror looked at her and saw her sobbing, the enormity of what they had done fully hit him, and he started vigorously punching the button to close the doors.

Indeed, the media generally did not fare well in the jurors' commentary. Jurors would describe how, after the trial, they had read news accounts of the trial, and, "Frankly, they don't look like the same trial." One juror described with incredulity how after the jury had announced a death sentence and jurors were leaving the courtroom, a reporter yelled out, "Do you believe he should have received the death penalty?" The juror thought the question unbelievably stupid: "Well, my goodness, we just voted on that, what do you think?"

Nor did the sense of isolation necessarily disappear once the jurors returned to their everyday routines. They discovered an abundance of what one juror termed "armchair jurors," acquaintances and coworkers who were quick to offer up their critiques despite not having heard a minute of testimony. Sometimes the feedback, although positive on its surface, only reinforced the juror's feeling that no one began to understand what he or she had been through. Jurors who had returned death sentences, for instance, would arrive at work and have coworkers congratulate them because the jury "had fried the s.o.b." or they would "want the gory details" about the crime. These people did not realize that the juror was secretly recoiling at the comments and thinking about how little others comprehended the emotional toll of having to condemn someone to death.

Life jurors, on the other hand, usually were subjected to critical second-guessing, especially if the crime had been in a smaller community where the victim was well known. Although no interviewed jurors were subjected to death threats or had acid thrown into their work lockers, as has happened elsewhere,[6] they found themselves having to defend their life verdict to friends and fellow employees. One juror told of feeling a tremendous sense of relief that her jury service was finally over, only to return to work and have "a lot of people ask me why I didn't fry him." This juror also had the misfortune of attending a dinner party where, to her discomfort, the case came up in conversation. Her discomfort soon turned to horror as one of the guests indignantly identified herself as a close friend of the victim's family and began harshly criticizing the juror for not returning a death sentence.

Both death and life jurors typically resented these "armchair jurors," feeling that it was impossible to understand their decision unless the person had served as a capital juror herself. One death juror explained, "You develop all these theories about the death penalty and the criminal justice system, but being in it is different. You come to grips with what you really think and feel. There wasn't a day I didn't think about it." Jurors sometimes expressed identification with jurors from high-profile cases, such as the O. J. Simpson or Rodney King beating cases, who had been criticized for their decisions. One of the *Brown* jurors recounted how he had "a lot of people rage at me 'How could you not find death for this guy?' because they had read the newspaper about how he had tortured people," which had given the juror "an appreciation how in a case like the Rodney King case you've got to be there to understand. Like with George Brown, you had to have seen the sister testify and hear about the father's rapes and how he took a hot iron and burned this kid and the child abuse stories that kept going on and on and on." It was as if jury service on a trial that subjected the jurors to public second-guessing acted as an instant fraternal bond with jurors in similar cases, the secret handshake consisting of being criticized by the uninitiated.

Nor was the experience one that readily could be stashed away in the subconscious after the trial. Not only were coworkers and friends posing questions, but it seemed as if reminders of the case abounded like little Post-its pasted everywhere. Sometimes it was a mundane event that triggered a disturbing memory, like the juror from the *Brown* case who related that "Every time I see a Safeway grocery bag I think of a severed head" because the defendant had placed the victim's head in such a bag. A juror who served on a case where a victim was robbed at an ATM machine said simply the sight of an ATM card brought back disturbing memories of the trial. (He had destroyed his own ATM card.) And for another, a news story about a pending execution made the juror feel "like putting my head in the oven" as unwelcomed memories flooded back.

Although the comparison might seem odd at first, at times the jurors' stories were reminiscent of Vietnam veterans' descriptions of their experiences upon returning home. The comparison arises not simply because the jurors were drafted into service, but also because of what was asked of them in the name of civic duty. The jurors may not have seen firsthand the horrors of war, but they were forced to witness photos and exhibits that caused almost uniform revulsion. As one juror recalled,

"You think you're kind of sophisticated, then they show you, 'here's the neck wound,' and you want to leave the room." Just as disturbing was learning concretely about the terrible acts that people are capable of inflicting on other human beings and about the horrible circumstances that must pass for a childhood for some people. Perhaps it is good that jurors are exposed to the darker side of human behavior and the hardships that some must endure, but the effect often was shattering. As one juror lamented, "I lost a lot of faith in humanity as a whole."

Moreover, just as returning veterans sometimes were haunted by what they discovered about themselves out on the battlefield, jurors occasionally discovered insights about themselves that they would have rather not confronted. In a newspaper interview, a juror recalled discovering "[a] horrifying capacity for anger that I didn't know was within me," warning future capital jurors "to be ready to find out all kinds of things about yourself and your society, including some things you don't want to know."[7] Her sentiments were echoed by other jurors, some of whom were alarmed to find themselves using phrases like "gas him" in the jury room. One juror, who with evident self-reproach confessed to letting some of the "vernacular creep into" his jury room deliberations, immediately expressed resentment that the process makes it feel "natural" to talk about "frying" the defendant.

And although the jurors never were forced to point a gun at someone, they were required to live with the responsibility of having passed judgment on whether another person should live or die. Not all jurors, of course, went through Peggy's emotional turmoil, although a number expressed surprise that the court did not offer any counseling after such a traumatic experience. One juror bluntly stated, "I think that it sucks that they don't offer counseling to the jury for all this bullshit. I definitely would have taken them up on it. . . . It's like, 'Okay, thank you, good-bye.' You know, I've just given you four months of my life and now you're just kicking me out."

Even jurors who had achieved peace of mind talked about the heavy weight that the decision had placed on them and the personal strife it had caused. Sometimes they referred to themselves as victims: "I came to the conclusion that the jurors ended up being as much a victim as the victim's family, because we had to sit there and make a decision about someone's life, whether they were going to live or die." Another juror observed that the defendant "takes a part of your life, too, by his acts, and I don't think it will ever go away. It was one of the most intense things I've ever done." This juror added, "But I would do it again—I'm the kind of person who doesn't like to back down from difficult things."

And, of course, for no jury member was the clash between the utopian vision of the jury and the reality of jury duty greater than for Peggy. Eventually she emerged from her depression able to face the world again but still with many questions and a lingering sense of self-recrimination. For months after the trial she replayed what had happened in her mind and asked herself what she might have done differently. Had she done the right thing in telling Mark that she did not want him to continue voting life just to support her? What would have happened if she had broken the cold silence that had greeted her announcement that the jury was deadlocked by saying "Okay, let's buzz the court and tell them we're finished,' rather than offering this nice 'I wonder what happens now?'" Or, she wondered, what if she had been able to read the instructions with a calm mind and realized that a hung jury would not lead to a life sentence? Her biggest regret was that she had not "trusted myself and my convictions. I was part of a group that recommended an execution I don't believe was appropriate." Now, Peggy realized, she should have recognized herself as "someone who counts, who represents the part of society that would have sympathy."

Although Peggy identified actions she could have done differently, she also had questioned whether the criminal justice system and the lawyers could have found a way to throw her a lifeline that would have enabled her to keep from voting for a death sentence she did not believe in. She thought it important that a lawyer tell jurors, "'You may find yourself alone and, if you do, it could get very confusing and mind boggling.' The lawyer should talk something about the process, even saying 'It has been our experience that not all of you will have the same opinion.'" Peggy also believed it important that jurors should be alerted by the court that "a person faced with a group of people often change their views, . . . but you have a legal responsibility to the defendant to state your opinion." Because Peggy had been devastated by the fact that "not one person validated my opinion in any positive way, no one said . . . 'You're entitled to your opinion, people have different opinions,'" she urged attorneys and judges to encourage jurors to accept the idea that a juror with a different opinion is not doing anything wrong. And finally Peggy suggested that a lawyer should let the jurors know that "panels deadlock and that can be the right answer—I mean [for our jury] it was like 'We've got to get the right answer!' [A lawyer] should stress that voting by your conviction is what is right, instead of the goal is to have a unanimous decision. [In our case], I think that the jurors really felt, 'We're going to fail if we deadlock.'"

What was striking about Peggy's crash course on how a defense lawyer might reach out to a juror who finds herself alone was how closely her observations resembled the practices of the best capital defense attorneys. These are lawyers who invariably possess a keen sense of human nature and understand the power of the majority. From their first contact with jurors, they work in anticipation that any jurors arguing for life may find themselves in the minority. They also understand that those most able to defend a minority position in a group situation are persons who are confident that they possess the information necessary to make the correct decision.[8] Consequently, these lawyers work to reassure jurors that they possess the information they need to reject the death penalty and that their role in arguing for life in the jury room, even against majority sentiment, is valued by the judicial system and community. This means stressing to jurors as early as jury selection that they are legally and morally entitled to their individual opinions and gently warning them to be prepared for the likelihood that arguing the case for life in the jury room may be hard to express in logical terms. As a lawyer in one case explained in his closing argument to the jury knowing that a juror like Peggy might find herself alone in defending feelings favoring a life sentence: "[The judge] will tell you that . . . you can consider any reason for life at all that you think is fair. . . . The sort of reason that you can't express, except you feel in your heart that [a death sentence] is not the right thing to do. . . . That is not violating the law. That is not violating your oath. That is following the law. That is being faithful to your oath."[9]

Peggy's continual reflections after the trial on how the process had unfolded and what had gone wrong eventually proved cathartic. Ultimately she came to view her ordeal as a step, albeit a painful one, in her growth as a person. Peggy's complex view of the world may have set her at odds with her fellow jurors, but after the trial it allowed her to at least partly accept her experience as an event from which she would have to learn and grow, even if she might not quite appreciate why she had been forced to endure it. She also had drawn on her intrinsic optimism that people can change as a way of viewing her own difficult time as a catalyst for positive change in herself. The trial, for instance, had caused her to become more religious and spiritual, as she frequently had looked to

God as a source of strength and comfort both during the trial itself and in its aftermath.

In the end, Peggy thought that the most important change that the trial had brought about in her was a greater inner strength. At first that statement sounds like a motivation poster gone badly awry. The idea that Peggy had become stronger by voting to execute someone whom she believed deserved life would push even the most ardent advocate of positive thinking to the limits. Peggy related these final thoughts, however, without trying to make it sound as if she had suddenly emerged from her post-trial depression to discover herself in the ending of *It's a Wonderful Life*. She still deeply regretted her change of vote and still felt a great deal of anger with herself, but she also had come to believe that her views had been right and proper all along. She had concluded that her failure was not in her judgment but in her inability to believe in herself, a mistake that Peggy vowed she would never make again in her life. The learning process had not been an easy or welcomed one, but, Peggy concluded, "The experience has taught me that I can trust myself."

CHAPTER SEVEN

CONCLUSION

HOWEVER ONE FEELS ABOUT THE DEATH PENALTY, THE JURORS' stories lead to one indisputable conclusion: At bottom, a jury's effort to decide between life and death is a distinctly human endeavor infused with emotion and moral judgment. Despite the efforts of legislatures and courts to make the death penalty decision a legal judgment that is reached by following a series of rules, in the end the determination of whether the defendant lives or dies results unavoidably from the intersection of twelve jurors' individual beliefs and views. Nor will the importance of who is sitting in the jury box manifest itself solely through the values and beliefs that each juror brings to the decision. As the accounts of both the *Lane* and *Brown* cases vividly illustrate, each juror's personality plays a role in how the jury as a group resolves the collision of differing views. And as the jury struggles to reach unanimity, all of the qualities that make us human, both the appealing and unappealing, will be brought into full relief.

It is this human dimension to the death penalty decision that is the strongest argument for using juries to make the capital punishment decision. If a sentence of death is to be announced in society's name, it should be drawn from the views of ordinary citizens who will bring into the jury box a cross-section of views of justice and mercy. This is especially true given that the decision of whether someone should live or die is not a question of expertise, such as solving a complex mathematical equation, but rather an effort to express the community's moral sense of what constitutes a just punishment based on the defendant's acts and life story. After the evidence is heard, the jury room may become a scene of angry exchanges and emotional outbursts, but that should be expected if we are asking individuals to decide the monumental question of whether someone should live or die and to make the decision by drawing upon their most basic values and beliefs. What would be astonishing is if capital juries did not experience emotional turmoil in trying to make their collective decision.

The great advantage, therefore, in placing the death penalty decision with a jury rather than with a judge is that a properly constituted jury will bring together a number of perspectives to test the evidence and arguments rather than letting one person's viewpoint dictate the outcome. Judges may bring to the decision a better understanding of legal concepts, but if they alone decide whether a defendant should live or die, they would make the moral judgment without being forced to listen to the clamor of other voices in the jury room. Not only would this make one person the sole voice for the community's conscience, but it would raise the distinct possibility that the death penalty could be imposed based on the judgment of one person who is out of step with the majority's viewpoint. In almost every case studied where the jury chose a life sentence, even cases where the vast majority of jurors favored life from the outset, at least one juror strongly insisted on a death sentence and usually was quite surprised to discover that he or she was virtually alone in that view. In all likelihood, if the juror favoring a death sentence had been acting as the sole decision maker, the defendant would have been sentenced to death.

By requiring a jury of twelve individuals to make the decision, therefore, we can at least have the confidence that a death sentence is not solely the result of one person's viewpoint. And lest someone who opposes the death penalty think that judges on whole will be less likely than jurors to favor the death penalty in most cases, the lesson from the handful of states that have allowed judges to "override" jury recommendations for a life or death sentence teach that such an assumption is hazardous at best.[1] Even more fundamentally, if the death penalty decision is to reflect the community's conscience, the accuracy of the reflection will be enhanced the more the decision maker can incorporate the full range of voices in the community.

To say that a jury is the best choice as a decision maker if we are to have capital punishment does not, however, answer the most basic question of whether capital juries are fairly administering the death penalty. The first inclination is to think of this question primarily as one of *factual accuracy*, an inclination which is understandable given that DNA testing has revealed a startling number of innocent individuals who have been convicted and condemned to death. In the wake of these revelations, various reforms have been proposed to reduce the risk that innocent individuals will be wrongfully convicted and sentenced to death. One set of proposals, for example, would allow a jury to consider a sentence of death only in cases where scientific evidence exists that "strongly corroborates" the defendant's guilt and would require that the scientific evidence be reviewed by an independent panel of experts.[2] Not surprisingly, disagreement exists whether a system can be devised that guarantees that no innocent person would be subjected to the death penalty.[3]

But even if the legal system successfully eliminated the possibility that an innocent person could be sentenced to death, another crucial inquiry would remain about the fairness of the death penalty. This inquiry centers on the idea of *moral accuracy:* Can the legal system guarantee that the death penalty is being consistently and fairly imposed from case to case based on each defendant's moral culpability and not because of other factors? In other words, just as we must have confidence in the jury's factual determination that the defendant was the true killer, we also must be confident that the jury's moral determination that the defendant deserves to die is not influenced by factors unrelated to the defendant's culpability.

The difficulty in answering this question, of course, is that no equivalent to a DNA test exists that enables us to determine if a jury's decision to impose a death sentence was morally accurate. Ultimately the decision of whether a defendant like Steven Lane or George Brown deserves to die is a deeply personal one, and to label the juries' decisions in those cases as right or wrong requires each individual to use his or her own sense of justice and mercy as the answer key.[4] Some might believe that Steven Lane's crime, while horrible, simply cannot compare with the depravity of George Brown's two murders involving torture, so that it is unjust that Lane ends up on death row and Brown serves a life sentence. Others may counter that George Brown's horrendous childhood makes a life sentence understandable, while Steven Lane's background does not call out for the same type of mercy, making a death sentence for Lane justified based on his taking of an innocent life. And some—although they would not be allowed to sit on a capital jury because of their beliefs—would argue that society's use of the death penalty for any individual, no matter how terrible his or her crime, is immoral and should never be allowed, making any death sentence wrong.

In one sense, therefore, the deeply personal nature of the death penalty decision makes it difficult to label a death sentence as right or wrong in the same way that we might assess that a jury's determination that the defendant was the actual killer was right or wrong. We can, however, ask whether cracks exist in the capital punishment system through which influences can enter that might threaten the moral accuracy of a jury's penalty decision. And although this book does not pretend to answer the moral accuracy question fully, the jurors' stories do raise several matters worth reflecting on in trying to find an answer. Raising these issues is not a way of casting doubt on the ability or sincerity of those who are called to capital jury duty—every indication suggests that capital jurors undertake their jury service with great seriousness and diligence. The issues that arise are not about the individual jurors themselves, but about whether the legal system can provide the means for jurors to fulfill their desire to act justly, fairly, and consistently.

In undertaking this inquiry, it is important to keep in mind that the decision of many capital juries will be delicately balanced between life and death. As the stories of jurors from different cases reveal over and over, relatively few death penalty decisions are "easy" in the sense that all twelve jurors quickly agree on the verdict. In almost every case, jurors face important forks in the road that are critical to making their ultimate moral decision: for instance, deciding whether or not the defendant will always pose a danger; determining if they can trust the criminal justice system to not release the defendant; debating whether the defendant ever had the chance to choose the "high road"; grappling with what justice and mercy require. And at almost every one of these forks, additional evidence or a different argument might lead the jury to choose a different answer, which, in turn, could result in a different verdict.

That the decision between life and death is a close call for many juries raises the possibility that even relatively minor changes in how a trial is conducted might alter the outcome. Consider the George Brown case as an example of how disparity in the quality of legal representation might change the outcome of a case. Imagine if less dedicated lawyers had not uncovered in detail Brown's tragic childhood and the abuse he suffered. Not only would the jury have likely come to a verdict of death because of the missing information, but the jurors would have felt shocked if they had learned later that they had made their decision without the benefit of having heard such compelling evidence.

Nor need we posit a sleeping or incompetent lawyer to recognize that the quality of representation might have a wildcard influence on a jury's decision. Even those states that require a lawyer to meet certain training criteria before they are allowed to handle a capital case inevitably will experience discrepancies in how well lawyers represent their clients at the penalty phase. As we have seen, the effective presentation of a defendant's case for life in many ways is more about Shakespeare than Blackstone, and even with the same facts, lawyers will vary considerably in their ability to tell a defendant's life story in a compelling manner. The problem of disparity is not, of course, isolated to capital trials, but given the uniqueness of the penalty phase question—whether the defendant morally deserves to die—it tends to accentuate the differences in lawyers' abilities to communicate a defendant's life story to a jury. When it comes to the question of legal representation and moral accuracy, therefore, the legal system and society must ask how much risk it is willing to tolerate that a different lawyer in a death penalty case might have obtained a different verdict.

The jury itself is another area that must be examined as a possible opening for inconsistency to creep into the death penalty decision. At a minimum, if the jury is acting as the moral voice of the community, it is fair to ask that it be representative of all segments of the community. The presence of minorities on a jury provides the most obvious example of how different perspectives and backgrounds can affect a jury's deliberations. The black jurors in the *Brown* case serve as striking examples of how jurors with a particular background can provide a context for those who had a different upbringing. Jurors told of similar instances in other cases where minority jurors played a key role in shaping the jury's debate over the meaning of evidence.[5] And, as noted earlier, emerging research has demonstrated that the presence of minority jurors, especially black males, can dramatically shape the jury's viewpoint.

Historically, though, trying to achieve representative juries in capital cases has proven to be an elusive goal. In almost nine out of every ten capital cases that have resulted in executions since 1977, African Americans were significantly underrepresented on the juries that had sentenced the defendant to death, and at least one out of every five blacks who have been executed were sentenced to death by all-white juries.[6] Nor is the problem of underrepresentation of minority jurors limited to the deep South. A 1999 study of Illinois's death row found that "of 65 death penalty cases . . . with a black defendant and white victim, the jury was all-white in 21 of them, or nearly a third."[7]

This systematic underrepresentation is caused in part because jury lists still do not fully reflect the number of African Americans in the population.[8] Another major culprit, however, has been the use of peremptory challenges by prosecutors to remove blacks and other minorities from capital juries. Sometimes prosecutors state their bias openly; the jury-selection manual prepared by a senior prosecutor and circulated in Dallas County, Texas in the 1960s instructed prosecutors to "not take Jews, Negroes, Dagos, Mexicans or a member of any minority race on a jury." As late as the 1980s, a training guide actively used in the same county warned against selecting jurors from minority races, people with "physical afflictions," and Jews, because they "usually empathize with the accused."[9]

Such open discrimination is unlikely to occur today, because the Supreme Court in 1986 held in *Batson v. Kentucky* that prospective jurors can be removed only for "race neutral" reasons.[10] Considerable doubts exists, however, about *Batson's* ability to effectively eliminate the more subtle influence of race on the exercise of peremptory challenges. After reviewing a number of cases involving allegations of race-based peremptory challenges, Justice Thurgood Marshall ultimately concluded that *Batson* was "ineffective against all but the most obvious examples of racial prejudice," because prosecutors only have to provide a plausible nonracial reason for dismissing a minority juror.[11] Consistent with Justice Marshall's observation, a recent study on the use of peremptory challenges in capital cases found that courts were extremely reluctant to find that a peremptory challenge had been exercised on the basis of race.[12]

Addressing problems that keep juries from being representative of the community, therefore, is a necessary step in trying to achieve moral accuracy. Perhaps the most difficult question when it comes to the jury, however, is whether the very nature of the jury poses a hurdle to consistent imposition of the death penalty. Although the moral assessment required by the death penalty decision presents the strongest argument for using juries as the voice of the community, it is the moral quality of the decision that also creates one of the greatest threats to moral accuracy: the potential that a defendant's death sentence will always partly depend on whose names are chosen by a spin of the jury wheel. The question quite simply is whether we can ever be certain of consistency where the addition or subtraction of a Hope juror or a fundamentalist juror or a minority juror might alter the interaction of the jury as a whole.

As the stories of Ken, Peggy, and Frank powerfully demonstrate, a jury is not a static collection of interchangeable drones but an intriguing jumble of different personalities and viewpoints that comprise a whole. This fascinating intermix of individuals at times is so strong that juries seem almost to assume a living essence of their own with a personality created from the dynamic interaction of the various jurors. This dynamic aspect of the jury does not pose a problem, at least in theory, if the jury is asked only to determine facts, such as whether a defendant *in fact* killed the victim. A series of randomly chosen juries should consistently reach the same factual conclusion when looking at the same evidence, just as randomly chosen math students should always agree that four times four equals sixteen. This proposition has not proven to be quite so straightforward in practice, as social scientists have discovered that jurors' backgrounds and beliefs will affect how much credence they assign to certain types of evidence.[13] Still, when juries deliberate in their traditional role of deciding whether the defendant is factually guilty, we know that a correct answer exists (the defendant either *did* or *did not* kill the victim) against which the jury's verdict can be measured.

The intensely personal and moral nature of the death penalty decision, on the other hand, raises the concern that whether a defendant is sentenced to death will vary from jury to jury depending upon each jury's dynamic. Although a jury of twelve individuals is more likely than a single judge to express the community's conscience, it remains a relatively small deliberative body that can change "personality" with even a minor variation in the mix of individual members. How concerned should we be, then, that if Peggy had been joined on the jury by even one more Hope juror looking into the evidentiary kaleidoscope, the two might have formed an alliance that would have led her to not change her vote and, perhaps, even have led the other jurors to vote for life to avoid being a hung jury? Or, in George Brown's case, that replacing the black jurors with white jurors, especially if they were of a fundamentalist bent, might have created a strong majority sentiment on the first ballot for a death sentence that ultimately would have prevailed?

The criminal justice system tries to minimize this danger of inconsistency by providing legal rules that are intended to guide jurors as they make what the Supreme Court has characterized as a "reasoned moral response" to the evidence arguing for life and death.[14] But whether the legal system can channel successfully the powerful dynamic of jury deliberations that attaches to such a deeply moral and emotional issue is a question that has bedeviled the courts since the death penalty was reinstituted in the 1970s.

Part of the difficulty, as we have seen, centers around the jury instructions that are intended to communicate to the jurors the legal rules governing the death penalty. From a juror's point of view, the legal system's attitude toward jury instructions often appears as incomprehensible as many of the instructions themselves. Currently, the legal system seems more concerned with whether an instruction makes "legal sense" than with whether ordinary citizens can understand what is being asked of them. An appellate court far removed from a jury room may say that the word "heinous" satisfies the Constitution's demand that only the "worst of the worst" be subject to the death penalty, but can the legal system claim the death penalty is being consistently applied without knowing whether a layperson called to jury duty can meaningfully define what "heinous" means?

Several Supreme Court cases have bordered on the surreal when they have rejected arguments that a jury instruction was too confusing to allow the death penalty to be imposed. These cases have upheld the death sentences on the assumption that "reasonable jurors" would have understood the meaning of the contested instructions, even though the *actual jurors* in the cases had complained to the trial judge that they were confused and needed clarification.[15] In making these rulings, the Court recited the system's traditional concern of not wanting to intrude into the jury's deliberations. Certainly, though, it is a different matter when jurors themselves are telling the trial judge that they are perplexed by what they are being asked to do.

If the legal rules governing the death penalty truly are too difficult or elusive that we cannot provide answers to jurors who ask for clarification, then the legal system needs to openly acknowledge the impossibility and face the consequences of not being able to provide consistent guidance to juries in deciding between life and death. If, however, the criminal justice system believes that it can formulate coherent rules to achieve moral accuracy, the legislature and courts need to write those rules and allow them to be explained to juries in ways that make certain that juries are not being forced to "fill in the blanks" for the legal system.

Telling jury members that they should do their best when they are confused or that they should not concern themselves with a question that clearly has them very concerned is to invite arbitrary responses as jurors attempt to fill the void with their own definitions or with "folk wisdom" garnered from watching *Law & Order*.

After two decades of grappling with an endless succession of death penalty cases, one Supreme Court justice finally concluded near the end of his time on the Court that the death penalty could never be consistently and fairly administered. As a result, Justice Harry Blackmun declared:

> From this day forward, I no longer shall tinker with the machinery of death. For more than twenty years I have endeavored—indeed, I have struggled—along with a majority of this Court, to develop procedural and substantive rules that would lend more than the mere appearance of fairness to the death penalty endeavor. Rather than continue . . . I feel morally and intellectually obligated simply to concede that the death penalty experiment has failed. It is virtually self-evident to me now that no combination of procedural rules or substantive regulations ever can save the death penalty from its inherent constitutional deficiencies. The basic question—does the system accurately and consistently determine which defendants "deserve" to die?—cannot be answered in the affirmative. . . . The problem is that the inevitability of factual, legal, and moral error gives us a system that we know must wrongly kill some defendants, a system that fails to deliver the fair, consistent, and reliable sentences of death required by the Constitution.[16]

Even those justices who disagree with Justice Blackmun that the death penalty is a failed experiment have agreed that the effort to establish consistency through legal rules remains a central difficulty of the capital punishment system.[17]

Undoubtedly, the debate as to whether a system can ever be devised that enables juries to impose the death penalty in a consistent manner will continue for as long as we have capital punishment. Whatever the answer to this larger question, however, looking at the death penalty decision from the juror's perspective makes clear that capital juries cannot ever hope to achieve fair and consistent results unless they are at least provided with certain basic tools. If we are to have a death penalty, all jurors should be entitled to serve on a jury that is representative of the community and to hear from lawyers who are able to provide the jurors with a complete picture of the defendant and the case. Jurors also must be provided with instructions that are worded in a manner that everyday citizens can understand, and they should have reasonable questions about their duties and the evidence answered as fully as possible.

The policy questions that are raised by the jurors' stories are important to think about as part of the broader debate about the future of capital punishment in America. It should come as no surprise, however, that the final words of this book are about the jurors themselves. If we are to have a death penalty and ask juries to choose between life and death, it is important that we neither overly romanticize the jury nor demonize it, but acknowledge the jury as a collection of twelve individuals who bring to the jury box all the strengths and faults of being human. And of all the lessons to be gained from talking with jurors, perhaps the most valuable is the need to remember that as the national policy debate over the death penalty rages, ultimately it is these twelve individuals, who do nothing more than answer a jury summons, who must bear the tremendous demands of implementing the death penalty.

Arguments about capital punishment understandably tend to focus on the victim and the defendant and on what moral and legal balance society should strike in finding a fair and just punishment. Yet while this tug-of-war is going on in ornate statehouses and appellate courtrooms around the nation, at any one time twelve jurors are being marched off to cramped jury rooms and being told to decide a person's fate. They do their best with what they have been given, although what they are given varies dramatically depending on the skill of the lawyers and the judge's rulings. And once the verdict is announced, often with the jury box full of crying jurors holding hands, they are sent back home. At this point, the legal system acts as if the jurors' task is finished once they exit through the courthouse door because those twelve individuals no longer formally bear the title "juror."

As some individuals who were called on to undertake their civic duty as capital jurors have discovered, however, the sense of responsibility does not end so easily with the turning in of the juror's badge. As one juror who had struggled with the aftermath of having sentenced someone to death put it: "The whole process is very disturbing; it wasn't easy, and I've been trying to get rid of the memory. Knowing that this person has to live with what we've decided is very difficult—I don't think I was put on this earth to play God." And because we ask so much of capital jurors—everyday citizens like Ken, Peggy, Frank, and the Chorus members—it is only fair that the next time an argument springs up over the death penalty, we also listen to the jurors' voices and what they tell us fairness and justice require.

NOTES

CHAPTER ONE

1. Sir Patrick Devlin, *Trial by Jury*, London: Stevens (1956): 156.
2. In most states, the jury is not asked to find the special circumstance or aggravating factor until the penalty phase itself. In those states, a conviction for first-degree murder alone will trigger the penalty hearing and the jury will be asked to find whether an aggravating factor exists as its first task during penalty deliberations. If jury members do not find that the prosecution has proven that an aggravating factor exists, then they must return a life sentence.
3. *Furman v. Georgia*, 408 U.S. 238 (1972). In 1972 the legal assault on the unguided discretion given to capital juries came to fruition in a challenge spearheaded by the NAACP Legal Defense and Educational Fund. In the landmark case of *Furman v. Georgia*, by the narrowest of margins, five of the nine justices of the Supreme Court found that the process of simply instructing the jury that they must decide between a life-or-death sentence without any further instructions had led to "arbitrary and capricious" death sentences in violation of the Eighth Amendment's ban against "cruel and unusual punishments." *Furman* was to mark the beginning of the Court's struggle over the coming decades to constitutionally explain to the states and the public when and how the death penalty could be imposed.

    In striking down the death penalty as then practiced, a majority of the Court said that under the current system of unguided discretion, no rational explanation existed as to why some defendants received the death penalty while others in similar circumstances did not. As Justice Potter Stewart vividly explained: "These death sentences are cruel and unusual in the same way that being struck by lightning is cruel and unusual. . . . [The Constitution] cannot tolerate the infliction of death under legal systems that permit this unique penalty to be so wantonly and so freakishly imposed."

    Moreover, to the extent explanations did exist as to why some defendants were singled out for death row and not others, several justices argued that the likely explanations were the repugnant ones of race and class. Justices Thurgood Marshall and William O. Douglas pointed out that although blacks were a minority of the general population, well over half of those who had been executed since 1930 were blacks. Justice Douglas also pointed out that "[o]ne searches the chronicles in vain for the execution of any member of the affluent strata of this society."

Furman's effect on capital punishment in America was the legal equivalent of the Big Bang. With one decision, the Court invalidated every death penalty statute in America and overturned the death sentences of over 600 inmates sitting on the nation's death rows. The legal puzzle that state legislatures now were faced with in drafting new capital statutes—how to control the sentencer's discretion so as to no longer produce arbitrary and capricious death sentences—was seen by some as an unsolvable one. Indeed, in a case just one year before *Furman*, Justice John Harlan had expressed the belief that such an effort was likely to be futile because "identify[ing] before the fact those characteristics of criminal homicides and their perpetrators which call for the death penalty" in terms that juries could apply was "beyond present human ability." "The infinite variety of cases and facets to each case," he contended, "would make general standards either meaningless 'boiler-plate' or a statement of the obvious that no jury would need."

In 1976, four years after *Furman*, a majority of the Supreme Court in *Gregg v. Georgia*, 428 U.S. 153 (1976), gave new life to the death penalty in America by upholding statutes that had adopted a "guided discretion" approach that, among other procedures, used special circumstances or aggravating factors to limit who was eligible for the death penalty. The Court agreed with the states that the guided discretion schemes now had a constitutional checkpoint in place that ensured that the only individuals who passed through to the penalty phase were those whose acts arose to a particularly high level of reprehensibility. By using special circumstances, the majority ruled, the states had successfully cured the problem of the death penalty being imposed with the same arbitrary targeting of lightning strikes: The criminal justice system could now look any defendant receiving the death penalty in the eye and say that he or she had been singled out for death because the defendant had committed an especially egregious crime that constituted a special circumstance. Moreover, by limiting the death penalty's availability to the most egregious cases, the Court hoped to also limit the possibility that arbitrary reasons like racism would creep into the jury's decision.

4. *Stewart v. Commonwealth*, 427 S.E. 2d. 394, 409 (1993).
5. David Baldus, "Arbitrariness and Discrimination in the Administration of the Death Penalty: A Challenge to State Supreme Courts," *Stetson Law Review* 15 (1986): 133, 138.

6. The Supreme Court has attempted to partly rein in the scope of the felony-murder factor, for instance, by not allowing it to apply to a get-away driver who believes his or her cohorts are unarmed. *Edmund v. Florida*, 458 U.S. 782 (1982).

7. Baldus, 138–39.

8. States vary as to whether the killing during the felony-murder must be intentional or not, and the law can change over time within a state. In Lane's trial, the trial judge instructed the jury that they must find that Steven Lane had intended to rob and kill Castillo.

9. Professor Stephen Garvey has elegantly used Portia's speech to examine what role mercy should play in structuring the death penalty decision. Stephen Garvey, "'As the Gentle Rain From Heaven': Mercy in Capital Sentencing," *Cornell Law Review* 81 (1989): 1996.

10. *Lockett v. Ohio*, 438 U.S. 586 (1978).

11. Even when a case moves into murkier areas of the criminal law, the law still attempts to phrase the inquiries in a way that makes the jury's determination amoral and objective. With an insanity defense, for example, the jury is not asked to decide whether the defendant was so mentally ill that he or she should be held criminally responsible, but, rather, is asked to decide whether the defendant *in fact* understood the difference between right and wrong when the criminal act was committed.

12. California, for example, lists ten specific factors that the jury is "to take into account" in deciding between life and death. Factors include a defendant's prior record, the defendant's age, and whether the defendant was a major or minor participant in the killing. But just as one begins to think that specific guidance is being given, along comes the completely open-ended final factor stating that the jury is to consider "any other circumstance which extenuates the gravity of the crime even though it is not a legal excuse," a concession to the impossibility of listing in advance every circumstance that might mitigate against a sentence of death.

13. As former Justice Joseph Grodin writing for the California Supreme Court eloquently observed: "In [the death penalty context], the word 'weighing' is a metaphor for a process which by nature is incapable of precise description. The word connotes a mental balancing process, but certainly not one which calls for a mere mechanical counting of factors on each side of the imaginary 'scale,' or the arbitrary assignment of 'weights' to any one of them. Each juror is free to assign whatever moral or sympathetic value he is permitted to consider. . . . Thus the jury, by weighing the various factors, simply determines under the relevant evidence which penalty is appropriate in the particular case." *People v. Brown* (Brown I), 40 Cal. 3d. 512, 541 (1985), reversed on other grounds, 479 U.S. 538 (1987).

14. *Witherspoon v. Illinois*, 391 U.S. 510 (1968).

15. In addition to "for cause" dismissals, each side is given a limited number of peremptory challenges that may be used to dismiss jurors whom the attorneys believe will be unsympathetic to their side. The number of peremptories for a capital case varies widely from state to state. In California, for instance, each side in a capital case is entitled to twenty peremptory challenges (compared to ten in a noncapital case); in Virginia, each side is given only four peremptories for a capital case, the same as in a noncapital case.

16. One concern has been that removing these potential jurors because their views would affect their ability to be fair at the *penalty phase* alters the fairness of the jury composition at the *guilt stage*. Indeed, a number of social science studies have found that a "death-qualified jury"—that is, one composed of jurors who have been asked the *Witherspoon* questions and is now composed only of individuals whose beliefs would allow them to impose the death penalty—is more likely to convict at the guilt stage, is more distrustful of defense attorneys, and is more skeptical of certain types of defenses (such as insanity) than a jury composed of jurors who have not been death qualified. Moreover, of the 11 percent to 17 percent of jurors estimated to be excluded because of the *Witherspoon* question, a disproportionate number are women and African Americans. See generally, Claudia Cowan, William Thompson, and Phoebe Ellsworth, "The Effects of Death Qualification on Jurors' Predisposition to Convict and on the Quality of Deliberation," *Law and Human Behavior* 8 (1984): 53 (finding that jurors' attitudes toward the death penalty affects their predisposition to convict); *Lockhart v. McCree*, 476 U.S. 651 (1986) (citing studies).

   These types of studies eventually spawned legal challenges arguing that while a death-qualified jury might make the jury "more fair" at the penalty phase, it makes it "less fair" to the defendant at the guilt stage because the jury is more conviction-prone and not fully representative of the community. Proponents of this argument envisioned a capital case as having two separate juries: a guilt-stage jury that, as in any other criminal case, would not be death qualified, and a penalty-phase jury that would be death-qualified but decide the penalty only if the defendant was convicted of capital murder. The two-jury vision, however, turned into a mirage once the issue reached the Supreme Court. In *Lockhart v. McCree*, a majority of the Court held that death-qualified juries violate neither the defendant's constitutional right to an impartial jury nor the right to a jury drawn from a fair cross-section of the community.

17. *Hance v. Zant*, 696 F.2d 940 (11th Cir. 1983).

18. A similar upside-down *voir dire* can occur where the potential juror responds to the reverse-*Witherspoon* questions with answers suggesting that he or she might automatically impose the death penalty for murder. The defense attorney likely will be pushing the person to say

that he or she thinks the death penalty is always justified for murder so that the juror will be dismissed "for cause," while the prosecutor will try to show that a scenario exists where the person could find that mitigating circumstances called for a life sentence ("What if the defendant had been whipped and sexually molested every day by an alcoholic father?"). Even if a juror is not dismissed "for cause," the juror still can be dismissed if one side exercises a peremptory challenge. Attorneys, however, like to save their peremptories if at all possible and prefer to have an unsympathetic juror dismissed "for cause" if they can convince the judge to do so.

CHAPTER TWO

1. The reference to Hunter S. Thompson's *Fear and Loathing in Las Vegas: A Savage Journey to the Heart of the American Dream* is owed to Professor William Geimer, who founded the Virginia Capital Case Clearinghouse at Washington & Lee University, a student-run clinic for assisting capital counsel. He began his training of incoming students with the premise that the key to successful capital defense was to be found in counteracting the two basic emotions found in the title of Thompson's book. The jurors' interviews that form the basis of this work confirmed the wisdom of his advice.

2. This is not to say that contesting guilt is always a bad tactical decision in a capital case. First and foremost, a defendant in fact may be innocent despite apparent evidence of guilt, requiring the attorney to wage an all-out battle for acquittal. As the alarming number of innocent people who have been sentenced to death has begun to come to light, especially because of the increased availability of DNA evidence, it has become apparent that despite evidence sufficient to find someone guilty beyond a reasonable doubt, a defendant's protestations of innocence may indeed be genuine. By the late 1990s, for instance, Illinois seemed to offer a Pulitzer Prize opportunity to any journalist who wanted to demonstrate that an innocent man had been condemned to death row. By the time Governor George Ryan, a death penalty proponent, declared a moratorium on executions in 1999, as many individuals had been freed from Illinois's death row because of their innocence as had been executed. Four years later Governor Ryan commuted all 164 death sentences because he concluded after extensive review that "the Illinois capital punishment system is broken. It has taken innocent men to a hair's breadth escape from their unjust execution." Nationwide, in the thirty years since the death penalty was reinstituted in 1973, over 100 inmates under a sentence of death have been released because of evidence of their innocence, and one study has concluded that over 400 people sentenced to death during the twentieth century in fact were innocent, including 23 who were

executed. Michael Radelet, H. A. Bedeau, and C. E. Putnam, *In Spite of Innocence: Erroneous Convictions in Capital Cases*. Boston: Northeastern University Press (1992). Although the authors' conclusion that 23 innocent people have been executed has been challenged by several commentators, no one disputes that a number of individuals who undoubtedly were innocent have come within hours of being executed. See Stephen J. Markman and Paul G. Cassell, "Protecting the Innocent: A Response to the Bedeau-Radelet Study," *Stanford Law Review* 41 (1988): 121. See also H. A. Bedeau and Michael Radalet, "The Myth of Infallibility: A Reply to Markman and Cassell," *Stanford Law Review* 41 (1988): 161 (defending the methodology of the study).

3. The problem of doubting jurors is even greater in other states providing for life without parole, with only 10 to 17 percent of jurors reporting that they believed that "life" was the true alternative sentence to death. Thus even in the states where life without parole is the only other option to the death penalty, jurors still estimate on average that a defendant receiving a life sentence actually would serve only 16.3 years. William J. Bowers and Benjamin D. Steiner, "Death by Default: An Empirical Demonstration of False and Forced Choices in Capital Sentencing," *Texas Law Review* 77 (1998): 605, 648–50.

4. Peter Blumberg, "Costly Death Penalty," *San Francisco Daily Journal*, December 12, 2000. In most instances, four justices of the California Supreme Court would have to concur if a governor ever should decide to recommend commutation to a sentence less than life without parole. Article 5, Section 8 of the California Constitution bars a governor from commuting a sentence of a twice-convicted felon without the approval of four justices, and it is the rare capital defendant who has not had at least one prior felony conviction.

5. While it is true that both Manson and Sirhan receive periodic parole hearings despite the notoriety of their crimes, their cases do not provide a reason to be skeptical when a sentence of life without parole is imposed today. Both were sentenced to death but had their death sentences reduced to life sentences after the death penalty was briefly declared unconstitutional in the 1970s. At the time their death sentences were overturned, all life sentences in California included parole eligibility, which is why they continue to have parole hearings. If they were given a life sentence today for their crimes, it would be without parole.

6. As part of the interview, jurors were asked: "How many defendants sentenced to death in California were likely to be executed?" Jurors were then given choices ranging from "very few" to "nearly all." An eye-opening 84 percent of the interviewed jurors chose the "very few" answer, with only 3 percent thinking that "nearly all" would be executed and barely 10 percent thinking that even half of those sentenced to death will ever have their sentence carried out.

7. The argument that the courts were anti–death penalty became the centerpiece of a bitter political campaign waged in 1986 to oust several California Supreme Court justices. Much of the campaign focused on the fact that the Court (known as the Bird Court after Chief Justice Rose Bird) had reversed 66 of the 69 death sentences that it had reviewed between 1977 and 1985. The campaign was successful in achieving its goal, as three justices lost their seats on the court.

    Since 1986 the California Supreme Court has reversed 10 percent of death sentences compared to a 90 percent rate from 1977 to 1986. Although the California Supreme Court's current reversal rate of death sentences is one of the lowest among state courts, the Ninth Circuit Court of Appeals, the federal appellate court that ensures that California death sentences do not violate the United States Constitution, has to some extent stepped into the void, reversing 62 percent of the California death sentences that it had reviewed through 2002. (By comparison, federal courts on average had reversed 40 percent of the state death sentences that they had reviewed through 1995.) Howard Mintz, "State, U.S. Courts at Odds on Sentences," *San Jose Mercury News*, April 15, 2002. For a thorough review of the rates of reversal on the state and federal levels, see James Liebman, Jeffrey Fagan, and Valerie West, "A Broken System: Error Rates in Capital Cases," *Texas Law Review* 78 (2000): 1839.

8. Surprisingly, though, juries often used their skepticism that the defendant would be executed as a way to break deadlocks in favor of a life sentence. One juror, for instance, explained that the rarity of executions led her to change her vote from death to life: "I just brought up that if death is given, they don't get death, they just sit on death row. I ended up feeling, yeah, he's going to get life anyway." Interestingly, while a few jurors said that they used the argument that the death penalty would never be carried out "as an out from the death penalty," others jurors maintained that they wanted the death penalty but simply thought that the small probability of an execution did not justify triggering the elaborate and lengthy process that follows a sentence of death. As one juror colorfully put it, "I think he deserved the death penalty if they'd shoot him right on the spot like in the Western days, hang him. But, no, if it takes time and money, then let him sit in jail."

    This sentiment—that in the end a death sentence really would end up just being a life sentence—was seen as particularly compelling where the jurors thought that a life sentence would short-circuit the defendant's ability to appeal a conviction and sentence. In several cases, the jury incorrectly believed that giving a life sentence meant that the defendant could not appeal at all and, therefore, that voting for life was in fact the best way "to make sure the defendant never got out." Although a life sentence generally will mean fewer appeals and certainly will not result in the dramatic last-minute legal maneuvering that often accompanies the days preceding a scheduled execution, a defendant sentenced to life without parole is fully entitled to appeal the conviction through the state courts. Where jurors' perceptions were more in accord with reality was in the belief that a defendant sentenced to life was less likely than a death row inmate to have access to the same level of resources to challenge the conviction or to obtain as extensive a review of the conviction by the state and federal courts. Peter Blumberg, "Habeas Resources: A Mere Life Sentence Means Far Fewer Funds and Opportunities to Challenge a Conviction," *San Francisco Daily Journal*, December 13, 2000.

9. Scott E. Sundby, "The Capital Jury and Empathy: The Problem of Worthy and Unworthy Victims," *Cornell Law Review* 88 (2003): 343. On the other end of the spectrum, the jurors in the cases involving nonrandom victims often dealt with fact scenarios in which they were unlikely to imagine themselves confronting someone like the defendant. Sometimes this was because the nonrandom victim had been engaged in high-risk behavior, such as making a drug deal with the defendant. This lack of identification with the victim, however, was true even in the nonrandom cases that did not involve victims engaged in high-risk behavior, because these cases often involved matters particular to the defendant's relationship with the victim, such as a soured romantic relationship or a troubled family situation. Consequently, jurors in the nonrandom cases were almost twice as likely to return sentence of life rather than death, with the chances of a life sentence increasing with the jury's perception of the victim as having been reckless or careless.

10. The trial of the Menendez brothers for the murder of their parents garnered considerable attention because of their defense that the murders had been provoked by years of sexual abuse. To establish their claim, they relied on expert testimony that one legal commentator called "pretentious babble" that would be "laughable" except "there is a serious risk that when an expert takes the stand, recites her qualifications, and the judge 'qualifies' her as someone who can speak with authority, she can influence a jury's deliberations." George Fletcher, *With Justice for Some: Protecting Victims' Rights in Criminal Trials*, Reading, Massachusetts: Addison-Wesley Publishing Company (1995): 234. The phrase "Twinkie defense" was coined after the 1978 trial of Dan White for killing San Francisco Mayor George Moscone and City Supervisor Harvey Milk. Although his claim that he was suffering from a "diminished capacity" when he committed the killings was based on a number of factors, one of the defense experts testified that White's consumption of sugary junk foods might have contributed to his violent behavior. Ibid., 31. White was convicted of two counts of manslaughter rather than murder, and the press made much of the "Twinkie defense" even though it is not clear

that it played much of a role in the jury's decision. Ibid., 32. See also, Alan M. Dershowitz, *The Abuse Excuse: And Other Cop-Outs, Sob Stories, and Evasions of Responsibilities*, New York: Little Brown and Company (1984), (describing the problem of "psychobabble" and arguing "we must not be seduced by the jargon of experts, particularly 'experts' who are really advocates for a particular political position or worldview").

    Not everyone agrees that a trend of "abuse excuse" is occurring. Professor Richard Bonnie has argued that such claims are "unadorned hyperbole" if the cases and their facts are closely examined. Richard J. Bonnie, "Excusing and Punishing in Criminal Adjudication: A Reality Check," *Cornell Journal of Law and Public Policy* 5 (1995): 1, 7–9.

11. Senate Floor Amendment 1 to Senate Bill 459, 42nd Leg., 1st Session (New Mexico 1995).

12. In one case, the defendant's uncle made a particular impression on a juror simply through his constant presence at the trial and the fact that he cared about the defendant. The juror often noticed the uncle in the hall reading a Bible (the uncle was also a pastor) and at one point saw him crying. The juror was impressed that the uncle cared enough about his nephew to attend everyday, which convinced the juror that the defendant did have some "good" in him.

13. Phillip G. Zimbardo and Michael R. Leippe, *The Psychology of Attitude Change and Social Influence*, Philadelphia: Temple University Press (1991): 320–322. Psychologists call the phenomenon "group polarization," which can be slightly misleading, because the tendency is not to split groups into two poles but for individuals to move more strongly in the direction of their initial tendencies. Psychologists attribute this tendency to two factors: The more discussion that occurs in favor of a particular view, the greater the number of reasons that are generated for group members favoring that position, and, as some people discover that others in the group share their perspective, they will become more extreme in their views as a way to establish their individuality within the group.

14. Jurors as a whole tended to see their decision as a matter determined primarily by the defendant's actions and the law's requirements. When asked to rank who was "most responsible for the defendant's punishment," jurors consistently chose by a significant margin "the defendant because his conduct is what actually determined the punishment" (50 percent) or "the law" (26 percent), distantly followed by "the jury" (9 percent), "the individual juror" (9 percent), and "the judge" (5 percent). Professor Joseph Hoffmann has expressed concern that findings like these suggest that jurors may not fully understand that the law places primary responsibility for the decision on the juror's personal determination of the proper punishment. Joseph Hoffmann, "Where's the Buck?—Juror Misperception of Sentencing

Responsibility in Death Penalty Cases," *Indiana Law Journal* 70 (1995): 1137, 1155–1160. See also William Bowers, "The Capital Jury Project: Rationale, Design, and Preview of Early Findings," *Indiana Law Journal* 70 (1995): 1043, 1093–1098. After examining a number of questions that shed light on the jurors' sense of responsibility, Theodore Eisenberg, Stephen Garvey, and Gary Wells have concluded that "jurors generally accept responsibility for the sentence they impose," while adding the important caveat that "the data also suggest ample room for improvement." Eisenberg, Garvey, and Wells, "Jury Responsibility in Capital Sentencing: An Empirical Study," *Buffalo Law Review* 44 (1996): 339, 379.

CHAPTER THREE

1. Solomon Asch, "Effects of Group Pressure Upon the Modification and Distortion of Judgments," in E. E. Macoby, T. M. Newcombe, E. L. Hartley (eds.), *Readings in Social Psychology* (New York: Holt, Rinehart and Winston 1958):178; Solomon Asch, "Studies of Independence and Conformity: A Minority of One Against a Unanimous Majority," 70 *Psychological Monograph* 70 (1956): 1.
2. Morton Deutsch and Harold B. Gerard, "A Study of Normative and Informational Social Influences Upon Individual Judgment," *Journal of Abnormal and Social Psychology* 51 (1955): 629, 634.
3. Asch, "Effects of Group Pressure," 180.
4. Philip G. Zimbardo and Michael R. Leippe, *The Psychology of Attitude Change and Social Influence* (New York: McGraw Hill 3rd Ed. 1991): 59.
5. Samuel M. Kassin, "The American Jury: Handicapped in the Pursuit of Justice," *Ohio State Law Journal* 51 (1990): 704 & nn. 74–75.
6. R. Wolosin, S. J. Sherman, and A. Cann, "Prediction of Own and Other's Conformity," *Journal of Personality* 43 (1975): 373–376.
7. Julie Woodzicka and Marianne LaFrance, "Real Versus Imagined Gender Harassment," *Journal of Social Issues* 57 (2001):15.
8. Naomi I. Eisenberger, et al., "Does Rejection Hurt? An fMRI Study of Social Exclusion," *Science* 302 (2003): 290; Associated Press, "Brain Pain the Same for Ego Blow, Physical Punch," October 9, 2003 (quoting Dr. Eisenberger).
9. *McDonald v. Pless*, 238 U.S. 264, 267–68 (1915).
10. *Tanner v. United States*, 483 U.S. 107, 120 (1987).
11. Ibid.
12. *McDonald v. Pless*, 238 U.S., 268.
13. *Tanner v. United States*, 483 U.S., 120.
14. Ibid., 117. The jury's bacchanalia was first brought to the court's attention by one of the nonrevelers who was upset that the beer-drinking jurors had generally slept through the afternoon's testimony

following their lunchtime imbibing. The full extent of the jury's revelry, however, was detailed by one of the revelers who showed up at the defense lawyer's office after the trial. This juror wanted "to clear my conscience. . . . I felt . . . that the people on the jury didn't have no business being on the jury. I felt . . . that Mr. Tanner should have a better opportunity to get somebody that would review the facts right."

15. Ibid., 120. In making its decision, the Supreme Court was interpreting a rule of evidence that applies only to federal courts. A state court could decide to allow inquiries into a jury's "internal processes" under state law or rules of evidence. In explaining its decision, however, the Supreme Court documented the legal system's long-standing general aversion to allowing postverdict examination of the jury's decision making.

16. Frank Green, "Jurors Seek Execution Block," *Richmond Times-Dispatch*, October 10, 2001.

CHAPTER FOUR

1. For one juror, the connection was having a stepson who was becoming mixed up with a gang, a personal struggle that led the juror to repeatedly state his admiration for the defendant's father, who had tried so hard to keep his son out of trouble. A juror in another case said she had felt deeply for the defendant's mother, who attended the trial every day, in part because the defendant "made me think of my own son." The juror then revealed that "my son had a few run-ins with the law. . . . I've had a few problems with him, so maybe it hit me a little closer, I mean, my son went to juvenile hall for a week or so, so I mean he's straightened himself out, but they can go this way or that. It's so hard these days."

2. A South Carolina state senator and strong death penalty supporter once worried that if the state made the jury's choice one of between death and life without parole instead of between death and life with parole, it would spell the end of the death penalty; he argued, "If we pass [life without parole], let's close the death house . . . [and] transfer the chair to the state museum. . . . [A] juror considering the death penalty will think, 'I can put that person away forever, and my conscience will be clear.'" Petition for a Writ of Certiorari to the Supreme Court of South Carolina, *Simmons v. South Carolina* (October term, 1992), quoting "Senate OKs Amended Crime Bill," The State (Columbia, S.C.), March 20, 1986, 8C. Because jurors are not influenced solely by concerns of future dangerousness, South Carolina's adoption of life without parole has not seen an end to the imposition of the death penalty in South Carolina or any other state that uses life without parole.

3. Professors Bowers, Sandys, and Steiner report that 43.9 percent of early pro-death jurors stated that they made the guilt and punishment decisions based on "similar considerations" compared to 17.6 percent of jurors who were undecided after the guilt phase and 31.8 percent of jurors who were leaning toward life after the guilt phase. William Bowers, Marla Sandys, and Benjamin Steiner, "Foreclosed Impartiality in Capital Sentencing: Jurors' Predispositions, Guilt-Trial Experience, and Premature Decision Making," Cornell Law Review 83 (1998): 1476.

4. Slightly more than a quarter of the California jurors (26 percent) emerged from the guilt phase—*before* they had heard any evidence at the penalty phase—already leaning toward a death sentence. (By comparison, 16 percent of jurors were leaning toward a life sentence and 58 percent were undecided.) Moreover, about 42 percent of the death-leaning jurors were "absolutely convinced" and 56 percent were "pretty sure." Nationwide, the breakdown is similar: 28.6 percent of jurors favor death after the guilt phase, 19.7 percent lean toward life, and 51.7 percent are undecided. Ibid.

   An analysis by Bowers, Sandys, and Steiner has found that such "early pro-death jurors" exhibit a view of the death penalty consistent with the fundamentalist's viewpoint: They were "decidedly more likely to agree that the death penalty should be required for a serious intentional killing" and that the death penalty would deter if used more often. The early pro-death jurors also had far fewer moral doubts about the death penalty as a punishment than other jurors.

5. A mere 1 percent of jurors who sat on juries that returned a death sentence said that "feelings of vengeance or revenge" were "very important" to their punishment decision; only an additional 4 percent said it was "fairly important." Paradoxically, jurors who served on life juries were slightly more likely than death jurors to say that feelings of vengeance were important to their decision: 4 percent of life jurors reported that feelings of revenge were very important and an additional 10 percent stated that it was fairly important.

6. Thirty-two percent of the death jurors identified the principle of an "eye for an eye" as "very" or "fairly" important to their punishment decision (14 percent stating that the principle was "very" important and 18 percent that it was "fairly" important). By comparison, only 23 percent of life jurors agreed that the principle was fairly or very important to their decision (6 percent of the life jurors identified the principle as "very" important with an additional 17 percent identifying it as "fairly" important).

7. Jurors sometimes expressed the idea that prison life was not so bad ("He won't have to worry about where his meals are coming from, he'll have a job, he'll have a TV in his cell"), as well as a sense that the defendant would not find prison particularly harsh ("He didn't look

like he would have a hard time in prison—he looked like the kind of person who would get along"). This perception of prison as not being a sufficiently severe punishment often was exacerbated by the fact that many of the defendants had been in and out of prison before ("Going to prison for him is just like going home again; it really wouldn't be a punishment at all").

8. One juror who sat on a case involving an inmate killing a fellow prisoner, for example, was fully convinced after the guilt phase that "life without parole is a horrible sentence, it's a hideous way to live, especially in the conditions that I saw." This juror, however, wanted a death sentence, because although "life is a harsh punishment, it didn't fit the crime. You should have to suffer something other than what you're used to, even if it's living in filth with a bunch of other criminals."

9. Sir James Fitzjames Stephen, "Capital Punishments," *Fraser's Magazine* 69 (1864): 753, 763.

10. Bowers, Sandys, and Steiner have determined that a significant percentage of capital jurors decide for death as early as the guilt stage, a determination that creates doubts whether capital jury selection is effectively filtering out potential jurors who are unable to consider a life sentence as required by the Supreme Court. Bowers, Sandys, and Steiner, "Foreclosed Impartiality in Capital Sentencing" *Cornell Law Review* 83 (1998): 1476.

CHAPTER FIVE

1. William Bowers, Benjamin Steiner, and Marla Sandys, "Death Sentencing in Black and White: An Empirical Analysis of the Role of Jurors' Race and Jury Racial Composition," *University of Pennsylvania Journal of Constitutional Law* 3 (2001): 171; Theodore Eisenberg, Stephen Garvey, and Martin T. Wells, "Forecasting Life and Death: Juror Race, Religion, and Attitude toward the Death Penalty," *Journal of Legal Studies* 30 (2001): 277–311.

2. A host of nightmare cases of capital lawyers failing to provide adequate representation are described in Stephen Bright, "Counsel for the Poor: The Death Sentence Not for the Worst Crime but for the Worst Lawyer," *Yale Law Journal* 103 (1990): 1835; Vivian O. Berger, "The Chiropractor as Brain Surgeon: Defense Lawyering in Capital Cases," *New York University Review of Law & Social Change* 18 (1990): 18.

3. "The Death of Fairness? Counsel Competency & Due Process in Death Penalty Cases," *Houston Law Review* 31 (1994): 1105, 1132 (panel discussion, remarks of Stephen Bright on Alabama case of Judy Haney).

4. *Romero v. Lynaugh*, 884 F. 2d 871 (5th Cir. 1989).

202 / A LIFE AND DEATH DECISION

5. *Fisher v. Gibson*, 282 F. 2d 1283 (10th Cir. 2002).

6. Randall Coyne, *Capital Punishment and the Judicial Process*, Durham: Carolina Academic Press (2001): 148 (teacher's manual).

7. One juror's comments capsulizes how the free-will notion often trumped even very emotionally compelling mitigating evidence: "He had a pretty bad childhood. The mother blew her brains out in front of him, he was a very young kid. The mom was a drug addict. She used to stay up all night and sleep all day. . . . So the sister who was just a couple of years older than he—she did all the cooking, she did all the cleaning. And I remember at one point I began crying because I had two little kids and I just, it just tore my heart out that the sister made his lunches, his first day at kindergarten, his sister, just two years older, took him to school and stood in line for him to get into kindergarten. It just tore me up. I thought he got a raw deal starting off. But he had many, many chances, okay . . . he chose to take that path."

8. A similar unintended evidentiary side effect helped convince a jury in another case that prison was a harsh punishment. The trial involved the killing of an inmate, and the jury had to tour the prison as part of the evidence of the crime scene. The jury was taken aback by how terrifying the prison felt and the conditions in which the prisoners lived. This jury had no trouble in agreeing that sentencing the defendant to life in prison was a just punishment for his crime.

9. A judge who is asked such a question will be hard-pressed to give an answer that is both truthful and coherent. While the statute does not allow parole, it is still theoretically possible that the governor could commute a life sentence to a lesser sentence. A judge who briefly acknowledges the governor's commutation power over both death and life sentences but tells the jury not to take the power into consideration essentially is telling the jury to ignore the elephant in the jury room. If the judge declines to answer the question (sometimes by saying the law does not allow him or her to answer the question), jurors show a marked inclination to see the refusal to answer as a covert acknowledgment that the defendant may someday be released.

   Yet if a judge states that the defendant will never be released, he or she can be accused of not candidly acknowledging the governor's commutation power; some juries ask specifically whether the governor can commute a life sentence. Then again, if the judge does acknowledge the commutation power, fairness argues that he or she also must provide the information that of the more than 2,500 inmates given life without parole since 1978 in California, not one has ever had a life sentence commuted to a lesser sentence. Peter Blumberg, "Costly Death Penalty," *San Francisco Daily Journal*, December 12, 2000. Indeed, the California Constitution bars a governor from commuting the sentence of a twice-convicted felon without the approval of four justices of the California Supreme Court, and most capital defendants will have at least one prior felony conviction (California Constitutional Article 5, Section 8.) The issue of prison release is an area where trial judges must recognize that what they say—or do not say—will be listened to very carefully. Judges should also recognize that if guidance is not forthcoming from the bench, it is likely to come from other sources, like the jurors' assumptions coming into the trial.

10. Eisenberg, Garvey, and Wells, "Forecasting Life and Death." Death sentences tended to be an all-or-nothing affair based on the outcome of the first ballot. If eight or more jurors vote for death on the first ballot, a death sentence almost always results. On the other hand, if fewer than eight jurors vote for death on the first ballot, the result almost invariably preordains a life sentence. This means, of course, that the threshold to obtain a life sentence on the first ballot is far lower. Eisenberg, Garvey, and Wells have observed, therefore, that "death verdicts are . . . relatively more difficult to orchestrate [than life verdicts]."

11. Juries with one black male juror returned death sentences in 42.9 percent of the cases, a rate far lower rate than the 71.9 percent of the cases where no black males were on the jury. Bowers, Steiner, and Sandys, "Death Sentencing in Black and White." It was the seating of at least one black male juror that was the key in precipitating the drop in the rate of death sentences, as the presence of additional black males on the jury only brought the death sentence rate down marginally. (Juries with two or more black males returned death sentences in 37.5 percent of the cases.) Also important was the independent effect of the number of white males on the jury. Juries that served on cases with a black-on-white killing and had four or fewer white males on the jury returned a death sentence in 30 percent of the cases, but if the jury included five or more white males, the chances of a death sentence increased "dramatically," with 70.7 percent of such cases resulting in death sentences.

   Professor David Baldus's earlier study of Philadelphia capital juries also had found that black defendants were treated more severely as the number of whites on the jury increased, particularly in cases of a black defendant killing a white victim. The Philadelphia research additionally discovered that black defendants fared better as the number of young black males and middle-age females on the jury increased. Baldus et al., "The Use of Peremptory Challenges in Capital Murder Trials: A Legal and Empirical Analysis," *University of Pennsylvania Journal of Constitutional Law* 3 (2001): 69–73.

12. Bowers et al., at 203–244. Female jurors of both races fell in the middle between the perceptions of the black and white male jurors, with black female jurors closer to the black males' views and white female jurors closer to the white males' views.

13. Ibid., 203–204. The concern over racism in the death penalty has plagued the American death penalty from colonial days. Although the legal system has eliminated the overt forms of racism that once infected capital punishment—laws such as the infamous Black Codes, which allowed blacks to be executed for crimes that whites could not, and rules that barred blacks from testifying against whites or from serving on juries—the extremely troubling question of racism continues to haunt the legal system.

The raw numbers of the nation's death row population certainly create discomfort. Although African Americans comprise just under 13 percent of the U. S. population, at the beginning of the year 2003, 43 percent of death row inmates were black. By comparison, although whites constituted 82 percent of the general population, only 45 percent of the death row population were white. Not surprisingly, then, the proportion of black inmates who have been executed also far exceeds the representation of blacks in the general population. Since 1976 when the Supreme Court first approved of guided-discretion death penalty statutes following its 1972 decision in *Furman* striking down the death penalty because no guidance was being given to juries, 35 percent of the inmates who have been executed have been black (compared to 13 percent of the population) and 57 percent have been white (compared to 82 percent of the population)

As researchers have delved further into the role that race has played in capital punishment, they have discovered that even more than the defendant's race, the race of the victim is the portal through which bias gains its entry: Someone who kills a white victim is far more likely to be sentenced to death than someone who kills a black victim. Again, the raw numbers quickly highlight the problem, especially where a cross-racial killing is involved. Since 1976 only 12 executions have involved a white defendant who murdered a black victim, while 178 black defendants have been executed for murdering a white victim. (If one examines executions on American territories between 1608 and 1997, the figure becomes even more eye-popping: out of more than 16,000 executions, only 31 have been of whites for killing a black person.) Mark Costanzo, *Just Revenge*, New York: St. Martin's Press (1997): 80.

Further study has revealed a number of points where the victim's race influences the administration of the death penalty. The first juncture is simply the prosecutor's decision on whether to seek the death penalty when a homicide has occurred. Professor Hugo Bedau notes that while each year between 2,000 and 4,000 murders are committed for which a prosecutor could seek the death penalty, only about 250 death sentences are actually imposed. He attributes a large part of the "enormous attrition" from death eligible cases to actual death sentences to "the prosecutor's decision." Hugo A. Bedau, *The Death*

Penalty in America: Current Controversies, Oxford: Oxford University Press (1997): 31–32. One study discovered that even after accounting for twenty different factors that might influence a prosecutor's decision to seek the death penalty in a particular case, prosecutors asked for the death penalty five times more often in cases where the victim had been white than where the victim was black. David C. Baldus, George G. Woodworth, and Charles A. Pulaski, *Equal Justice and the Death Penalty: A Legal and Empirical Analysis,* Boston: Northeastern University Press (1990).

The possibility that juries also might be reacting to the victim's race was brought to light dramatically in a study that has become known as the Baldus study. In a study of nearly 600 Georgia cases decided over a six-year period, Baldus, Woodworth, and Pulaski found that even after accounting for over 230 factors that might influence whether a defendant received the death penalty, the murderer of a white victim was 4.3 times more likely to be sentenced to death than the murderer of the black victim. Nor was the defendant's race irrelevant: Among those who killed white victims, black defendants were sentenced to death at a rate of more than seven times the rate of whites who murdered blacks. Ibid. Studies of other states similarly have found that, even after taking into account the crime's characteristics, the killer of a white victim, especially if the murderer is black, is far more likely to receive the death penalty. Samuel R. Gross and Robert Mauro, *Death and Discrimination: Racial Disparities in Capital Sentencing,* Boston: Northeastern University Press (1989). The findings of the Baldus study and others underscore the need to look carefully at who is making the death penalty decision.

14. J. H. Baker, *An Introduction to English Legal History,* Virginia: Lexis Law Publishing (3rd Ed. 1990): 39.
15. *United States v. Bailey,* 468 F. 2d 652, 665 (5th Cir. 1972).
16. Ibid., 665 (summarizing cases).
17. Ibid., 666. A typical dynamite charge would provide: "You have informed the Court of your inability to reach a verdict in this case. At the outset, the Court wishes you to know that although you have a duty to reach a verdict, if that is not possible, the Court has neither the power nor the desire to compel agreement upon a verdict. The purpose of these remarks is to point out to you the importance and the desirability of reaching a verdict in this case, provided, however, that you as individual jurors can do so without surrendering or sacrificing your conscientious scruples or personal convictions. You will recall that upon assuming your duties in this case each of you took an oath. The oath places upon each of you as individuals the responsibility of arriving at a true verdict upon the basis of your opinion and not merely upon acquiescence in the conclusions of your fellow jurors. However, it by no means follows that opinions may not be changed by

conference in the jury room. The very object of the jury system is to reach a verdict by a comparison of views and by consideration of the proofs with your fellow jurors. During your deliberations you should be open-minded and consider the issues with proper deference to and respect for the opinions of each other and you should not hesitate to re-examine your own views in the light of such discussions. You should consider also that this case must at some time be terminated; that you are selected in the same manner and from the same source from which any future jury must be selected; that there is no reason to suppose that the case will ever be submitted to twelve persons more intelligent, more impartial or more competent to decide it, or that more or clearer evidence will ever be produced on one side or the other. You may retire now, taking as much time as is necessary for further deliberations upon the issues submitted to you for determination."

18. In one such rare case, the holdout for life made a passionate final speech for life, only to conclude "But I'm not going to be the one person to cause a hung jury, and I've said my piece and I'm going to change my vote [to death] to be a unanimous vote." Even in that case, though, one of the majority jurors recalled that the holdout's statement came only after much "table pounding" and "yelling," and the majority juror was left with the distinct feeling that the holdout was "sorry" that he changed his vote.

19. The father's moving testimony about the terrible grief that Brown caused when he murdered his son is a form of what is referred to as "victim impact evidence," evidence about the victim and the family's sorrow over the killing. In Brown's case, the jury did not hear the father testify at the trial itself; at one time, this was true for all capital cases because the Supreme Court had prohibited victim impact evidence from being introduced at the trial. The Court was concerned that such evidence would draw the jury's attention away from what the Court viewed as the proper focus of the death penalty decision—the defendant's culpability—and instead place it on factors over which the defendant had no control, such as whether the victim was religious or had family members who could articulate their grief in an emotionally wrenching manner. Because a majority of the Court at the time believed that such facts were "fortuitous," they held that victim impact evidence made the death penalty decision arbitrary and capricious and violated the Eighth Amendment. *Booth v. Maryland,* 482 U.S. 496 (1987).

As a result, capital juries often heard very little about the victim. A juror in one case where victim impact evidence was not allowed voiced his frustration over the paucity of information about victims: "They were presented as slabs of meat—as far as we knew, they didn't have families, they were just dropped here out of an airplane." As often happens when juries are denied information, they regularly speculated to fill the void, such as whether the victim's family was in the courtroom. Some jurors in cases where victim impact evidence was not allowed angrily saw the lack of information about the victim as unfairly tipping the balance toward the defendant, especially when contrasted with a well-presented case in mitigation about the defendant's life.

Following a change in the Supreme Court's personnel, the Court reconsidered the issue and ruled that evidence about the victim and the murder's effect on the family can now be presented to the jury without violating the Constitution. *Payne v. Tennessee*, 501 U.S. 808 (1991). In reversing course, the majority of the Court, like some of the jurors, saw the limitations on evidence about the victim as unfairly "turning the victim into a 'faceless stranger at the penalty phase of a capital trial'" while the defendant is able to fully present his life story. States are not required to allow victim impact evidence to be introduced at the penalty phase, but thirty-three of the thirty-eight states that have the death penalty and the federal government now allow the jury to hear such evidence. If victim impact evidence is not introduced at the trial itself, a court generally will allow the victim's family to testify at the formal sentencing hearing after the jury already has rendered its verdict, as happened in the *Brown* case.

It is unclear whether the Court's decision to allow victim impact evidence at the penalty phase has resulted in many juries returning death sentences in cases that otherwise would have ended in a life sentence. In many cases, the impact of such evidence appears primarily to reinforce juries already leaning toward a death sentence rather than changing a jury's decision from life to death. If victim impact evidence is likely to tip a jury's decision toward death from life, it would be in a case like *Brown* where most of the jurors saw both the aggravating and mitigating evidence as strong, thus producing a number of undecided jurors who might have found that victim impact evidence tilted the balance toward death. See generally, Theodore Eisenberg, Stephen P. Garvey, and Martin T. Wells, "Victim Characteristics and Victim Impact Evidence in South Carolina Capital Cases," *Cornell Law Review* 88 (2003): 306; Scott E. Sundby, "The Capital Jury and Empathy: The Problem of Worthy and Unworthy Victims," *Cornell Law Review* 88 (2003): 343.

CHAPTER SIX

1. Katherine E. Finkelstein, "Tempers Grow Shorter in the Jury Room," New York Times, August 3, 2001. While contentious jury deliberations are not a new phenomenon, some observers believe that they are becoming more frequent.

2. Alexis de Tocqueville, "Journal Entry, October 11, 1831," *Democracy in America*, New York: The Colonial Press (1899).
3. About one in five life jurors (19 percent) and one in ten death jurors (9 percent) stated that they were more opposed to the death penalty after having served on a capital jury.
4. The confusion and frustration that the jurors reported with the jury instructions in their cases is consistent with studies that have found poor comprehension of capital sentencing instructions using potential jurors as test subjects. These studies generally have found that less than half of the tested subjects have been able to apply the instructions correctly, and people seem to have particular trouble understanding instructions on how they are to consider mitigating circumstances. James Luginbuhl, "Comprehension of Judges' Instructions in the Penalty Phase of a Capital Trial: Focus on Mitigating Circumstances," *Law and Human Behavior* 16 (1992): 203; *Free v. Peters*, 806 F. Supp. 705 (N.D. Ill. 1992) (summarizing research of Hans Zeisel); Sheri Diamond and Judith Levi, "Improving Decisions on Death by Revising and Testing Jury Instructions," *Judicature* 79 (1996): 224. In one study, revised instructions aimed at making the instructions on mitigation clearer did improve comprehension from 52 percent to 67 percent (and with improved comprehension, the jurors were more likely to vote for life). Even a 67 percent rate, however, means that almost one-third of those tested were still applying the law incorrectly. Ibid., 232.

The problems associated with jury instructions are not isolated to the death penalty context, and interesting research is being conducted on how to improve juror understanding. Courts are experimenting with rewriting instructions to rid them of legalese and with other methods to enhance juror comprehension. One reform involves instructing the jury members on the law *before* they hear the evidence, which makes eminent good sense. Not being told what criteria you will be using to judge the case is similar to being told that you are to judge a contest with forty contestants but that you only will be told the criteria for judging *after* you have watched all forty contestants do their presentations.

In one case where the judge did explain the law to the jurors before they heard the penalty phase evidence, the jurors reported far less confusion: "[The judge] explained about aggravating and mitigating evidence before the attorneys even presented evidence . . . [and] he explained the different events that were going to occur . . . before he started the penalty phase of the trial." The jurors on this case felt far better prepared to try and understand the penalty phase evidence by knowing beforehand what they were going to be asked to decide. And obviously any techniques that improve juror understanding of the law is for the good; leaving jurors on their own to puzzle out the instructions' meaning can lead to deadly mistakes.

5. As frustrated as many of the jurors were with the judge's refusal to clarify the jury instructions, the primary fault lies with the instructions themselves. Trial judges tread on judicial eggshells when juries ask for a clarification on a jury instruction. One observant juror noted that after they had asked the judge to clarify an instruction, "It was real clear that he had to be real careful how he worded things—he'd check with both attorneys and then answer specific questions I didn't really want." As this juror correctly surmised, trial judges are extremely cautious when dealing with jury instructions, because faulty jury instructions are a major ground for appeals, especially in death penalty cases. Because appellate courts usually have approved the jury instructions that the trial judge reads to the jury, trial judges know that if they stick with the instructions they first gave the jury, they are not likely to be reversed later based on a flawed instruction. When a jury asks a trial judge to further explain what an instruction means, therefore, even if the judge may want to be helpful and rephrase the instruction in more familiar terms, the judge's safest route is simply to reread the instruction (although certainly not to treat the jury in a demeaning manner that shuts down further communication between judge and jury).

6. In a Georgia case, a judge publicly identified the juror who had deadlocked the jury by insisting on life. Afterward, the juror had "acid thrown into his locker at work and received several death threats over the phone." D. Ranii, "Judge Is Criticized for Identifying Holdout Juror," *National Law Journal* 2 (January 4, 1982):14.

7. Angelo Figueroa, "Agonizing over the Death Penalty: Jury Selection for Murder Case Takes Its Toll," *San Francisco Examiner* (November 24, 1989, quoting juror Robin Lakoff).

8. Zimbardo & Leippe, 60–63.

9. This excerpt comes from David Bruck's closing argument at the penalty phase that convinced the jury to spare the life of Susan Smith, the South Carolina woman who killed her two young children by driving them into a lake. Court of General Sessions, Sixteenth Circuit, Union County, South Carolina, July 28, 1995, 94-GS-44-906 and 94-GS-44-907.

CHAPTER SEVEN

1. Florida's procedure, for example, asks the jury to recommend a "life" or "death" sentence, which a trial judge can override only if he or she finds the recommendation unreasonable. Between 1972 and 1992, Florida judges imposed death sentences over a jury's recommendation of life in 134 cases, but overrode a jury's recommendation of death in only about 50 cases. In Alabama cases the disparity was even more striking: As of 1995, a trial judge had imposed a death sentence over

the jury's recommendation of life in 47 cases, but had reduced a jury's recommendation of death in only 4 cases. Harris v. Alabama, 513 U.S. 504 (1995) (Justice Stevens dissenting). See also, Michael L. Radelet and Michael A. Mello, "Death to Life Overrides: Saving the Resources of the Florida Supreme Court," *Florida State University Law Review* 20 (1992): 195–96, 210–11. Where the judge who makes the death penalty decision is elected, the concern arises that an upcoming election will make the judge more inclined to impose a death sentence. A study of capital cases in Chicago between the years 1870 and 1930, for example, found that defendants who were sentenced by judges were 15 percent more likely to receive the death penalty in a judicial election year. Richard R. W. Brooks and Stephen Raphael, "Life Terms or Death Sentences: The Uneasy Relationship Between Judicial Elections and Capital Punishment," *Journal of Criminal Law and Criminology*, 92 (2002): 609. See generally, Nancy King, "Jury Sentencing in Capital and Non-Capital Cases Compared," *Ohio State Journal of Criminal Law* 2 (Fall 2004).

2. Proposals 6 & 8, Massachusetts Governor's Council on Capital Punishment: Final Report, Massachusetts Governor's Office (May 3, 2004). The final report of the Governor's Council on Capital Punishment consists of ten proposals that are intended to "allow creation of a fair capital punishment statute that is narrowly tailored, and as infallible, as humanly possible." The proposed reforms include: separate juries for the guilt and penalty phases (Proposal 4); a requirement that a jury find that there is "no doubt" that the defendant is guilty (Proposal 7); and extending broad powers to appellate courts to set aside death sentences (Proposal 9).

3. Symposium, "Toward a Model Death-Penalty Code: The Massachusetts Governor's Council Report," *Indiana Law Journal* 80 (Winter 2005).

4. Certain events, of course, would make the death penalty wrong under any person's standard, such as a jury that engaged in racial discrimination or a defense attorney who failed to present important mitigating evidence.

5. In one case, for instance, the sole black juror was from the area where the killings had occurred. He provided background to understand the evidence that the jury heard, making him, as a white juror said, "kind of . . . our advisor." With this knowledge came influence on the jury, and because the black juror was convinced that the defendant's role in the killing resulted from the defendant being forced to deal with the realities of "street life," his views helped pushed the jury toward a life sentence.

6. Equal Justice Initiative of Alabama, Informational Pamphlet; Amnesty International, "Death by Discrimination: The Continuing Role of Race in Capital Cases," Report, April 24, 2003.

7. "Death Row Justice Derailed," *Chicago Tribune*, November 14, 1999.

8. State task forces in Pennsylvania, California, Oregon, Ohio, New York, and New Jersey have all found that ethnic and racial minorities were underrepresented in their jury pools. Final Report of the Pennsylvania Supreme Court Committee on Racial and Gender Bias in the Justice System, Report (2003) (summarizing findings of various states).

9. *Miller-El v. Cockrell*, 537 U.S. 322 (2003) (describing the practices in the Dallas District Attorney's Office designed to exclude African Americans from serving on juries).

10. *Batson v. Kentucky*, 476 U.S. 79 (1986).

11. *Wilkerson v Texas*, 493 U.S. 924 (1990) (Justice Marshall dissenting from denial of certiorari). Another federal judge also wrote that he had been troubled by a series of cases "where the *Batson* issue has been raised and where superficial or almost frivolous excuses for peremptory challenges with racial overtones have been proffered and accepted. I fear that *Batson* is fast coming to offer a theoretical right without an effective remedy." *United States v. Clemmons*, 892 F. 2d 1153 (3rd Cir. 1989) (Judge Higginbotham concurring).

12. David C. Baldus et al., "Use of Peremptory Challenges in Capital Murder Trials: A Legal and Empirical Analysis," *University of Pennsylvania Journal of Constitutional Law* 3 (February 2001): 3.

13. See generally, Claudia Cowan, William Thompson, and Phoebe Ellsworth, "The Effects of Death Qualification on Jurors' Predisposition to Convict and on the Quality of Deliberation," *Law and Human Behavior* 8 (1984): 53 (finding that jurors' attitudes toward the death penalty affect their predisposition to convict).

14. *California v. Brown*, 479 U.S. 538, 545 (1987) (Justice O'Connor concurring).

15. In a Virginia case, for example, the jurors sent out a question asking whether it was required to impose the death penalty if jurors found that an aggravating factor existed, or whether they could still consider mitigating evidence. The defense lawyer asked the judge to clarify for the jury what everyone agreed was the correct answer: The jury was *not* required to impose the death penalty simply because they found an aggravating factor and *should* consider the mitigating evidence. The trial judge, however, simply referred the jury back to the jury instruction that the jury had said it was confused by. With many of the jurors openly weeping in the jury box, the jury then returned a sentence of death. A majority of the Supreme Court upheld the death sentence on the theory that no reasonable likelihood existed that the jury misunderstood the instruction. *Weeks v. Angelone*, 528 U.S. 225 (2000). A study replicating the facts of *Weeks* and using a mock jury concluded that the jurors probably never understood the instruction, meaning that "The [Supreme] Court got this one wrong, both on the facts and the law." Stephen Garvey, et al., "Correcting

Deadly Confusion: Responding to Jury Inquiries in Capital Cases," *Cornell Law Review* 85 (2000): 627.

16. *Callins v. Collins*, 510 U.S. 1141 (1994) (Justice Blackmun dissenting).

17. Supreme Court Justice Antonin Scalia, for instance, while agreeing with Justice Blackmun that the Court's efforts to regulate the death penalty have been less than successful in bringing consistency, argues that "[Justice Blackmun] unfortunately draws the wrong conclusion from the acknowledgment." From Justice Scalia's viewpoint, the problem of inconsistency is created because the Court gives defendants too much leeway in presenting mitigating evidence. Ibid., 1141. Justice Scalia's solution would be to move to a mandatory death penalty or to at least allow states to limit what can be introduced in mitigation. *Walton v. Arizona*, 497 U.S. 639, 647 (1990) (Justice Scalia concurring).

ARTICLES AND BOOKS BASED ON THE CAPITAL JURY PROJECT

Bentele, Ursula, and William J. Bowers, "How Jurors Decide on Death: Guilt is Overwhelming; Aggravation Requires Death; and Mitigation is No Excuse." *Brook Law Review* 66 (2001): 1011.

Bienen, Leigh B. "Helping Jurors Out: Post-Verdict Debriefing for Jurors in Emotionally Disturbing Trials." *Indiana Law Journal* 68 (1993): 1333.

Blume, John H., Theodore Eisenberg, and Stephen P. Garvey, Lessons from the Capital Jury Project." In *Beyond Repair? America's Death Penalty*, ed. Stephen P. Garvey. Durham, NC: Duke University Press, 2003: 144.

Blume, John H., Stephen P. Garvey and Sheri Lynn Johnson, "Future Dangerousness in Capital Cases: Always at Issue." *Cornell Law Review* 86 (2001): 397.

Bowers, William J., "The Capital Jury: Is it Tilted Toward Death?" *Judicature* 79 (1996): 220.

Bowers, William J. "The Capital Jury Project: Rationale, Design, and Preview of Early Findings." *Indiana Law Journal* 70 (1995): 1043.

Bowers, William J. And Wanda D. Foglia, "Still Singularly Agonizing: Law's Failure to Purge Arbitrariness from Capital Sentencing." *Criminal Law Bulletin* 39 (2003): 51.

Bowers, William J., Marla Sandys and Thomas W. Brewer, "Crossing Racial Boundaries: A Closer Look at the Roots of Racial Bias in Capital Sentencing When the Defendant is Black and the Victim is White," *DePaul Law Review* 53 (2004): 1497.

Bowers, William J. and Benjamin D. Steiner, "Choosing Life or Death: Sentencing Dynamics in Capital Cases." In *America's Experiment with Capital Punishment: Reflections on the Past, Present and Future of the Ultimate*

Penal Sanction (First Edition), eds. James R. Acker, Robert M. Bohm, and Charles S. Lanier. Durham, NC: Carolina Academic Press (1998).

Bowers, William J. and Benjamin D. Steiner, "Death by Default: An Empirical Demonstration of False and Forced Choices in Capital Sentencing," *Texas Law Review* 77 (1998) 605.

Bowers, William J., Benjamin D. Steiner, and Michael E. Antonio, "The Capital Sentencing Decision: Guided Discretion, Reasoned Moral Judgment, or Legal Fiction." In *America's Experiment with Capital Punishment: Reflections on the Past, Present and Future of the Ultimate Penal Sanction (Second Edition)*, eds. James R. Acker, Robert M. Bohm, and Charles S. Lanier. Durham, NC: *Carolina Academic Press* (2003).

Bowers, William J., Benjamin D. Steiner, and Marla Sandys, "Death Sentencing in Black and White: An Empirical Analysis of the Role of Jurors' Race and Jury Racial Composition," *Univ. of Pennsylvania Journal of Constitutional Law* 3 (2003): 171.

Bowers, William J., et al, "Foreclosed Impartiality in Capital Sentencing: Jurors' Predispositions, Guilt-Trial Experience, and Premature Decision Making," *Cornell Law Review* 83 (1998): 1476.

Eisenberg, Theodore, and Martin T. Wells, "Deadly Confusion: Juror Instructions in Capital Cases," *Cornell Law Review* 79 (1993): 1.

Eisenberg, Theodore, Stephen P. Garvey & Martin T. Wells, "Jury Responsibility in Capital Sentencing: An Empirical Study," Buffalo Law Review 44 (1996): 339.

———. "But Was He Sorry? The Role of Remorse in Capital Sentencing," *Cornell Law Review* 83 (1998): 1599.

———. "The Deadly Paradox of Capital Jurors," *Southern California Law Review* 74 (2001): 371.

———. "Forecasting Life and Death: Juror Race, Religion, and Attitude Toward the Death Penalty," *Journal of Legal Studies* 30 (2001): 277.

———. "Victim Characteristics and Victim Impact Evidence in South Carolina Capital Cases," *Cornell Law Review* 88 (2003): 306.

Foglia, Wanda D. "Arbitrary and Capricious After All These Years: Constitutional Problems with Capital Jurors' Decision Making." *The Champion* 25 (2001): 26.

Foglia, Wanda D. "They Know Not What They Do: Unguided and Misguided Decision-Making in Pennsylvania Capital Cases." *Justice Quarterly* 20 (2003): 187.

Garvey, Stephen P. "Aggravation and Mitigation in Capital Cases: What Do Jurors Think?" *Columbia Law Review* 98 (1998): 1538.

———. "The Emotional Economy of Capital Sentencing," *New York University Law Review* 75 (2000): 26.

Garvey, Stephen P., Sheri Lynn Johnson and Paul Marcus, "Correcting Deadly Confusion: Responding to Jury Inquiries in Capital Cases." *Cornell Law Review* 85 (2000): 627.

Hoffmann, Joseph L. "How American Juries Decide Death Penalty Cases: The Capital Jury Project." *In The Death Penalty in America: Current Controversies,* ed. Hugo Adam Bedau. New York: Oxford University Press (1997).

Hoffmann, Joseph L., "Where's The Buck?—Juror Misperception of Sentencing Responsibility in Death Penalty Cases," *Indiana Law Journal* 70 (1995): 1137.

Luginbuhl, James and Julie Howe, "Discretion in Capital Sentencing Instructions: Guided or Misguided?" *Indiana Law Journal* 70 (1995): 1161.

Sandys, Marla, "Cross-Overs—Capital Jurors Who Change Their Minds about the Punishment: A Litmus Test for Sentencing Guidelines," *Indiana Law Journal* 70 (1995): 1183.

Sandys, Marla and Scott McClelland, "Stacking the Deck for Guilt and Death: The Failure of Death Qualification to Ensure Impartiality." In *America's Experiment with Capital Punishment: Reflections on the Past, Present and Future of the Ultimate Penal Sanction (Second Edition),* eds. James R. Acker, Robert M. Bohm, and Charles S. Lanier. Durham, NC: Carolina Academic Press (2003).

Sarat, Austin, "Violence, Representation, and Responsibility in Capital Trials: The View from the Jury," *Indiana Law Journal* 70 (1995): 1103.

Steiner, Benjamin D. "Before or Against the Law: Citizens' Legal Beliefs and Experiences as Death Penalty Jurors." *Studies in Law, Politics and Society* 27 (2003): 115.

Sundby, Scott E., "The Jury as Critic: An Empirical Look at How Capital Juries Perceive Expert and Lay Testimony," *Virginia Law Review* 83 (1997): 1109.

———. "The Capital Jury and Absolution: The Intersection of Trial Strategy, Remorse, and the Death Penalty," *Cornell Law Review* 83 (1998): 1557.

———. "The Capital Jury and Empathy: The Problem of Worthy and Unworthy Victims," *Cornell Law Review* 88 (2003): 343.

Steiner, Benjamin D. "Narratives of the Death Sentence: Toward a Theory of Legal Narrativity." 36 (2002) *Law and Society Review* 549 (2002).

Steiner, Benjamin D., William J. Bowers and Austin Sarat., "Folk Knowledge as Legal Action: Death Penalty Judgments and the Tenet of Early Release in a Culture of Mistrust and Punitiveness." *Law and Society Review* 33 (1999): 461.

INDEX